Shirley
Burnett

THE Introvert Advantage

How to Thrive in an Extrovert World

Marti Olsen Laney, Psy.D.

WORKMAN PUBLISHING • NEW YORK

Library of Congress Cataloging-in-Publication Data

Laney, Marti Olsen.
The introvert advantage/Marti Olsen Laney.
p. cm.
Includes bibliographical references and index.
ISBN 0-7611-2369-5 (alk. paper)—ISBN 0-7611-2589-2
1. Introversion. 2. Interpersonal relations. I. Title.
BF698.35.I59 L36 2001
155.2'32—dc21   2001026987

Workman Publishing Company, Inc.
708 Broadway
New York, NY 10003-9555

www.workman.com

Printed in the United States of America

First printing: September 2002
10 9 8 7 6 5 4 3 2 1

Dedication

Feeling gratitude and not expressing it
is like wrapping a gift and not giving it.
—WILLIAM A. WARD

To my husband of thirty-eight years, Michael, who dragged me out into extroverting and enlarged my universe. I dedicate this book to you for coaching me to keep breathing through the long labor of the book birthing process. And you are awarded the Highest Medal of Husbandry Honor for devoting so many hours to read page after page about introverts (more than any mortal extrovert should ever have to). Last, but not least, a final thank-you for delivering nourishing meals to me as I sat staring and pecking at my computer.

To my daughters and their families, whom I love very much and who have enriched my life in countless ways:

Tynna, Brian, Alicia, and Christopher DeMellier

Kristen, Gary, Kaitlin, and Emily Parks

I also dedicate this book to all of my clients who have courageously let me into their lives.

Acknowledgments

I would like to thank everyone I've met in my life.
—Maureen Stapleton

It takes a lot of midwives to birth a book. I would like to thank my dear friend Valerie Hunter, for knowing I could write before I did. Sylvia Cary, for confirming I was pregnant with a book idea and giving me invaluable feedback about the neonate. My agent, Andrea Pedolsky, for recognizing the possibilities in the book proposal and her ongoing encouragement throughout the elephantine labor. Peter Workman and Sally Kovalchick, who were aware that introverts needed a book to be born about them. My editors, Margot Herrera and Kitty Ross, for combing through my right-brained manuscript and untangling snarls with their left-brained minds. Tia Maginni, who must have ESP to be able to decode the arrows, cross-outs, and smudged ink on the manuscript. Thank you to all those at Workman Publishing, for laboring until the book was born.

A special thank-you to all those introverts I interviewed for this book. I would also like to thank all the dedicated scientists and researchers in the many fields who strive to help all of us to understand the "simply complex" humans we are.

Contents

Part I: A Fish Out of Water

Part II: Navigating the Extroverted Waters

Part III: Creating the "Just Right" Life

Prelude

It is the chiefest point of happiness
that a man is willing to be what he is.

—ERASMUS

Growing up, I was often puzzled about myself. I was full of confusing contradictions. An odd duck. I did so poorly in first and second grade that my teachers wanted me to repeat, yet in third grade I did very well. Sometimes I was very animated and talkative, making crisp, informed comments. In fact, if it was a subject I knew about, I could talk someone's arm and leg off. Other times I wanted to speak, but my mind was blank. Or I would think of something to say in class, raise my hand—thrilled that I might improve the 25 percent of my grade that was based on class participation—but when I was called on, my comment would disappear into thin air. My internal screen would go dark. I wanted to crawl under my desk. Then there were the times when my remarks would come out in some halting, unclear form, making me sound much less knowledgeable than I was. I developed all sorts of techniques for avoiding the teacher's eyes when she was scanning the class for someone to answer a question. I couldn't rely on myself; I never knew how I would react.

Confusing me further was that when I did express myself out loud, people often told me I was well spoken and concise. Other times my classmates treated me as if I were mentally disabled. I didn't think I was stupid, but I didn't think I was sharp as a tack either.

The way my brain worked puzzled me. I couldn't figure out why I could think of lots of comments after the fact. When I gave my opinion about something that had happened earlier, teachers and friends would ask, in an irritated tone, why I hadn't spoken up before. They seemed to think I was purposely withholding my thoughts and feelings. I found my thoughts were like lost airline baggage; they arrived some time later.

As I grew up, I began to think of myself as a stealth person, running silent, deep, and invisible. Many times I would say something, and no one would respond. Later, another person might say the *same* thing and he or she would be acknowledged. I would think there was something wrong with the way I spoke. At other times, when people heard me speak or read something I wrote, they would look at me with a stunned expression. It happened so many times that the "look" had become very familiar to me. It seemed to say, *You* wrote this? I felt mixed about this reaction because I liked being acknowledged but I also felt overwhelmed by the attention.

Socializing was also a confusing experience. I enjoyed people, and people seemed to like me, but I often dreaded going out. I would go back and forth deciding whether to show up at a party or public event. I concluded I was a social chicken. Sometimes I felt awkward and uncomfortable; at other times I felt okay. Even when I was having a wonderful time, I was eyeing the door and fantasizing about snuggling in bed in my pajamas.

Another source of pain and frustration was my low energy. I got fatigued easily. I didn't seem to have the same stamina as my friends and family. When I was tired, I walked slowly, ate slowly, and talked slowly, with lots of agonizing gaps in my conversation. On the other hand, if I was rested, I could chat so fast, jumping from thought to thought, that the people I was with may have felt blitzed. In fact, some people thought I had a lot of energy. Trust me, I didn't (and still don't).

Yet even with my slow pace I trudged along until I ended up accomplishing most of what I wanted with my life. It took me years to discover that all of my puzzling contradictions actually made sense. I was a normal introvert. This discovery brought me such relief!

Overture

Democracy cannot survive without
the guidance of a creative minority.

—Harlan F. Stone

Remember when we were kids and compared belly buttons? Back then it was considered better to be in "innie" than an "outie." Nobody wanted a belly button that stuck *out,* so I was glad mine went in.

Later, when "innie" came to mean "introvert" in my mind, and "outie" came to mean "extrovert," it was the opposite. Extrovert was "good." Introvert was "bad." Since no matter how hard I tried I didn't have those extroverted qualities, and I thought something was wrong with me. I didn't understand many things about myself. Why did I feel overwhelmed in environments that thrilled other people? Why did I come away from outside activities feeling as if I were gasping for air? Why did I feel like a fish out of water?

Why Are Outies the Cultural Ideal?

Our culture values and rewards the qualities of extroverts. America was built on rugged individualism and the importance of citizens speaking their minds. We value action, speed, competition, and drive.

It's no wonder people are defensive about introversion. We live in a culture that has a negative attitude about reflection and solitude. "Getting out there" and "just doing it" are the ideals. In his book *The Pursuit of Happiness,* social psychologist Dr. David Myers claimed that happiness is a matter of possessing three traits: self-esteem, optimism, and extroversion. Dr. Myers based his conclusions on studies that "prove" extroverts are "happier." These studies required participants to agree or disagree with such statements as, "I like to be with others" and "I'm fun to be with." Introverts don't describe happiness in the same way, so they are perceived as unhappy. For them, statements like "I know myself" or "I'm comfortable in my own skin" or "I am free to pursue my own path" are the benchmarks for a feeling of personal contentment. But they are not asked their reaction to these statements. An extrovert must have developed these studies.

When extroversion is taken for granted as the natural outcome of healthy development, introversion can't help but become the "dreaded other." Somehow introverts have failed to achieve appropriate socialization. They are doomed to isolated unhappiness.

Otto Kroeger and Janet Thuesen are psychological consultants who use the Myers-Briggs Type Indicator (more on this later). In their book *Type Talk,* they discuss the plight of the introvert: "Introverts are outnumbered about three to one. As a result, they must develop extra coping skills in life because there will be an inordinate amount of pressure on them to 'shape up,' to act like the rest of the world. The introvert is pressured daily, almost from the moment of awakening, to respond and conform to the outer world."

I think the playing field of life needs to be evened out a little. Extroverts get most of the good press. It's time that introverts realize just how unique and special they are. We are ripe for a cultural shift toward the okayness of introversion. It's all right for us to stop trying to fit in and to "shape up." We need to appreciate our own shape as it is. This book aims to help us do this. In it you will learn three basic things: (1) how to determine if you're an introvert (you may be surprised); (2) how to understand and appreciate your introverted advantages; (3) how to nurture your valuable nature with numerous useful tips and tools.

Nothing Is Wrong with Me, I'm Just Introverted

What a lovely surprise to finally discover how unlonely being alone can be.
—ELLEN BURSTYN

When I was in my thirties, I made a career change from children's librarian to psychotherapist (two introverted occupations that require social skills, you may note). Although I enjoyed many aspects of being a librarian, I wanted to work on a more personal level with people. Facilitating individual growth and development to help others live more satisfying lives felt like a gratifying life purpose for me. In graduate school, I learned about the phenomena of introversion as a distinct temperament or style for the second time. As part of my coursework, I took a few personality tests, and, on several of them, I came out as an introvert. I was surprised. When my professors discussed the results, they explained that introversion and extroversion are on opposite ends of an energy continuum. Where we fall on that continuum predicts how we derive our life energy. People on the more introverted end of the continuum focus inward to gain energy. People on the more extroverted end of the continuum focus outward to gain energy. This fundamental difference in focus can be seen in practically everything we do. My professors emphasized the positive aspects of each temperament and made it clear that each was okay—just different.

The concept of different energy requirements clicked with me. I began to understand my need to be alone to recharge my batteries. I didn't feel quite as guilty for wanting breaks from my children. It finally dawned on me that nothing was wrong with me; I was just introverted.

As I became informed about the strengths and weaknesses of introverts, I felt less ashamed. When I learned the ratio of extroverts to introverts—three to one—I realized I lived in a world structured for all those "outies." No wonder I felt like a fish out of water. I was living in a sea of extroverts!

I also began to have insights into why I hated the large staff meetings I was required to attend every Wednesday evening at the counseling center where I was an intern. I understood why I rarely spoke in group supervision, and why my mind would often vapor lock whenever I was in a room with more than a few people.

Being an introvert in a world geared toward extroverts affects all aspects of a person's life. Psychoanalyst Carl Jung developed theories about introversion and extroversion and thought that we are attracted to our opposite to help strengthen and complete what's missing in each of us. He thought introversion and extroversion were like two chemicals: When they are combined, each can be transformed by the other. He also saw this as a natural built-in way for us to appreciate complementary qualities in one another. This concept doesn't apply to everyone, but it has certainly proved true in my marriage of thirty-eight years.

Initially, my husband, Mike, didn't understand my introversion, and I couldn't comprehend his extroversion. I remember when the two of us went to Las Vegas after we were first married. I staggered through the casino, my brain numbed. Colors danced everywhere, and lights exploded in my eyes. The clanking of winners' coins tumbling into metal catchers pounded in my head. I kept asking Mike, "How much farther is it to the elevator?" (They do that tricky thing in Las Vegas, making you walk through a maze of shiny machines, misted in cigarette smoke, to get to the elevator and the quiet oasis of your room.)

My husband, the extrovert, was ready to rock and roll. His cheeks were rosy, and his eyes sparkled—all the noise and action excited him. He didn't understand why I was heading up to the room. I was pea green and felt like a trout I once saw lying on a bed of crushed ice in a fish market. At least the trout got to lie down.

Later, when I woke up from my nap, I was surrounded by two hundred silver dollars Mike had won. Obviously, extroverts have many charms. And they are a good balance for us introverted types. They help us go out and about. We help them slow down.

Why I Wrote This Book

Come forth into the light of things,
Let Nature be your Teacher.
—WILLIAM WORDSWORTH

One afternoon, Julia, an introverted client, and I were brainstorming about how she could manage an upcoming training workshop. "I am dreading it," she told me. We developed several strategies to help her get through it, and, as she got up to leave, she lowered her head and looked me intently in the eye. "I still hate schmoozing, you know," she said. As if she thought I expected her to be a social butterfly. "I know," I said, "I still hate it myself." We sighed together in a knowing way.

As I closed my office door, I thought about my own struggle with introversion. In my mind's eye I pictured the faces of all the introverted clients I have worked with over the years. I thought about how where a person falls on the introvert/extrovert continuum affects all areas of life. I heard clients blaming themselves for qualities they have that they don't like. I would think, Oh, I wish they realized that nothing is wrong with them. They are just introverted.

I remembered when I first ventured to say to a client, "I think you're introverted." Her eyes widened in surprise. "Why do you think that?" she asked. Then I explained that introversion is a collection of traits that we are born with. It's not about disliking people or even being shy. She looked so relieved. "You mean there's a reason I'm like this?" she said. It's amazing how many people are introverts and don't even know it!

As I discussed my ideas about introversion with other therapists, I was surprised to discover that many didn't really understand the original theory of introversion. They thought of it in terms of pathology, not temperament. When I submitted my dissertation for my psychoanalytic degree on the subject, I was moved to tears by the incredible response I got, and I was excited by the comments I received from many of my colleagues. "I am now looking at all of my patients in terms of the introvert/extrovert continuum," one said, "and it has really helped me to understand and not pathologize the ones who are more introverted. I realize I've been looking at them through an extroverted lens."

I know how powerful it can be when the shame of being introverted is lifted. It's a great relief to stop trying to be who you're not. Once I made this connection, I realized I had to write a book to help people understand introversion.

How I Wrote the Book

Quiet people are often found
to have profound insights.
The shallow water in a brook or river runs fast:
The deep water seems calmer.

—JAMES ROGERS

Many introverts don't feel as if they know enough about a subject until they know almost everything, and that's the way I approached this project. This happens for three reasons. First, introverts can imagine the vastness of any subject. Second, they have had the experience of their brain locking, so in an attempt to avoid that awful blank-mind moment, they overprepare by accruing as much information as they can. Third, since they often don't talk about what they are thinking, they receive no feedback to help them gain perspective about how much they already know.

Although I had worked with introverts for years and studied introversion in depth, I wanted to know what new research was available about the physiology and genetics of introverted brains. My first step, as a former librarian, was to check the Bio-Med Library at UCLA. When I typed in the subject heading of introversion, I was surprised to find that more than two thousand journal citations appeared in the fields of personality, temperament, neurophysiology, and genetics. Most of the research had been conducted in European countries, where introversion is more accepted as a form of inborn temperament. In Chapter 3, I will discuss some of the research findings that explain introversion in terms of genetic and physiological endowment.

My second step was to check out the Internet, since I thought lots of "innies" might hang out there. I found several hundred sites about introversion. Many of the websites were linked to the Myers-Briggs Type Indicator, a widely used personality assessment based on four aspects of temperament. The first and most statistically valid of these is the introversion/extroversion continuum. Developed by Isabel Myers and Katharine C. Briggs, and based on Jung's original theories, the main strength of this inventory is that it does not pathologize any personality type. Rather, it looks at innate preferences. Introversion is also included on several sites about giftedness, as there is a correlation between introversion and intelligence. (And in case you're interested, there's a rock band named Introversion—its performance schedule can be found on the Internet.)

The library and Internet research were very useful and illuminating, but I learned the most about introversion from my own experiences and those of my clients, and from the people I interviewed for this book. I interviewed more than fifty people from many walks of life including writers, ministers, therapists, historians, teachers, artists, college students, researchers, and computer professionals. (Names and some identifying details have been changed.) A number of interviewees had taken the Myers-Briggs Inventory, and so they knew they were "innies."

Even though they were not selected with any specific career criteria in mind, a surprising number were in what Dr. Elaine Aron calls "advisor class" positions—people who work independently, who wrestle with decisions, who have had to learn how to put themselves in other people's shoes and communicate with people. These workers are creative, imaginative, intelligent, and thoughtful. They are observers. Their work often impacts many people and they have the courage and perspective to say unpopular things. In her book *The Highly Sensitive Person*, Dr. Aron states that the other class, the warrior class, are the doers of the world. They need counsel from the advisors, and the advisors need warriors to take action and make things happen. Many theorists feel that that is why only 25 percent of the population consists of introverted people—fewer introverts are needed.

In many interviews, I heard introverts criticizing themselves for their introverted qualities, especially if they didn't even know they were introverted. They were confused about why they felt disregarded and unseen. Since I know introverts like to have time to think about their experiences, I did follow-up calls several weeks after the interview to see if the person had any further thoughts he or she wanted to add.

I was surprised and encouraged to find that after our conversation many felt much better about *who* they are. "Just by learning that my brain is different and that I live in a sea of extroverts, I feel calmer about being me," many of them said. Having proof in the form of scientific research that it's okay to be different was a powerful force that reduced guilt, shame, and other negative views people had developed of themselves. These experiences fueled my motivation to get this book published.

I am writing this book primarily for introverts. I want innies to understand that there are valuable reasons behind their sometimes-puzzling temperament. I would also like them to know they are not alone.

However, there are two valuable reasons for extroverts to read it, too. First, they can gain an understanding of those mysterious introverts in their lives. Second, extroverts, especially as they enter midlife, need to balance the physical limitations of aging by enhancing their pause-to-reflect self. This book can open the door to a whole new way for extroverts to think about introverts and to develop self-reflective aspects of themselves.

Read It Your Way

No furniture is so charming as books.

—SYDNEY SMITH

Since introverts often feel as if something is wrong with them, they try to figure out the "right way" to do things. Although we live in an extroverted world, the right way isn't always right for innies. So read this book cover to cover, or dip into it anywhere you like. Learning to break new information into bite-size pieces is one way to manage feeling overstimulated. By this I mean a physical and mental feeling of *too muchness,* of being keyed up like a car with the idle set too high, leaving you unable to take in any more stimuli.

I have designed this book in small morsels. You can read it chapter by chapter. Or let the book fall open and just read that page. Personally, I like to start books at the end. It's a habit that shocks some of my friends. Use the book any way you feel works best. Remember, it is meant to be a helpmate to you.

If the information in a given chapter seems relevant to you, great. If something seems less pertinent, that's okay, too. This is a tool for you to understand yourself and any introverts you may know. Play means creating a space for something new to happen. This book, like life, is meant to be played with.

Once you understand your own introversion (or the introversion of someone close to you), it is such a relief. So *that's* all it is! You are not weird or hopeless or alone. There are other introverted fish in the sea.

This book will help you learn how to recharge yourself. You can create a plan for tackling everyday life—maybe not the way extroverts do it, but the way that works for innies. Celebrate your introvert advantage.

Points to Ponder

- 75 percent of the world is extroverted.
- Being introverted affects all areas of your life.
- Nothing is wrong with you.
- Introverts feel drained and overstimulated.
- Being introverted is something to be celebrated.

PART I A Fish Out of Water

I am what I am.

—Popeye

CHAPTER 1

What's an Innie?
Are You One?

The exception that proves the rule . . .

—PROVERB

Introversion is at its root a type of temperament. It is not the same as shyness or having a withdrawn personality, and it is not pathological. It is also not something you can change. But you can learn to work *with* it, not *against* it.

The strongest distinguishing characteristic of introverts is their energy source: Introverts draw energy from their *internal world* of ideas, emotions, and impressions. They are energy conservers. They can be easily overstimulated by the external world, experiencing the uncomfortable feeling of "too much." This can feel like antsyness or torpor. In either case, they need to limit their social experiences so they don't get drained. However, introverts need to balance their alone time with outside time, or they can lose other perspectives and connections. Introverted people who balance their energy have perseverance and the ability to think independently, focus deeply, and work creatively.

What are the most obvious characteristics of extroverts? They are energized by the *external world*—by activities, people, places, and things. They are energy spenders. Long periods of hanging out, internal contemplation, or being alone or with just one other person understimulate them. However, extroverts need to balance their time *doing* with intervals of just *being*, or they can lose themselves in a whirlwind of anxious activities. Extroverts offer much to our society—they express themselves easily, they concentrate on results, and they enjoy crowds and action.

Introverts are like a rechargeable battery. They need to stop expending energy and rest in order to recharge. This is what a less stimulating environment provides for introverts. It restores energy. It is their natural niche.

Extroverts are like solar panels. For extroverts, being alone, or *inside*, is like living under a heavy cloud cover. Solar panels need the sun to recharge—extroverts need to be out and about to refuel. Like introversion, extroversion is a hard-wired temperament. It cannot be changed. You can learn to work *with* it, not *against* it.

The Main Differences Between Innies and Outies

Appreciate your uniqueness.
—Captain Kangaroo

Energy creation is the most salient difference between introverts and extroverts, but there are two other primary differences: their response to stimulation and their approach to knowledge and experience. Extroverts thrive on a variety of stimuli, whereas introverts can find it too much. Similarly, outies generally cast a wide net when it comes to accruing knowledge and experience, whereas innies like a narrower, more in-depth focus.

Refueling

Let's talk a little more about energy. As I said earlier, the primary difference between introverts and extroverts is how they recharge their batteries. Extroverts are energized by the outer world. Most extroverts like talking to people, engaging in activities outside of themselves, and working around people, activities, and things. Contrary to most of our perceptions about extroverts, however, they are not necessarily more outgoing or lively than an introvert, but their focus is outside themselves.

Extroverts spend energy freely and often have trouble slowing down. They can refresh themselves easily by doing something in the outer world, especially since there is so much to choose from today. Extroverts may experience loneliness and a feeling of being drained when they are not in contact with people or the outside world. They may be the ones who are raring to go *after* a party, asking, What shall we do next? Often the harder part for them is relaxing and giving their bodies a rest.

Introverts, on the other hand, are energized by the internal world—by ideas, impressions, and emotions. Counter to our stereotypes of introverts, they are not necessarily quiet or withdrawn, but their focus is inside their heads. They need a quiet, reflective place where they can think things through and recharge themselves. Whew! It was great to catch up with Bill, but I am so glad the party is over! they say with relief.

Creating energy isn't so easy for introverts, especially in today's fast-paced world. It takes more time for introverts to restore energy, and it flows out faster than an extrovert's energy. Introverts need to calculate how much energy something will take, how much they need to conserve, and plan accordingly.

For example, the day *before* she goes out for a hectic day of driving from sales call to sales call in Los Angeles, my client Sandra (a saleswoman who works from home), sets aside a quiet day doing paperwork with few outside interruptions. She goes to bed early and eats a good breakfast before she hits the road. Throughout the day she schedules breaks where she can be alone and revive herself. In this way she plans for her energy needs so she won't be depleted.

Stimulation—Friend or Foe?

The second difference between the introvert and the extrovert is how they experience external stimulation. Extroverts like to experience a lot, and introverts like to know a lot about what they experience.

For introverts who have a high level of internal activity, anything coming from the outside raises their intensity level index quickly. It's kind of like being tickled—the sensation goes from feeling good and fun to "too much" and uncomfortable in a split second.

Introverts, often without realizing why, attempt to regulate experiences of overstimulation through limiting external input. My client Katherine wants to plant a garden in her backyard. She is a teacher, and her job requires most of her focus and energy. New to gardening, she sits down to read the *Basic Book of Weekend Gardening*. As she reads, the scope of the project slowly dawns on her. She will need to learn about shade plants, soil pH, mulching, watering, insect control, and sun exposure. She foresees the complexity and energy requirement involved in going to the nursery and picking out plants in the glaring sun—so many choices to sort through. She thinks of the time it will take to prepare the soil, plant the plants, weed the space, massacre insects, chase away snails, and water every day. Her feeling of enjoyment is receding. There's so much to know, so much to do, that she begins to feel as if it will be too much. Her head is whirling, and she feels overwhelmed. She decides she will limit her garden to a smaller piece of her yard.

Introverts enjoy complexity when they can focus on one or two areas, without pressure. But if they have too many projects, they easily feel overwhelmed. In later chapters I will discuss ways to manage the experience of overstimulation.

Just being around people can be overstimulating to introverts. Their energy is drained in crowds, classes, or any noisy and invasive environment. They may like people very much, but after talking to *anyone*, they usually begin to feel the need to move away, take a break, and get some air. This is the reason for the mind/vapor-lock experience I mentioned on page 8. When overstimulated, the introvert's mind can shut down, saying, No more input, please. It goes dark.

Extroverts need breaks, too, but for different reasons.

If they go to the library, they can spend only a short time in a study mode (an internal process) before they need to take a walk around the stacks, head to the vending machines, or talk with the librarian. They like a lively environment "where the action is." Extroverts itch for refueling the more they feel *under*stimulated inside. But, just as breaks can increase extroverts' stimulation, breaks can decrease introverts' stimulation. When innies are studying, for example, they may be taking in so much information that it becomes overwhelming, as was the case with Katherine planning her garden.

How Deep Is the Ocean, How Wide Is the Sky?

The third way extroverts and introverts are different involves the concept of breadth and depth. By and large, extroverts like breadth—lots of friends and experiences, knowing a little bit about everything, being a generalist. What they take in from the outside environment does not generally expand internally as they process the experience. They are on to the next experience. As an outie friend told me, "I love to flit around a party and just catch the highlights from each conversation." She doesn't like to miss out on anything. For extroverts, life is about collecting experiences. Extroverts view the world as an extensive Sunday brunch. They can graze at the banquet and fill up on all sorts of tasty treats, leaving when they are full to bursting. They want to wring every drop of stimulation they can from life. Variety is stimulating and energizing.

Introverts like depth and will limit their experiences but feel each of them deeply. Often, they have fewer friends but more intimacy. They like to delve deeply into topics and look for "richness" more than "muchness." This is why it's necessary to limit their topics to one or two, or they can become overwhelmed. Their mind absorbs information from the outside environment and then reflects on it and expands it. And long after they have taken in the information, they are still munching and crunching it—a little like cows chewing their cud. How would anyone other than an introvert have had the patience to study the mating patterns of the South African tsetse fly? This is also why introverts resent being interrupted, as I will discuss later. It's difficult to pull themselves up and out of their deep well of concentration. And regaining that concentration takes lots of extra energy that they often don't have.

Different Strokes for Different Folks

A good example of these differences between introverts and extroverts is how my husband, Mike, and I decide on our vacations.

As I've mentioned, Mike is an extrovert, and I am an introvert. We don't agree on what constitutes a "fun," satisfying vacation at all.

Our favorite ways to holiday are so opposite, we take turns choosing our destination. One year I pick; the next year he picks. The year after Mike picked a "nine countries in nine days" vacation, I picked a vacation in which we did nothing but explore the historic mining area of Leadville, Colorado. Sitting by the fire at the hotel the first afternoon, we read the Chamber of Commerce's one-page flyer, What to See in Leadville. My stomach was tingling with excitement. Mike had dozed off.

Ever since I saw the movie *The Unsinkable Molly Brown,* I have wanted to see where Horace Tabor discovered silver. Leadville has the Tabor Opera House, the Heritage Museum, the National Mining Hall of Fame, and the Matchless Mine Museum, not to mention the Leadville Railroad and tours of the actual mines. Who could ask for anything more? Mike said, "Looks like we'll be done seeing Leadville by two tomorrow afternoon; what are we going to do after that?"

I had planned to take in one attraction per day. I wanted to get a feel for how the miners lived a century ago. Mike said, "Look, we're only fifty-nine miles from Aspen; we can drive there tomorrow afternoon."

"Whoa, Nelly," I said. "Whose vacation pick is this, anyway?"

Leadville was really one of my favorite vacations. I have gladly endured years of teasing from Mike about the four days in Colorado that seemed like four years to him. "Well, aren't you lucky," I say. "It's not everyone who gets their sense of time expanded, especially when they're on vacation."

Carl Jung's
Original Innie and Outie

*The pendulum of the mind oscillates between
sense and nonsense, not between right and wrong.*
—C. G. JUNG

In the early 1900s, psychoanalyst Carl Jung was working with
Sigmund Freud and Alfred Adler, two other pioneering psychoanalytic theorists, when he noticed something puzzling. When Freud
and Adler discussed the same case histories of patients, they focused on
very different information. They also had developed almost opposite
theories. Jung thought they had *both* captured something valuable. Jung
gave it some thought (guess which Jung was, an introvert or an extrovert?) and developed his own theory.

Jung thought Freud was extroverted because his personal orientation was outward toward the world of people, places, and things. Many
of Freud's theories were developed in conjunction with extensive corre-
spondence and discussions with numerous colleagues. Freud believed
that the goal of psychological development was to find gratification in
the world of external reality. Jung thought Adler was introverted, since
his theory and focus were inward toward one's own thoughts and feelings. Adler's theories were based on the internal struggle to overcome
the feelings of helplessness expressed in his term "inferiority complex."
He saw people as creative artists shaping their own lives.

Freud's theoretical differences with Adler and Jung ended in
bitterness. The three parted company and each went his own way.
At that point, Freud began to use the concept of introversion as a
negative, implying a turning inward away from the world, in his writ-
ings about narcissism. This shifted the evolution of the concept of

introversion away from healthy and toward the unhealthy, a misconception that remains to this day.

Jung continued to develop his theory, and he surmised that we are born with a temperament endowment that locates us somewhere on a continuum between very introverted and very extroverted. He

What Twins Tell Us About Temperament

In her book *Entwined Lives,* preeminent twins researcher Nancy Segal, Ph.D., writes about the incredible findings during her years at the University of Minnesota Center for Twin and Adoption Research. Fascinating studies compared personality similarities in identical (same egg) and fraternal (different eggs) twins raised apart and raised together. As fifty *reunited* twins passed through the center, the similarities were astounding. Twins reared apart showed an amazing array of specific shared traits, especially identical twins. One such set of twins loved to discuss their favorite subject, raising horses and dogs. Another pair of identicals were both volunteer firefighters, and both were known for their impatience with inferior cuisine. Another pair who had never before met drove up to the reunion in light blue Chevrolets. Still another pair used the same rare toothpaste from Sweden. As the center studied more reunited twins, it became apparent that their temperaments were more similar than expected. Dr. Segal writes, "A surprise was that Traditionalism, the endorsement of traditional family and moral values, did not show common family effects. In other words, living with someone does not lead to agreement on standards of conduct or parenting practices." Studies also showed that fraternal twins raised together are *much less* alike than identical twins that have been raised separately. These studies reveal what Jung was saying so long ago: we are born with an innate temperament. Dr. Segal goes on to say, "The bottom line is that living together does not make people in a family alike and that similarities are explained by shared genes."

believed that there was a physiological foundation for these disposi-
tions. Science is now finding his intuition was right! He realized we
could adapt best in the world if we could move easily on the continuum, introverting and extroverting when needed. However, he recognized that humans don't seem to work that way: We are oriented or
pulled in one direction more than the other. He concluded that we all
have a "natural niche" where we function best. Jung also thought that,
apart from either extreme, any place on the continuum is healthy.
Jung believed that it is harmful to push a child outside of the natural
range of his or her temperament, thinking this would "violate the
individual's innate disposition." In fact, he thought this was the cause
of some mental illness.

However, he pointed out that the other aspects of the continuum
are still available to us. Our ability to move on the continuum can
improve with our awareness of the process. For example, you can learn
to store up energy, and thereby have a reserve to enable you to use
your less natural side. Think about writing all day with your less dominant hand. You could do it, but you would use more exertion and
concentration to focus. Jung thought this was what it is like to function outside your natural niche. You can do it, but it will consume
extra energy without creating any new energy.

Are You an Introvert?

*To see what is in front of one's nose
requires a constant struggle.*
—GEORGE ORWELL

Here's the fun part. Are *you* a fish out of water? The IRS gives us
taxpayers the choice of short forms and long forms for our tax

returns, and I am giving you the same option. Take the Quickie Quiz that follows or the longer Self-Assessment for Introversion below, whichever strikes your fancy. Or take them both, and see what you come up with.

Quickie Quiz

Look over the list of key qualities below. Which list feels more like you, or is more like you *most* of the time? (Not every characteristic on a list will fit.) Answer as you *are,* not as you would like to be. Go with your first impression.

Qualities A

Like to be in the thick of things

Relish variety, bored with sameness

Know lots of people, consider them friends

Enjoy chitchatting, even with strangers

Feel stoked after activity, eager for more

Speak or act without needing to think first

Are generally quite peppy

Tend to talk more than listen

Qualities B

Prefer to relax alone or with a few close friends

Consider only deep relationships as friends

Need rest after outside activities, even ones you enjoy

Often listen but talk a lot about topics of importance to you

Appear calm, self-contained, and like to observe

Tend to think before you speak or act

Experience mind going blank in groups or under pressure

Don't like feeling rushed

Which list of qualities describes you best? If it's list A, you're extroverted. If it's B, you're introverted. You probably won't have *all* of the qualities on the list, but one list will fit better than the other. Since we all live in a culture biased toward extroversion, and your job and family demands may require you to function as an extrovert quite a bit, it may be difficult to decide which portrait seems more like you. If you are undecided, then ask yourself this question: "Am I refreshed more often after quiet time [innie] or active time [outie]?" If you are still uncertain, take the longer Self-Assessment For Introverts below.

Self-Assessment for Introverts

Take the test for introversion on a day when you are feeling relaxed and not stressed out. Pick a cozy nook where you won't be interrupted. Consider each statement in terms of what is generally true or false for you, not how you wish you were or how you are some of the time. Don't analyze or think too deeply about each statement. Your first impression is usually the best. For an outside view of yourself, it can be enlightening to have a partner or friend answer for you. Compare your results with your friend's score. If the two tallies differ, talk about both of your views.

Answer the following questions T or F, then add up your True answers and check the scoring at the end of the list to see if you're an introvert, fall in the middle of the continuum, or are an extrovert.

_____ When I need to rest, I prefer to spend time alone or with one or two close people rather than with a group.

_____ When I work on projects, I like to have larger uninterrupted time periods rather than smaller chunks.

_____ I sometimes rehearse things before speaking, occasionally writing notes for myself.

_____ In general, I like to listen more than I like to talk.

_____ People sometimes think I'm quiet, mysterious, aloof, or calm.

_____ I like to share special occasions with just one person or a few close friends, rather than have big celebrations.

_____ I usually need to think before I respond or speak.

_____ I tend to notice details many people don't see.

_____ If two people have just had a fight, I feel the tension in the air.

_____ If I say I will do something, I almost always do it.

_____ I feel anxious if I have a deadline or pressure to finish a project.

_____ I can "zone out" if too much is going on.

_____ I like to watch an activity for a while before I decide to join it.

_____ I form lasting relationships.

_____ I don't like to interrupt others; I don't like to be interrupted.

_____ When I take in lots of information, it takes me awhile to sort it out.

_____ I don't like overstimulating environments. I can't imagine why folks want to go to horror movies or go on roller coasters.

_____ I sometimes have strong reactions to smells, tastes, foods, weather, noises, etc.

_____ I am creative and/or imaginative.

_____ I feel drained after social situations, even when I enjoy myself.

_____ I prefer to be introduced rather than to introduce others.

_____ I can become grouchy if I'm around people or activities too long.

_____ I often feel uncomfortable in new surroundings.

_____ I like people to come to my home, but I don't like them to stay too long.

_____ I often dread returning phone calls.

_____ I find my mind sometimes goes blank when I meet people or when I am asked to speak unexpectedly.

_____ I talk slowly or have gaps in my words, especially if I am tired or if I am trying to speak and think at once.

_____ I don't think of casual acquaintances as friends.

_____ I feel as if I can't show other people my work or ideas until they are fully formulated.

_____ Other people may surprise me by thinking I am smarter than *I* think I am.

Add up the number of Trues. Then read the following to see where you fall.

20–29 True: Pretty darn introverted. As a result, it is extremely important for you to understand how to keep your energy flowing and how your brain processes information. You relate to life through your ideas, impressions, hopes, and values. You are not at the mercy of your external environment. This book can help you use your inner knowledge to create your own path.

10–19 True: Somewhere in the middle. Like being ambidextrous, you are both introverted and extroverted. You may feel torn between needing to be alone and wanting to be out and about. So it's very helpful to notice when and how you consistently feel more energized. You judge yourself by your own thoughts and feelings and by the standards of other people. This gives you a broad view, but at times you may get caught up in seeing both sides of a situation and not know where you stand. It is important to learn to assess your temperament so you can maintain your energy and balance. I will talk more about this in Chapter 2.

1–9 True: You are more extroverted. You judge yourself in the light of the values and reality of others. You work within the bounds of what exists to bring about change. As you reach midlife and your body slows down, you may surprise yourself by wanting to take a break from socializing or needing time to yourself and then not knowing what to do. You can develop techniques to help yourself remember what is best for you to do when you need solitude. To do this you will have to balance your extroverting skills by learning more introverting skills.

If you're still not sure if you're an innie or an outie, consider the following question: In a crisis, do you tend to feel shut down and somewhat detached and to respond in slow motion? Or do you tend to move your body immediately, take action without even thinking? During a stressful event, we revert to our basic hard wiring. If you tend to pull back, a hush falling over you like a fog, then you are more introverted. If you are more extroverted, you react by propelling yourself forward into action. There's value in each reaction.

Innies and Outies
Are Both Valuable

It takes all sorts to make a world.
—PROVERB

For Jung the goal of a well-lived life was the attainment of whole-ness. Wholeness didn't mean *having* all parts but achieving har-mony through knowing and valuing your own personal strengths and weaknesses. As I have discussed, Jung thought of all positions on the introvert/extrovert continuum as healthy and necessary. While some of us are more innately extroverted or more innately introverted, everyone has a natural resting point where he or she can gain energy and expend less energy. As we age, most of us move closer to the center of the I/E continuum. But we need the strengths of each type of temperament to balance the world.

Throughout the book I will highlight and discuss the advantages and hidden strengths of introverts. Extroverts have received lots of good press all their lives. I won't be balancing every strength of an introvert with the strength of an extrovert. In fact, I will be focusing on how the advantages of introverts help to complement the limita-tions of extroverts. Each temperament supplies strengths where the other has constraints.

Remember, all humans have many facets. Introversion and extro-version are not the only qualities that have been separated into good and bad. It appears to be a human foible to divide ourselves into good and bad parts. For instance, in 1995 Dr. Daniel Goleman came out with his groundbreaking book, *Emotional Intelligence*. Until then, intelligence was thought of in terms of rational thinking. Emotions were thought of as irrational and less valuable. Humans were divided into the "head" and the "heart." However, we all realize that some people are highly intelligent, yet they seem to have little common sense or compassion for other people. Other people have great empathy and wisdom, yet they may not be so intellectual. Dr. Goleman asked this question: How can we bring intelligence to our emotions—and civility to our streets and caring to our communal life? We need the head and the heart. It's obvious we need to learn from people with opposing talents; our society benefits from all facets of humanity.

In the following chapters, I will focus on the advantages introverts have to offer. We bring important attributes to the party—the ability to focus deeply, an understanding of how a change will affect everyone involved, the capacity to observe, a propensity for thinking outside the box, the strength to make unpopular decisions, and the potential to slow the world down a notch. Of course, introverts would like to just drop these qualities off at a party and then skedaddle on home!

Points to Ponder

- Introverts are different and it's okay.
- We are different in three main ways:
    - Energy creation
    - Response to stimulation
    - Depth vs. breadth
- Innies do like people.
- The world needs introverts with their unique and precious qualities.

CHAPTER II

Why Are Introverts an Optical Illusion?

If we cannot now end our differences, at least
we can help make the world safe for diversity.

—JOHN F. KENNEDY

In the last chapter I explained what introverts *are*. They are people who need private space to refuel, who do *not* gain their primary energy from external activities, and who usually need time to reflect and think before they speak. In this chapter I will discuss what they are *not*. They are not scaredy cats, shrinking violets, or self-absorbed loners. Nor are they necessarily shy or antisocial. As a society we don't see introverts accurately because we are looking at them through a lens of incorrect assumptions. Most introverts don't understand their own temperament because they have grown up with their own misconceptions about introversion.

So let's polish up and correct that distorted lens.

Wallflowers They Are Not

First off, I want to do some myth busting about introverts being reclusive, retiring types. Contrary to popular belief, many public personalities are introverts, and these folks are definitely not sticking to any walls.

Take, for example, Emmy award–winning Diane Sawyer, co-anchor of *Good Morning America* and *PrimeTime Thursday*. She is included on Internet listings of famous introverts and in numerous Myers-Briggs Type books. She has also spoken in several interviews about her quiet temperament. "People assume you can't be reserved and be on television," she said. "They're wrong." Her bio on ABC's website states that she "decided to pursue a career in broadcasting because of her desire to write, and the challenge of breaking into a male-dominated field." It goes on to say she is "known for her coolly detached and professional demeanor." With a reputation for exhaustive research and her ability to interview headstrong politicians like Fidel Castro, Saddam Hussein, and Boris Yeltsin, she has become a leader in her field. Her interview subjects are sometimes taken by surprise when she asks a hard-hitting question in her softball style. "People think she's aloof, but Diane is funny as hell," says pal Oprah Winfrey. Friends say it's typical of Sawyer to e-mail them to say, "I'm thinking of you."

Picture Katie Couric, the extroverted newswoman who co-anchors *The Today Show*, and Diane Sawyer sitting together on a sofa. These two impressive women give a clear illustration of the energy differences between introverts and extroverts. Couric is peppy, spontaneous, and articulate. Sawyer is restrained, lower-keyed, and more deliberate. Both are effective in their jobs.

Award-winning actress Joan Allen is also a typical introvert, accomplished but not in a splashy, attention-grabbing way. She received an Oscar nomination for Best Actress for her portrayal of the vice president in *The Contender*, and she was nominated twice for Best Supporting Actress for her roles in *Nixon* and *The Crucible*. On Broadway she has won a Tony and an Obie. Asked about being nominated for an Academy Award, she said, "Winning an Oscar is not a goal in my life, but I know my mother would be thrilled." Her main concern is good scripts, which she finds hard to come by. Asked about aspects of her own personality that she brought to her role in *The Contender*, she said, "The issue of privacy is very big with me. I am a very private person." Known for the depth of her performances, she didn't leave Broadway and try films for a long time because, she said, "I tended to feel I'm the one not up to speed." She has come to appreciate her own slow but steady tempo. She named her production company Little by Little.

Some introverted people are forced into the limelight.

A Few Famous Introverts

- **Abraham Lincoln,** sixteenth president
- **Sir Alfred Hitchcock,** film director
- **Michael Jordan,** basketball player and celebrity
- **Thomas Edison,** inventor
- **Grace Kelly,** actress
- **Gwyneth Paltrow,** actress
- **David Duvall,** golfer
- **Laura Bush,** first lady
- **Bill Gates,** software pioneer
- **Candice Bergen,** actress
- **Clint Eastwood,** actor/director
- **Charles Schulz,** *Peanuts* cartoonist
- **Steve Martin,** comedian/actor/ writer
- **Harrison Ford,** actor
- **Michele Pfeiffer,** actress
- **Katherine Graham,** late owner of *Washington Post,* author

A Picture Is Worth a Thousand Words

Sometimes the answers to life's problems are in the movies.
—GARY SOLOMON

Many movies have themes about introversion and extroversion. A fun way to broaden your view of introverts is to watch a few. Many introverts see other people with more clarity than they see themselves. And some feel critical of their own actions but aren't critical when observing another person doing the same thing. Watching introverted characters can increase your appreciation of your positive qualities.

Amélie, introverted French gal quietly and cleverly pulls strings from behind the scenes of those around her and captivates an introverted guy

Bridget Jones's Diary, introverted gal, often embarrassed by foot-in-mouth disease, finally stumbles onto introverted good guy

Chocolat, introverted gal whips up remedies for others' lives, finally finds her own secret sauce

Driving Miss Daisy, introverted African American man is backbone of the film

Enchanted April, introversion is relished in sunny Italy

Gosford Park, introverted English maid figures out the plot but keeps mum

Notting Hill, introverted bookshop owner meets introverted actress; mishaps ensue and sparks fly

One True Thing, through illness, introverted daughter learns to understand her extroverted mother

Ordinary People, guilty introverted son comes to terms with mom favoring dead extroverted brother

Saving Private Ryan, introverted captain leads the pack

Sixth Sense, introverted boy is highly sensitive

Consider the life of Prince William, of the Royal Family in Great Britain. He dislikes having a fuss made over him and having his picture taken, and he cares more about privacy than any other royal. "I am uncomfortable with all the attention," he has said in interviews. Described as "laid back," one of his friends is quoted as saying, "He wants to be a normal guy." He prefers people to call him Wills or William. The palace, known for throwing family members to the hungry British press, is attempting to help him cope with the pressures of public life. Royal watchers write about his intelligence, sensitivity, and reflective nature. It has been reported that he influenced Princess Diana to give up her HRH title in the divorce. "I don't mind what you're called," he told her. "You'll always be Mummy." There is even some concern that he may eventually refuse the crown because he doesn't want the overwhelming attention that comes with the job. If he does become king, he could bring many introverted strengths to the throne.

Known for his love of solitude, Albert Einstein is an example of how harsh environments can impair introverts and undercut their potential. In Denis Brian's book *Einstein: A Life,* the author tells about how difficult schooling was for Einstein in Germany in the late 1800s. "He was quiet and withdrawn—the onlooker." He was actually thought to be mentally disabled or "dull-witted" because of his failure to learn by rote and his strange behavior. He never gave a *snappy* answer to a question like other students, but always hesitated. In fact, if he had stayed in German schools he may never have developed into a brilliant physicist. Fortunately (and ironically), his father's lack of business acumen propelled the family to Italy. Maja, Einstein's sister, was astounded by the change in her brother in just six months. "The nervous, withdrawn dreamer had become an amiable, outgoing young man with a tart sense of humor. Was it the Italian air? The warm-hearted people? His escape from purgatory?" she wondered.

Later, when Einstein went on to school in Switzerland, he was initially worried it would be a stifling atmosphere like Germany. But "Albert reveled in the relaxed atmosphere in which teachers freely discussed controversial topics with students, even politics—unthinkable in German schools—and encouraged them to devise and conduct their own chemistry experiments, short of blowing up the place." Einstein said later in life, "It's not that I'm so smart, it's just that I stay with problems longer." Introverts can access their talents, like the ability to concentrate and question, only in a fitting environment.

So introverts are definitely not wallflowers. However, what drives introverts onto center stage is often different from what drives extroverts. Introverts come into the limelight because of their quest for work that has meaning to them, an unusual talent, or extraordinary circumstances. They may enjoy brief stints in the glare that comes along with celebrity, but it is also a *big* energy drain. Julia Roberts is known to be a lively introvert. In an interview in *Time,* she said that when she is making a movie, she naps through most lunch breaks. "It makes me a much nicer person the rest of the day," she said. Many introverts with public lives must create time away from the dazzle.

Teasing Apart the Terms: Shy, Schizoid, and Highly Sensitive

Maybe being oneself is always an acquired taste.
—PATRICIA HAMPL

Shy, schizoid, and *highly sensitive* are fuzzy terms often used interchangeably with *introversion.* They are *not* the same as introversion, but I think each word captures some important aspect of human experience. Let me define each of the terms so it isn't so blurry and describe what each one illustrates. Both introverts and extroverts can be shy, schizoid, or highly sensitive.

Introversion: This is a healthy capacity to tune into your inner world. It is a constructive and creative quality that is found in many independent thinkers whose contributions have enriched the world. Introverts have social skills, they like people, and they enjoy some types of socializing. However, party chitchat depletes their energy while giving them little in return. Introverts enjoy one-on-one conversations, but group activities can be overstimulating and drain energy.

Shyness: Shyness is social anxiety, an extreme self-consciousness when one is around people. It may have some genetic roots (in the form of a highly reactive fear center), but it is usually learned from experiences at school, with friends, and in families. For some, it comes and goes at various ages and in certain situations. Shy people may feel uncomfortable with one-on-one conversations or in group situations. It is not an issue of energy; it is a lack of confidence in social situations. It is a fear of what others think of you. It produces sweating, shaking, red face or neck, racing heart, self-criticism, and a belief that people are laughing at you. It's a feeling that you are the only person standing in a giant beam of a klieg light and you wish the floor would open up and swallow you. Shyness is not who *you are* (like introversion), it is what you think *other* people think you are, and therefore it is responsive to behavior change. Extroverts who need to be with others to refuel can suffer greatly if they are shy. The good news is that learning strategies to alter your behavior can significantly reduce shyness. I have included several practical books on shyness in the Bibliography at the end of this book. Try some of the suggestions in these books. They work.

Schizoid: People with this disorder live in a painful dilemma. They need relationships, yet they fear close involvement with other people. In most cases, the individuals have grown up in traumatizing and/or neglectful homes and have withdrawn or detached to avoid any more pain from human contact. The schizoid personality disorder is a common diagnosis in the mental health field. Too many psychotherapists confuse it with introversion and shyness, as if they were all the same thing. They're not.

Introverted Characters

"Oh, Pooh! Do you think it's a-a-a Woozle?"
—PIGLET

Some of our most beloved literary, film, and television characters are introverted. Probably because so many writers and artists are introverted, so they include introverts in their work. Look over the list and think of the qualities like wisdom, the ability to think outside the box, the capacity to notice details, consideration for the needs of the group, and the ability to make difficult decisions.

- **Owl, Piglet** (shy introvert), and **Christopher Robin,**
  in *The Complete Tales of Winnie-the-Pooh*

- **Radar,** on M*A*S*H

- **Linus Van Pelt, Schroeder, Franklin,** and **Marcie,** from *Peanuts*

- **Jean-Luc Picard** and **Counselor Troi,** on *Star Trek, the Next Generation*

- **Ally McBeal,** in *Ally McBeal*

- **President Josiah Bartlet,** in *The West Wing*

- **Hercule Poirot,** detective

- *The Thinker,* sculpture

- **Atticus Finch,** in *To Kill a Mockingbird*

- **Jonas,** in *The Giver*

Highly sensitive: These are people who are born with a certain cluster of traits that is often described as a sixth sense. They are extremely perceptive, intuitive, and observant, with finer discrimination than most of us. They may stay away from social engagements because they dread the agonizing flooding of their senses. Introverts or extroverts can be highly sensitive, and Elaine Aron's excellent books on highly sensitive people are listed in the Bibliography.

If you are in psychotherapy, be sure your therapist knows the difference between all four of these terms.

Guilty as Charged, or Should the Charges Be Dropped?

Let's now take aim at two of the most common charges lobbed at introverts—that they are self-centered and unsociable. It's easy to see why introverts can appear self-absorbed or uninterested, because we shut down external stimulation when we have had enough. Why? We need to compare external experiences to our own internal experience, attempting to understand new information against our old information. We think, How did that experience effect me?

Rather than being self-centered, introverts are often really the opposite. Our ability to focus on our internal world and reflect on what we are feeling and experiencing allows us to understand the external world and other human beings better. What appears to be self-centeredness is actually the very talent that provides the capacity to understand what it's like to put ourselves in someone else's shoes.

Extroverts are also focused on the *self,* but in a different way. Extroverts like socializing and require the company of other people, but it's as much about the need to be stimulated—engage me, challenge me, give me something to react to—as it is to feel related. Since extroverts don't generate as much internal stimulation as introverts do, they need to get it from outside. Maybe this is why extroverts put introverts down—we annoy them because they feel we are withholding, and we threaten them because we don't shoot the breeze or socialize in the way they need.

This brings me to another major distortion about introverts—that they're antisocial. Introverts aren't unsocial—they are just social in a different way. Introverts need fewer relationships, but they like more connection and intimacy. Since it takes a great deal of our energy to engage with other people, we are reluctant to need to spend too much energy on socializing. That's why we don't enjoy idle chitchat. We prefer meaty conversations, which nourish and energize us. Such conversations give us a hit of what happiness researchers call "Hap Hits." When we munch on meaty thoughts, we get a good feeling of satisfaction and enjoyment. Energy conservation is also why we are very interested in other people but sometimes prefer to observe others rather than join them.

Self-Absorbed or Self-Reflective?

It's ironic that introverts are considered self-absorbed when often one of psychotherapists' major tasks when working with new clients is to help them *develop* the ability to be self-reflective. We struggle to get them to step back from outside activities so they can observe their own thoughts, feelings, and actions. Without self-reflection, it's all too easy for people to get caught up in a cycle of repeating the same behaviors over and over. For some strange reason, extroverts, who are usually much less skilled at self-reflection than introverts, are considered healthier than introverts, even in the field of psychology.

Extroverted brains release a few Hap Hits just by being in the crowd or sitting in the stands cheering madly for their team. Sitting quietly on the sidelines would make them wilt with boredom. Since extroverts get their energy from social sources and activities, they like being out on the town, flitting from flower to flower. They say, Just give me the stimulation jolt, and off I go. Again, it is just a *different* method of socializing, not a *better* method. Don't let people charge you with guilt for your temperament. You are not doing anything *to* extroverts because you are different. Drop the charges against yourself.

Shooting from the Lip

If nature intended us to talk more than listen,
she would have given us two mouths and one ear.
—ANONYMOUS

Extroverts, being the majority, influence the entire cultural view of introversion. Extroverts' verbal case intimidates introverts, making it even easier for them to conclude that they shouldn't speak. In his book *Psychology of Personality: Viewpoints, Research, and Applications,* Dr. Bernardo J. Carducci, one of the leading researchers on shyness, states, "Our founding fathers were rejected for their religious beliefs, so they took great pains to assure the freedom for all of us to speak our mind. Today we value boldness and individuality. 'Talkers' are perceived as influential and become role models. We place a great premium on verbal ability, courage and candor." It's interesting that "individuality" in this case means the qualities of an *extroverted* individual. Oration is valued in most Western societies. Think of popular television shows like the *McLaughlin Group, Crossfire,* or *Hardball.* Verbal jousting is the name of the game.

Introverts don't talk for talk's sake. When they speak, they speak their mind. Sometimes they withhold even that. One day several institute friends of mine were going to afternoon tea. Jamie, a smart, quiet gal, said, "I only allow myself two comments per seminar." "Please don't," everyone jumped in. "We love your comments." Jamie was so surprised. She would not have received that feedback if she hadn't mentioned her seminar strategy. She feared, as many introverts do, that she would take up too much space. We reminded her that we wanted to hear her valuable comments.

Our country places a high value on silver-tongued folks who appear confident and decisive. Introverts often exhibit the exact opposite qualities of these "in-charge types" we esteem so highly. This creates a gap between the introverts and extroverts filled with misunderstanding and faultfinding.

Why Innies
Unsettle Outies

One of the greatest necessities in America
is to discover creative solitude.
—Carl Sandburg

There are reasons why introverts sometimes feel so alien—as if our spacecraft landed on the wrong planet—and are so often misunderstood. Introverts reveal less of themselves and their actions; they can appear aloof and mysterious. And as we've seen, many societies extol the virtues of extroversion, and many extroverts cast a dubious eye on the gifts introverts bring to the world. Sadly, often we don't even comprehend our own contributions.

Let's look at some of the qualities of introverts that might contribute to extroverts' suspicions. As you look over this list, remember that introverts can be even more confusing; as their energy ebbs and flows, they may not appear consistent. One day their batteries may be well charged and they're chatty and outgoing. Another day they are draggin' their wagon and can barely talk at all. This can confuse and confound the people who know them.

Introverts are more likely to:

- Keep energy inside, making it difficult for others to know them
- Be absorbed in thought
- Hesitate before speaking
- Avoid crowds and seek quiet
- Lose sight of what others are doing
- Proceed cautiously in meeting people and participate only in selected activities
- Not offer ideas freely; may need to be asked their opinion
- Get agitated without enough time alone or undisturbed
- Reflect and act in a careful way
- Not show much facial expression or reaction

Looking at the list, it's easy to see why extroverts would think we are a bit mysterious. Three main differences between introverts and extroverts cause rifts to widen into vast misunderstandings.

1. Introverts Think and Talk Differently

Extroverts think and talk all at one time. It is effortless to them. In fact, things become clearer as they speak out loud. Introverts, on the other hand, need time to think and don't speak with spontaneity unless it's a familiar subject. Introverts can appear cautious or passive to extroverts. Extroverts are so used to speaking off the top of their heads that they may be distrustful of more reticent introverts. When introverts speak with hesitation, extroverts may feel impatient. Just spit it out, they think. Why don't they have more confidence in their own opinion? What are they trying to hide? Extroverts may experience an introvert as withholding information or ideas. After a meeting, for example, I have had several extroverted acquaintances ask me why I didn't speak up and tell them what was on my mind. Why didn't I participate and give my opinion?

Steeped in the Language

> How much easier it is to be critical
> than to be correct.
> —BENJAMIN DISRAELI

When perceptions are deeply held in cultures, they are woven into the language. Our language reflects the values and beliefs that we hold and that hold us. I looked up *introversion* in several dictionaries and a thesaurus. In the *Dictionary of Psychology* it is defined as: ". . . orientation inward toward the self. The introvert is preoccupied with his own thoughts, avoids social contact and tends to turn away from reality." *The International Dictionary of Psychology* states that introversion is: ". . . a major personality trait characterized by a preoccupation with the self, lack of sociability, and passiveness." In *Webster's New Collegiate Dictionary,* introversion is described as: ". . . the state or tendency toward being wholly or predominately concerned with and interested in one's own mental life." And now sit down for this one, *Webster's New World Thesaurus,* in which the introvert is said to be: ". . . a brooder, self-observer, egoist, narcissist, solitary,

I've never understood why in the world anyone would view me as hiding anything. But as I've mentioned, I have been told that I'm "mysterious." From my standpoint, when I do speak, I mean what I say. I reveal my thoughts and point of view. But apparently, in the extrovert's view, I take so darn long to say what I want to say that they think I'm holding something back *on purpose.*

Extroverts need to learn that introverts require time to form and articulate opinions. However, extroverts also ought to be aware that if introverts have carefully thought out their ideas on a subject, or know a lot about a topic, then watch out—the formerly quiet innies' lips will start flapping fast and furious.

lone wolf and loner." When I read this, I started picturing the Unabomber in his meager cabin in the woods.

When I looked up *extroversion* in the same reference books, it quickly became clear why most of us feel a little fishy about being introverted. In the *Dictionary of Psychology* it said: ". . . a tendency to direct the personality outward, the extrovert is social, a man [I'm sure they mean women, too] of action, and one whose motives are conditioned by external events." In *The International Dictionary of Psychology:* ". . . extroversion is marked by interest in the outside world, including confidence, sociability, assertiveness, sensation-seeking and dominance." In *Webster's New Collegiate Dictionary,* it reads: ". . . marked by obtaining gratification from what is outside the self, friendly, uninhibited." Finally, *Webster's New World Thesaurus* defines extroversion as: ". . . other-directed person, gregarious, life of the party, show-off." That's as bad as it gets for extroverts. Are you beginning to get the drift? When I sound a little bit as if I am tooting the horn for introverts in this book, I am. I'm just attempting to level the playing field. It's been uneven for too long.

2. Introverts Are Unseen

When introverts appear reluctant to speak or speak slowly, they often don't engage extroverts. Extroverts may think (introverts can think this, too) that the introverts don't have anything to contribute. Introverts dislike interrupting, so they might say something softly or without emphasis. Other times comments made by introverts have more depth than the general level of the conversation; because this may make people feel uncomfortable, they ignore the comment. Later another person may say the *same thing* and receive a great response. The introverted person feels unseen. It's frustrating and confusing for them.

From the outside, many introverts give no hint about the mental gears grinding and meshing inside. In social situations their faces may look impassive or uninterested. Unless they are overwhelmed or they really are disinterested (if the topic is too lightweight), they are usually just thinking about what people are saying. They will share their thoughts if asked. I have learned over the years to inquire about what introverted clients are thinking or feeling. Almost always they say something that expands what we have been talking about. But their faces are so blank I had no idea if they were a million miles away or not. Others in a group setting may start to exclude introverts if they don't keep eye contact and don't give clues that they are listening.

3. Introverts Pressure Extroverts to Stop and Think

The third reason extroverts are mistrustful of introverts is because we do something many extroverts hate—we dare to suggest that they stop reacting and start reflecting before barging ahead. It unnerves extroverts when introverts suggest that they slow things down, plan, think about consequences, and focus longer before acting. Extroverts can already see the end of the project, like new flowers freshly planted in the backyard. They are ready to go to the nursery and buy colorful plants. They're like racehorses; they whinny and tug at the reins if you try to restrain them. Slower-paced introverts, by contrast, like to stop and smell the roses. "Let's just sit and gaze at the backyard and think how we want to plant it first," they say. Trying to get them to "step it up" is like trying to speed up a tortoise. Even if you light a fire under their bellies, they just can't increase their pace. Innies and outies can definitely rub one another the wrong way.

Blamed and Defamed

To err is human; to blame it on
the other guy is even more human.
—Bob Goddard

Growing up constantly being compared to extroverts can be very damaging. Most introverted children grow up receiving the message overtly and covertly that something is wrong with them. They feel blamed—why can't they answer the question faster? And defamed— maybe they *aren't* very smart. Forty-nine of the fifty introverts I interviewed felt they had been reproached and maligned for being the way they were. However, number fifty, Greg, a minister, did not.

I had heard Greg give a talk in which he referred to himself quite casually as an introvert. And immediately afterward I asked him if I could interview him for this book. I wanted to find out why he appeared so unfazed about his introversion. As it turned out, he came from a whole family of introverts, so he never experienced that fish-out-of-water feeling. With a basic sense of accepting himself nurtured early, Greg has created a balanced introverted life.

This example shows how important a nurturing environment is for our nature. Unfortunately, most of us didn't grow up in families who accepted and nurtured introverted qualities.

Introverted children usually get the message loud and clear that something is wrong with them. In a study that was replicated three times with the same findings, introverts and extroverts were asked if they would prefer their ideal self to be extroverted or introverted. They were also asked if they would prefer their ideal leader to be introverted or extroverted. Reflecting the prejudices in our culture, both introverts and extroverts choose extroverts as their ideal self and their ideal leader. We live in a culture that caters to and extols extroverts. We definitely learn extroversion is the way we *should* be.

Blame Leads to Guilt and Shame

I have worked with a number of intelligent, introverted clients who thought they had a fundamental defect, that something was actually missing from their brain. To make matters worse, they felt shame and guilt. People often use the words guilt and shame interchangeably, but they are really different feelings, albeit sometimes difficult to distinguish.

Shame is an intensely mortifying and painful feeling that clings to your body like steamy tar stuck with feathers. It's hard to let go of the sicky, icky feeling. Clues that you are experiencing shame may include:

- an impulse to shrink or hide
- the wish to disappear
- the sense that your whole body is withering
- the feeling that speaking is even harder than usual

Shame is related to *being*. We feel shame when we think we are unworthy or innately flawed. The result of shame is the feeling of helplessness and hopelessness. Shame impels us to withdraw and conceal ourselves.

There are lots of sayings that reflect shame: *I wanted to crawl under a rock. Shame on you. I hoped the floor would open up and swallow me.* Shame is a crummy feeling. It squashes joy in sharing our inner world with those around us. Instead we feel that it hurts too much to be excited and show ourselves, that we need to stay hidden.

Shame is a complex and confusing feeling, and conditions have to be just right for it to be set off, much the way that specific atmospheric conditions need to exist for a flash of lightning to split the sky and a crack of thunder to be heard. In order for someone to experience shame, he or she must want to be engaged in *revealing* something deeply personal to another. Think of showing your friend something you are very proud of. This is the "atmospheric condition" needed for shame to be triggered—you intend to offer yourself up to be noticed. If, instead of appreciation, you receive a grimace or a look of disgust, anger, disapproval, or disregard, it can trigger an intense feeling of wanting to hide yourself. In other words, *shame.*

Although shame affects everyone, it is a double whammy for introverts. If we are shamed, we have few resources left to calm ourselves. We may withdraw and not show ourselves for a long time. This is a loss for everyone.

Guilt is a much less complex emotion, and it is connected with our actions. Guilt is an uncomfortable, nagging feeling of having *done something wrong*, like getting caught with your hand in the proverbial cookie jar.

We often feel guilt when we harm someone. Or when we have broken a rule or regulation and we are concerned about getting caught. Guilt motivates us to confess what we did wrong and to make restitution.

Too much guilt can cause introverts to withdraw. There are a number of reasons introverts may feel guilty. Many introverts see the bigger picture of how we are all interconnected, so they are concerned about how their actions affect others. Introverts may also think that what bothers them—for example, interruptions—bothers everyone. Since they are often quite observant, they may feel guilty over small indiscretions. Many times they are worried about mistreating others when they really haven't. Furthermore, to avoid doing something that might cause harm to another person, introverts sometimes retreat even more from the world, thereby reducing their own satisfaction with life. Society, too, is cheated of their contributions.

Antidotes to Guilt and Shame

Feelings are everywhere—be gentle.
—J. MASAI

Learning to manage shame and guilt is important for introverts; otherwise, we may spend a lot of time feeling miserable. Use these remedies to get yourself back on track.

■ If you feel guilty, try to find out if you *really* hurt someone. Sometimes we think we offended another person when we didn't. For instance, introverts don't like to interrupt people. If they do jump into a conversation and step on someone's words, they can feel guilty. But many people don't mind being interrupted. So before you assume you're responsible for upsetting someone, check with the person. Maybe she didn't react the way you thought she did. Say to yourself, "I was a little nervous about joining the conversation, and I interrupted Jane; she doesn't seem upset. It's okay."

- If you hurt someone, apologize sincerely. Then move on. "Oh Jane, I'm sorry, I didn't let you finish. What were you saying?" The main antidote to guilt is apologizing. We all make mistakes. Forgive yourself.

- If you feel the cringing, sticky feeling of shame, try to figure out what set it off. For instance, if a colleague asks you a question in a meeting and you want to respond but can't think of anything to say, it may trigger a feeling of shame in you. You feel yourself wanting to hide. I am no good; I'm not smart, you think. Stop. Say to yourself, "That is just how my brain works. I don't always have a quick answer. Neither did Albert Einstein. I can tell my colleague that I need to think the question over and get back to her." Then let it go. The main antidote to shame is self-esteem. Tell yourself that you are not flawed. Nothing is wrong with you. Your brain works in another way. Mulling is a useful activity. It's good to be you.

Taking Your Temperament Temperature

Keep high aspirations,
moderate expectations and small needs.
—H. Stein

The more introverted you are, the more likely you are to have encountered shame and guilt about who you are. And the more you have probably felt misunderstood, even by yourself. These experiences may have driven you to withdraw. There are two techniques that can help you guard against withdrawing too much: One is to learn to use the antidotes for guilt and shame described above. The second is to learn to read your temperament temperature. Like reading the mercury level on a thermometer, you can become adept at taking your energy temperature.

You can estimate your energy level each day. Then you can adjust your day or week or life in order to maintain a balance of supply and demand. In doing so, you can become a confident introvert, less vulnerable to getting overtired, experiencing a mind gone blank, or feeling shamed and blamed by others. Let's give it a try.

Has Aunt Vera been visiting? Did she follow you around the house talking eighty miles an hour for a week? Notice what you feel like. Leaden arms? Buzzing head? Exhausted body? Do your feet feel as if they are encased in cement boots? If so, you need to build lots of breaks into your days this week in order to recover your energy. Alternatively, have you been tucked up in your tranquil home all weekend? Your body feels energized. All sorts of ideas about what you want to do are buzzing in your head. You are raring to go. This is a good time to do some things you have been putting off.

Obviously, most of the time your energy level won't be this crystal clear, so here are some questions to ask yourself to get a reading:

- What is my mental energy level? Alert? Fuzzy? Brain dead?

- What is my body energy level? Pooped? Pert? Peppy?

- Do I feel overstimulated or understimulated?

- What do I have to do today? What is optional?

- Can I add anything if I have more energy?

- Can I put off anything if I'm running on low fuel? or empty?

- Can I put extra breaks in my schedule?

- Do I need time alone?

■ What kind of alone time do I need (e.g., reading, napping, staring out the window, sitting quietly inside, listening to music, watching television)?

■ Could I benefit from some external stimulation (seeing friends, going to a museum)?

■ What do I need today?

If you practice scanning your body and checking on your mental energy, you can learn to read your temperament temperature. If someone asks you to go out for Chinese food, you will feel more confident about saying yes if you are recharged. If you are low on fuel, then you can say no without feeling guilt or shame or fear that you will never go out again. You know you will accept the next time your fuel tank is topped off.

Points to Ponder

■ Even public figures are introverts.

■ Introverts are not necessarily shy, schizoid, or highly sensitive.

■ Most introverts have been blamed, shamed, and defamed. Learn the antidotes.

■ Learn to take your temperament temperature.

CHAPTER III

The Emerging Brainscape: Born to Be Introverted?

Within you there is a stillness and a sanctuary to which you can retreat any time and be yourself.

—HERMANN HESSE

How do we end up with a more introverted or a more extroverted temperament? The brain has been slow to yield its secrets. Until recently we could only understand what is happening in the brain by observing behavior and making inferences about what *might* be happening. Carl Jung made an informed "guess" that introversion and extroversion had a physiological foundation; in the early 1900s he had no way to be certain. Now, with the advancing technology of brain scans and imaging, we are closer to understanding the communication pathways in the brain and how they are reflected in human behavior. We can, for example, map the territory inside our brains and connect precise areas of brain activity to specific experiences and behaviors. Mind mapping also clarifies and validates which brain functions influence temperament.

Scientists are still in the exploration stages of brain travel, but it appears to be an incredibly complex landscape. This is reflected in the fact that almost every researcher has a slightly different theory about how the brain works. Some of the ideas I present in this chapter are still speculative. It will take years to gain more certainty. Still, we are on our way to unlocking the brain's marvelous and mysterious secrets.

Each of us is born with certain basic ingredients or inborn traits that make up our temperament. In her book *Molecules of Emotion*, Candice Pert attempts to tease apart temperament from other human characteristics: "The experts also distinguish among emotion, mood, and temperament, with emotion being the most transient and clearly identifiable in terms of what causes it; with mood lasting for hours and days and being less easily traced; and with temperament being genetically based, so that we're generally stuck with it (give or take certain modifications) for a lifetime." In addition to the fact that it is fairly stable over time and is under genetic influence, researchers agree that temperament has two other basic qualities: it varies among individuals and appears early in life.

There is no real consensus about the basic traits that constitute temperament. Nonetheless, introversion/extroversion is consistently included on every personality theorist's list of traits, and it is considered the most reliable construct of temperament.

Temperament Diversity

The most incomprehensible thing about the universe
is that it is comprehensible.
—ALBERT EINSTEIN

The current explosion in gene and brain mapping is creating a scientific window into the mysteries of human nature. Some of Charles Darwin's theories are being combined with those of psychology to form a new perspective called evolutionary psychology. Researchers in this field wonder if certain behavioral strategies increase our chances for survival and reproduction. Darwin studied the finches on the Galapagos Islands. He found that in response to environmental demands, the birds had adapted and developed specialized beaks. The diversity of beaks allowed them access to different feeding niches. Instead of eating only insects, they could now eat a varied diet consisting of insects, berries, seeds, and nuts. This increased the entire species' chances for survival.

When Jung, an admirer of Darwin, first wrote about introversion and extroversion, it was clear that he was thinking about temperament from an evolutionary perspective. He saw each variation of temperament as requiring its own optimal environment, a natural niche where it could flower. Having people who thrive in different optimal environments increases the chances of survival of the human race as a whole. It is nature's way to preserve her species.

Introverts, Jung wrote, conserve their energy, have fewer children, have more ways of protecting themselves, and live longer. Because they appreciate a simpler life, make intimate attachments, and plan and reflect on new ways of doing things, they encourage others to be prudent, develop self-reflection, and think before acting.

Jung thought extroverts, on the other hand, expend their energy, propagate more often, have fewer ways of protecting themselves, and die off faster. Extroverts act quickly when danger threatens and have the ability to get along with large groups. Because they have a quest for venturing farther afield to locate new land, food, and other cultures, they encourage far-ranging exploration.

Stability in nature is often based on tension between opposing forces. Quick-moving hares and slow-moving tortoises. Introverts and extroverts. Men and women. Thinking and feeling. Human beings are built to be adaptive. We are hardwired never to be completely balanced or satisfied, and this keeps us physiologically limber and desiring change. We have the capacity to conform to many diverse surroundings.

The human body's stability is based on the principal of adapting while remaining steady. The body has opposing regulatory mechanisms that maintain a fluid *balance*. Like teeter-totters, all body systems have an excite, or "turn up," side and an inhibit, or "turn down," side. Various set points in the body signal if something is out of whack. The signals travel through interconnected feedback loops, turning systems up or down until the body is back in a fluctuating homeostasis.

Since the beginning of humankind, people have attempted to explain the obvious differences among people, and often these differences were looked at through the lens of balance. Beginning in the fourth and fifth centuries B.C., the theory of humors was all the rage. For a balanced temperament it was thought the body needed equal amounts of four humors: yellow bile, black bile, blood, and phlegm. In China the balance was based upon the five forces of energy called *ch'i*—wood, fire, earth, metal, and water. Over the centuries many different categorizing schemes came in and out of fashion. The concept of innate temperament was forced underground for decades after the Nazis abused the concept by employing racial stereotypes as a pretext to murder Jewish people, Gypsies, homosexuals, and members of other groups. Only recently, with the technological advances in psychobiology, twin research, animal research, and studies of brain-injured patients has the notion of temperament been resurrected.

It has long been recognized that we all have a natural temperament climate in which we feel more comfortable, perform our best, and maintain a crucial balance for our species. What is new is that we are beginning to understand how temperament is a function of underlying brain mechanisms.

The Recipe for You

Nature is often hidden,
sometimes overcome,
seldom extinguished.
—SIR FRANCIS BACON

W here does our temperament come from? It begins with genes. We are shaped by our genes. Our genes are inherited chemical recipes that determine the makeup of each person: the cells, tissues, organs, and systems that create the intricate networks of our body and mind. All human beings have 99.9 percent of the same genetic prescription. Our individual differences come from the 0.1 percent of our genetic material that is *just us*. The genes of chimps and humans are 98 percent the same. It doesn't take much genetic material to make us quite different!

How do genes affect our temperament? Temperamental differences appear to be derived primarily from our neurochemistry. Our genetic inheritance includes a private reserve of about 150 different brain chemicals and recipes to formulate our neurotransmitters. Neurotransmitters guide messages from cell to cell, directing all brain functions. At present, about sixty neurotransmitters have been identified. The main ones are dopamine, serotonin, noradrenaline, acetylcholine, and endorphins. These neurotransmitters have certain pathways in the brain. As they travel along the pathway, they direct *where* the blood circulates and regulate *how much* of it flows to various brain centers. The route and quantity of blood flow influences what parts of the brain and central nervous centers are "turned on." Our response to the world and how we behave depend on what parts of the systems are activated.

In Your Genes

Let's trace the effect of one gene, D4DR, that influences temperament. Keep in mind that no *one* gene causes a specific temperament. However D4DR, or the "novelty-seeking gene," has been studied extensively, and the results are quite startling. It is housed on chromosome 11, which Matt Ridley, in his book *Genome, the Autobiography of a Species in 23 Chapters,* named the personality chromosome because of its influence on behavior. Studies of this gene began to unravel the differences in temperament between routine-loving Queen Victoria and thrill-seeking Lawrence of Arabia.

The D4DR gene affects the neurotransmitter dopamine, which controls excitement levels and is vital for physical activity and motivation. Dean Hamer, chief of gene structure and regulation at the National Cancer Institute in Bethesda, Maryland, studied the D4DR gene by testing families of people who like to bungee jump, skydive, and ice climb. Seeking experience for the sake of doing something new is their passion; they like far-out music, exotic travel, and anything novel. They can't stand repetitive experiences, routine work, and boring people. They can be impulsive and temperamental, and they may fall into addictions and risk burning out early in life. They are fast talkers and persuaders. They are willing to take risks to gain rewards. Their strengths are living life to the fullest and pushing the limits to new heights. The novelty seekers were found to have a long D4DR gene and were less sensitive to the neurotransmitter dopamine. Therefore, they need to experience life's thrills and chills in order to produce higher levels of dopamine.

Hamer then studied people whom he identified as "low-novelty seekers." He concluded that their D4DR genes were short and that they are highly sensitive to dopamine. Because they receive enough dopamine in quiet activities, they don't need as much "buzz" in their lives. They also receive a different kind of good feeling from another neurotransmitter that I will discuss later.

Low-novelty seekers tend to be reflective individuals who are perfectly content to live at a slower pace. They feel more discomfort than enjoyment from thrill seeking or risk taking. Orderly and cautious, they enjoy the comfort of routine and the familiar; thus, they don't

An Internal Life

Imagine having an active mind trapped inside a body that is entirely paralyzed except for the ability to move your eyes sideways and blink your eyelids. A few people are living in this nightmare, called Locked-In Syndrome. A mere millimeter makes the difference between ending up in a coma (unconscious) or in Locked-In Syndrome (conscious).

Both are caused by trauma to the brain stem (located at the base of the neck and involved in regulating basic body functions). If the trauma is to the front of the brain stem, the motor pathways are destroyed but patients are alert. Since the nerves for blinking and eye movement are at the back of the brain stem, they can still move their eyes. This tragic condition has given us an intriguing clue about the connection between acetylcholine and the enjoyment introverts gain from introspection. Although it seems as if people with Locked-In Syndrome should feel claustrophobic and terrified, researchers were shocked to find they don't. Although sad about their situation, these patients report a sense of tranquility and lack of terror about their loss of physical freedom. In these patients acetylcholine is blocked to the muscles but not to brain pathways, so their capacity to feel good about living in their internal world (the enjoyment from thinking and feeling) remains intact.

incur much risk. Low-novelty seekers like to see the big picture before plunging ahead, and they focus well on long-term projects. They are even-tempered, good listeners, and loyal.

As Hamer says in *Living with Our Genes*, "High and low novelty seekers don't differ in their desire to feel good—everyone likes to feel good—but they differ in what makes them feel good. High scorers need excitement for the brain to feel good. The same level of arousal makes a low scorer feel anxious. A steady predicable situation would bore a high scorer but comfort a low scorer."

Don't these low- and high-novelty seekers sound a lot like introverts and extroverts? Although not described by researchers in those terms, I think they come pretty close to characterizing the two extremes of the temperament continuum. Dopamine appears to play an important part in what brain pathways introverts and extroverts use and how those circuits affect their temperament and behavior.

Tracking Brain Tributaries

Turtle buries its thoughts, like its eggs, in the sand,
and allows the sea to hatch the little ones.
—NATIVE AMERICAN SAYING

Brain research has uncovered that the brain has separate pathways for different neurotransmitters. Many studies have traced the brain pathways associated with the personality dimension of introversion/ extroversion. However, until we could actually visually image the amount and location of blood flow in the brain, we were still in the educated-guess arena.

Dr. Debra Johnson reported in the *American Journal of Psychiatry* the first attempt to replicate, using positron emission tomography

(PET), earlier brain-function studies of introverts/extroverts. Dr. Johnson asked a group of introverts and a group of extroverts (who were determined by responses to questionnaires) to lie down and relax. Tiny doses of radioactivity were injected into their bloodstream. Then they were scanned to determine the most active part of the brain. On the scan, red, blue, and other bright colors revealed where and how much blood flowed in the brain.

The researcher discovered two findings that replicated what less sophisticated experiments had already suggested. First, introverts had *more* blood flow to their brains than extroverts. More blood flow indicates more internal stimulation. Anytime blood flows to an area of your body, like when you cut your finger, that area becomes more sensitive. Second, the introverts' and extroverts' blood traveled along different pathways. Dr. Johnson found the introverts' pathway is more complicated and focused internally. The introverts' blood flowed to the parts of the brain involved with internal experiences like remembering, solving problems, and planning. This pathway is long and complex. The introverts were attending to their internal thoughts and feelings.

Word Retrieval

Often introverts have trouble finding the word they want when they are speaking *out loud*. Our brains use many different areas for speaking, reading, and writing; therefore, information needs to flow freely between the separate areas. Word retrieval may be a problem for introverts because the information moves slowly. One cause of this is that we use long-term memory, so it takes longer and requires the right association (something that reminds us of the word) to reach back into our long-term memory to locate the exact word we want. If we are anxious, it may be even more difficult to find and articulate a word. Written words use different pathways in the brain, which seems to flow fluently for many introverts.

Dr. Johnson tracked the fast-acting brain pathway of extroverts, showing how they process input that influences their activity and motivation. The extroverts' blood flowed to the areas of the brain where visual, auditory, touch, and taste (excluding smell) sensory processing occurs. Their main pathway is short and less complicated. The extroverts attended externally to what was happening in the lab. They were soaking in sensory input. This study validated a key concept in the introvert/extrovert temperament puzzle. Dr. Johnson concluded that the behavioral differences between introverts and extroverts result from using different brain pathways that influence where we direct our focus—internally or externally.

As an extrovert, Dana is exuberant at a roaring football game, drinking in the sights and sounds. She is excited and uses her short-term memory to chat with her partner, Nathan, about the game during halftime, recounting all the plays. She feels energized and "up" as she leaves the stadium.

Peter, an introvert, is going to a museum, looking forward to seeing his favorite Monet. As he enters the museum, which is not crowded, he feels overwhelmed; he reduces his focus immediately, perhaps without even realizing it. Straightaway he heads for the room where the Monet hangs. He thinks about the Monet and his response to it, reaching back into his long-term memory, comparing the current experience with the last time he saw the painting. He imagines future visits and connects the gentle feelings of wistfulness and a tingle of excitement with the experience. Inside his head Peter talks to himself about the subtle pastels in the painting. He leaves the museum feeling good.

By learning the exact circuits of the brain that are activated by introverts and extroverts, we shed light on some of the reasons we behave the way we do. But the most valuable clue is yet to come.

Tracking Neurotransmitter
Paw Prints

Not only does introverts' and extroverts' blood travel on separate pathways, each pathway requires a different neurotransmitter. As we recall, Dean Hamer found that novelty seekers, based on their genes, need to pursue thrills to meet their greater demand for dopamine. I said they sounded a lot like extreme extroverts. And, it turns out, the pathway extroverts use is activated by dopamine. Dopamine is a powerful neurotransmitter most closely identified with movement, attention, alert states, and learning. In *Mapping the Mind*, Rita Carter states, "Too much dopamine seems to cause hallucinations and paranoia. Too little dopamine is known to cause tremor and the inability to start voluntary movement, and is implicated in feelings of meaninglessness, lethargy and misery. Low dopamine also results in lack of attention and concentration, cravings and withdrawal." Having the right amount of dopamine for your body is critical. And it has another important job. In *States of Mind*, Steven Hyman says, "One way of characterizing the job of this dopamine circuit is that it's a reward system. It says, in effect, 'that was good, let's do that again, and let's remember exactly how we did it.'" That is why cocaine and amphetamines are so addictive—they increase dopamine.

Since extroverts have a low sensitivity to dopamine and yet require large amounts of it, how do they get enough? Parts of the brain release some dopamine. But extroverts need its sidekick, adrenaline, which is released from the action of the sympathetic nervous system, to make more dopamine in the brain. So the more active the extrovert is, the more Hap Hits are fired and dopamine is increased. Extroverts feel good when they have places to go and people to see.

Introverts, on the other hand, are highly sensitive to dopamine. Too much dopamine and they feel overstimulated. Introverts use an entirely different neurotransmitter, acetylcholine, on their more dominant pathway. In *Wet Mind,* Stephen Kosslyn and Oliver Koenig site the brain pathway for acetylcholine, and guess what? It is the same pathway Dr. Johnson imaged for introverts. Acetylcholine is another important neurotransmitter connected to many vital functions in the brain and body. It affects attention and learning (especially perceptual learning), influences the ability to sustain a calm, alert feeling and to utilize long-term memory, and activates voluntary movement. It stimulates a good feeling when thinking and feeling. Much of the present research into acetylcholine strengthens our understanding of the introvert's brain and body.

Acetylcholine was the first neurotransmitter identified, but, as other neurotransmitters were detected, research focused on the newer ones. Recently, however, a connection was made between a deficiency of acetylcholine and Alzheimer's disease. This finding has prompted more research into acetylcholine and its connection with memory storage and dream processes. It seems that acetylcholine plays a large part in our sleep and dream states. We dream when we are in REM sleep. Acetylcholine switches on REM sleep, initiating dreaming, and then paralyzes us (disengages voluntary movement) so that we dream without "acting out" what we are dreaming. Researchers are finding that we need sleep to encode our memories, advancing them from short-term memories into long-term memories during REM sleep. As Ronald Kotulak says in his book *Inside the Brain,* "Acetylcholine is the oil that makes the memory machine function. When it dries up the machine freezes." One other interesting tidbit is that estrogen prevents a decline in acetylcholine. This is one of the reasons why during menopause, as their estrogen levels decline, women experience memory loss. So introverts require a limited range of not too much or too little dopamine, and a good level of acetylcholine, to leave them feeling calm and without depression or anxiety. It's a skimpy comfort zone.

Discovering what neurotransmitters introverts and extroverts use is pivotal because when neurotransmitters are released in the brain, they also engage the autonomic nervous system. This is the system that connects the mind and body and greatly influences our decisions about how we behave and react to our world. I think the link between which neurotransmitters travel what pathways and how they connect with different parts of the autonomic nervous center is the master key to unlocking the temperament puzzle. Whereas extroverts are linked with the dopamine/adrenaline, energy-spending, sympathetic nervous

---

The Nicotine Connection

A clue to the mystery about why introverts and extroverts feel different in contemplation and activity is derived from an odd source—research into why folks are addicted to smoking. In studies, smokers report they smoke because they feel as if they concentrate better, learn easier, remember better, and possess a "perked-up" feeling. Nicotine receptors in the brain mimic the action of acetylcholine. Pathways using acetylcholine, which increases attention, memory, and a sense of well-being, dominate introverts.

Nicotine also causes the body to release dopamine, and it influences the breakdown of serotonin and norepinephrine, all neurotransmitters that are activated in extroverts when they are active. Cigarettes trigger a sense of well-being from both sides of the introverted and extroverted continuum, so no wonder so many people smoke, even when they know the dangers.

---

system, introverts are connected with the acetylcholine, energy-conserving, parasympathetic nervous system.

Longer Introvert Acetylcholine Pathway

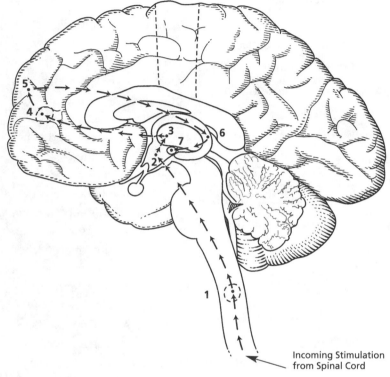

Incoming Stimulation
from Spinal Cord

1. Reticular Activating System - Stimuli enter here where alertness is regulated. Decreased in introverts

2. Hypothalamus - Regulates thirst, temperature, and appetite. Turns on the Throttle-Down System in introverts

3. Anterior Thalamus - Relay station—sends stimuli to frontal lobe and turns stimuli down in introverts

4. Broca's Area - Speech area where inner monologue is activated

5. Frontal Lobe - Where thinking, planning, learning, and reasoning are engaged

6. Hippocampus - Attuned to the environment and relays to long-term memory

7. Amygdala - Emotional center, where feelings are attached to thoughts in introverts

Shorter Extrovert Dopamine Pathway

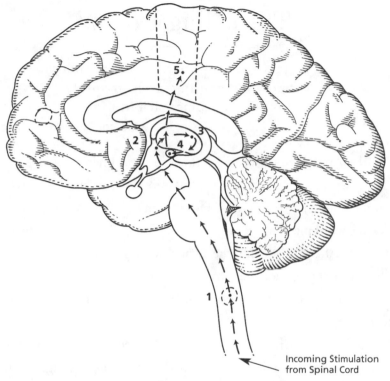

Incoming Stimulation
from Spinal Cord

1. Reticular Activating System - Stimuli enter here where alertness is regulated. Increased in extroverts

2. Hypothalamus - Regulates thirst, temperature, and appetite. Turns on the Full-Throttle System in extroverts

3. Posterior Thalamus - Relay station—sends increased stimuli to amygdala

4. Amygdala - Emotional center, where emotions are attached to actions in the motor area in extroverts

5. Temporal and Motor Area - Movement connects to working memory (short-term). Also the center for learning and processing sensory and emotional stimuli

Full-Throttling Ahead or
Throttling Down

Life begets energy—energy creates energy.
It is only by spending oneself wisely
that one becomes rich in life.

—ELEANOR ROOSEVELT

The hypothalamus, located at the base of the brain and only the size of a pea, regulates body temperature, emotions, hunger, thirst, and the autonomic nervous system. This system was named *autonomic* from a Greek word meaning "self-governing." There are two branches of the autonomic nervous system, the sympathetic and the parasympathetic. These act in opposition to each other, like the gas pedal and the brake in an automobile. They control involuntary, unconscious functions such as heart rate, respiration, and blood vessel regulation and are the most directly involved in maintaining our fluid homeostasis. They function in a feedback circle, sending messages back to the brain through the neurotransmitters that they release, regulating energy, mood, and health.

When mobility is required, the sympathetic system—often called the "fight, fright, or flight" system—leaps into action. I call it the Full-Throttle System. It is activated by the excitatory neurotransmitter dopamine in the brain. When withdrawal is required, the parasympathetic system, which I am calling the Throttle-Down System, relaxes the body and calms us down. It is activated by the inhibitory neurotransmitter acetylcholine in the brain.

It is my belief that these two powerful primary systems, the Full-Throttle (sympathetic) and the Throttle-Down (parasympathetic), are the basic foundations of introverted and extroverted temperaments. In his book *Affect Regulation and the Origin of the Self,* Dr. Allan Schore states that each person has a rest point between the two sides of these systems. The rest point is where we gain the most energy and feel the best. Throughout our lives we will fluctuate around our rest points. In a personal conversation with Dr. Schore, he stated that "temperament is key"; if we know our rest point, then we can adjust our energy to achieve our goals.

Supporting my conclusion, researchers David Lester and Diane Berry selected introverts and extroverts on the basis of questionnaires and then tested their physiological responses such as high or low blood pressure, physical activity level, moist or dry mouth, and frequency of hunger pangs. They reported in the journal *Perceptual and Motor Skills* that they found the parasympathetic branch of the autonomic nervous system to be dominant in introverts.

The Full-Throttle System

Let's say you are walking around the block at about nine P.M. and suddenly, out of the blue, a large coyote circles you, his head low, his eyes sizing you up for a tasty evening snack. Your body accelerates into the Full-Throttle System. Your pupils dilate to let in more light. Your heart pumps faster against your chest, and your blood pressure elevates to give your organs and muscles extra oxygen. Your blood vessels constrict to reduce bleeding in case you are wounded. Your brain is signaled to go on hyperfocused alert. Your blood sugar and free fatty acids are elevated to give you more energy. Your digestion, saliva, and elimination processes slow down. This fight, fright, or flight system is activated for emergencies, real or imagined. It is our active external coping system. It prepares us to make snap decisions to fight if needed or to head for the hills. Thinking is reduced, and the focus is on activity. In this situation, we need this system to wave our arms and yell at the coyote or, if all else fails, make fast tracks.

Full-Throttle/Throttle-Down Systems

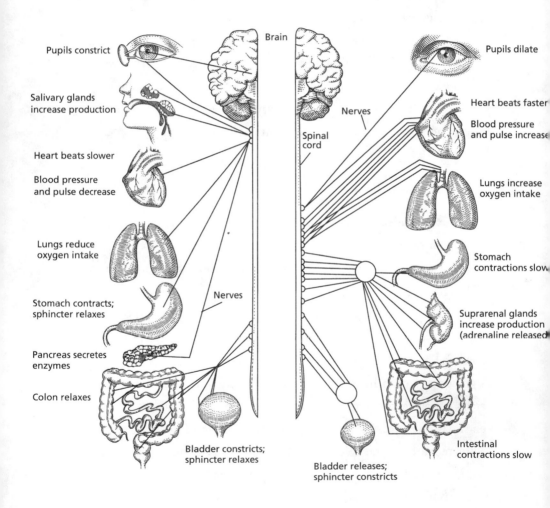

Parasympathetic (Throttle-Down) System

Sympathetic (Full-Throttle) System

Pupils constrict

Salivary glands increase production

Heart beats slower

Blood pressure and pulse decrease

Lungs reduce oxygen intake

Stomach contracts; sphincter relaxes

Pancreas secretes enzymes

Colon relaxes

Brain

Spinal cord

Nerves

Nerves

Bladder constricts; sphincter relaxes

Bladder releases; sphincter constricts

Pupils dilate

Heart beats faster

Blood pressure and pulse increase

Lungs increase oxygen intake

Stomach contractions slow

Suprarenal glands increase production (adrenaline released)

Intestinal contractions slow

Our bodies run primarily on this system until we are almost two years old. This gives us the energy and the enthusiasm to explore the world—what developmental psychologists call the "practicing phase." As adults, the sympathetic nervous system mobilizes us toward new things—food, new frontiers, and companionship, all of which we need for survival. When we are active, inquisitive, or daring, we are using this system. If we are sitting in the stands cheering for our favorite baseball team, this system releases energy by sending *feel good* neurotransmitters to our brain. It also releases glycogen and oxygen to our body for energy.

As we have seen, extroverts feel more energized by active behaviors. The Full-Throttle System is spending-oriented, and it doesn't restore the body. However, if extroverts don't learn to use the Throttle-Down System, they can burn out and damage their health. They can develop sleep and digestive problems, heart disease, and deficiencies in their immune system. The Throttle-Down System doesn't give extroverts the energy or Hap Hits (which I mentioned in Chapter 2), the Full-Throttle System does. By learning to use the Throttle-Down System by attending to thoughts, feelings, bodily sensations, and body messages, extroverts can balance their natural external strengths by developing internal capacities.

The Throttle-Down System

Picture yourself strolling down a dusty path in Big Sur. You lean on a rock to watch the tumbling waterfall. Suddenly you hear a rattle. It sounds very close. You slowly turn your head to spy a coiled diamondback rattlesnake quivering his rattle and staring beady eyes straight at you. Your body turns into petrified wood, and everything slows down. A lightbulb flashes on in your brain; what should you do? These are responses of the system responsible for energy conservation and storage, the parasympathetic nervous system. This system signals the body to conserve and withdraw. Your pupils constrict to reduce light. Your heart rate and blood pressure slow to reduce oxygen consumption; your muscles relax. Digestion, secretions, and elimination increase, which is why it is sometimes called the rest-and-digest system. Outward focus is reduced, and inward focus is increased. The mind is able to think and reflect. You decide to creep with micromovements away from the rock and the ominous snake.

This system becomes more active when children are around eighteen months to two years old. We learn to calm ourselves down in order to learn potty training and language. When you are lying in a hammock watching the clouds or just kicking back, this is the system

The Keys to Unlocking Your Long-Term Memory

Human memory is complex and uses many different areas of the brain. The brain stores memories in numerous locations and creates links between them called associations. Often we introverts think nothing relevant is in our head because we haven't triggered the association to our long-term memory. Our mind seems blank. This is why introverts can even forget what we like to do or what we are good at. We need to locate a connecting handle to yank an experience out of our memory. Here's the neat thing—most pieces of information in long-term memory were stored with several handles or keys (associations) for unlocking them. If we find just one key, we can retrieve the whole memory.

So let's say you like to paint or fish or walk around a park with flowers in bloom, but that information is locked in long-term memory. You have some free time, but you can't remember what you like to do. This may sounds nuts to an extrovert, but it is a you are engaging. Your body is storing, not spending, energy. Introverts' "feel good" neurotransmitters are firing as they relax in pensive contemplation. This system is restorative and prepares us to use the Full-Throttle System when it is required. The Full-Throttle System does not give introverts energy or Hap Hits, the way extroverts experience them. To people with an introverted physiology, all that dopamine and adrenaline usually feels too stimulating. Occasionally, it can be fun.

Introverts who stay in the Throttle-Down System too much can become depressed, unmotivated, or frustrated about not reaching goals they want to attain. They need to engage the Full-Throttle side of their system to get up and out. This requires learning to regulate anxiety and overstimulation, which I will be discussing later.

common problem of introverts. Remember, it takes only one key like a thought, emotion, or sensory association to open the whole memory.

Sit down, relax, and let your mind wander and associate to possible sensory keys, like smells, visual pictures, sounds, the feel of your body, or the taste of something pleasant. Or think of an emotional key, like how you felt the last time that you did something fun. Let your mind go anywhere it wants; jumping from association to association is okay.

Maybe the peaceful feeling of sitting in a park on a sunny day returns to you and with it the thought: I like Oak Park; I enjoyed going there. Now you could go to the park or relax and look for another memory. Write down the memories you find to use another day when you can't remember what you enjoy. Use these keys to unlock your memory to search for what you are good at, too.

The Full-Throttle and Throttle-Down Systems on the Road

Obviously, we need the ability to use the sympathetic and parasympathetic nervous systems at different times. But, under stress, our most dominant system is set into motion. For example, several years ago Mike and I were involved in a car accident. We were driving on a narrow, two-lane highway at night, and suddenly something huge flew at our windshield. Mike swerved over the double yellow line. Luckily, the oncoming lane was empty. The massive flying object missed us and hit the station wagon behind us. Mike pulled over to the side of the road and stopped. I didn't move; my body felt numb, and my breathing slowed. I didn't want Mike to get out of the car. In my mind I could see him getting hit by oncoming traffic. Mike, his heart racing, was thinking only of taking action. He opened his door and leaped out to see if anyone was hurt.

I went into my dominant system, the Throttle-Down (to halt and examine), while Mike was catapulted into his dominant system, the Full-Throttle (to bound out and *do* something).

It turned out that a mule had escaped his enclosure and meandered into the road. He had been hit by a pickup truck and crashed into its windshield. Then the ill-fated creature flew over us (because Mike dodged quickly, exhibiting good Full-Throttle reaction) and hit the hood of the car behind us. My Throttle-Down reluctance to get out of the car was sensible. It was a pitch-black night on a two-lane highway with cars strewn katywompus all over the road. It was dangerous. I wanted to assess the situation, a good strategy. Mike's Full-Throttle response, checking on the injured, was helpful. As it turned out, no humans were badly hurt. We were fortunate. Sadly, the mule wasn't so fortunate. Several of the men dragged the mule's body off the road before any other unsuspecting travelers could hit it.

To sum up, although we all need *both* of these systems for balance, we are genetically and environmentally wired to use one more than the other, especially under stress. I believe the two sides of the autonomic nervous system provide the introvert/extrovert continuum. Although we all engage both sides of the nervous system, our brains and neurotransmitters make one side dominant.

The Big Picture

If we combine the recipes from genetics, messages given by neurotransmitters, brain pathways, and functions of the autonomic nervous centers, what picture emerges? The complete process and feedback loop for each end of the introvert/extrovert continuum. Although I will simplify them, these are the basic components. Of course, we all have both systems, one to focus on the outside world and one to focus on the inside world; however, one will feel more restorative and energizing because of how our brains react to the neurotransmitters.

The Introverted Process

Introverts walk around with lots of thoughts and feelings in their heads. They are mulling—comparing old and new experiences. They often have an ongoing dialogue with themselves. Since this is such a familiar experience, they may not realize that *other* minds work in different ways. Some introverts aren't even aware that they think so much, or that they need time for ideas or solutions to "pop" into their heads. They need to reach back into long-term memory to locate information. This requires reflection time without pressure. They also need to give themselves physical space to let their feelings and impressions bubble up. During REM sleep or while dreaming, this

Our Physiology, Ourselves

You can observe a lot just by watching.
—YOGI BERRA

The terms introvert and extrovert have been used to describe people for almost a hundred years. Why? In part because being an introvert or extrovert is easy to read in many of our behaviors. And these behaviors stem from our physiology. Let's take a look.

Introvert Brain-Body Circuits

As we have seen, the introverted brain has a higher level of internal activity and thinking than the extroverted brain. It is dominated by the long, slow acetylcholine pathway. Acetylcholine also triggers the Throttle-Down (parasympathetic nervous) system that controls certain body functions and influences how innies behave.

The fact that introverts' brains are buzzing means that innies are likely to:
- Reduce eye contact when speaking to focus on collecting words and thoughts; increase eye contact when listening to take in information
- Surprise others with their wealth of information
- Shy away from too much attention or focus
- Appear glazed, dazed, or zoned out when stressed, tired, or in groups

The dominance of the l-o-n-g acetylcholine pathway means that introverts:
- May start talking in the middle of a thought, which can confuse others
- Have a good memory but take a long time to retrieve memories
- Can forget things they know very well—might stumble around when explaining their job or temporarily forget a word they want to use
- May think they told you something when they just have thought it
- Are clearer about ideas, thoughts, and feelings after sleeping on them
- May not be aware of their thoughts unless they write or talk about them

The activation of the parasympathetic nervous system means that introverts:
- May have trouble getting motivated or moving, might appear lazy
- May be slow to react under stress

- May have a calm or reserved manner; may walk, talk, or eat slowly
- May need to regulate protein intake and body temperature
- Must have breaks to restore energy

Extrovert Brain-Body Circuits

The extroverted brain has less internal activity than the introverted brain. It scans the external world to gather stimulation to fuel the shorter, quicker dopamine pathway. The signals from the brain travel to the Full-Throttle (sympathetic nervous) system that controls certain body functions and influences how outies behave.

The fact that extroverts' brains are constantly seeking new input means that outies are likely to:
- Crave outside stimulation; dislike being alone too long
- Increase eye contact when speaking to take in others' reactions; decrease eye contact when listening to notice what's happening in the environment
- Enjoy talking—and be skilled at it; feel energized by attention or the limelight

The dominance of the short dopamine pathway means that extroverts:
- Shoot from the lip, and talk more than listen
- Have a good short-term memory that allows quick thinking
- Do well on timed tests or under pressure
- Feel invigorated by discussion, novelty, experiences
- Make social chitchat easily and fluidly

The activation of the sympathetic nervous system means that extroverts are likely to:
- Act quickly under stress
- Enjoy moving their bodies and excercising
- Have high energy levels, not need to eat as often
- Be uncomfortable if they have nothing to do
- Slow down or burn out in mid-life

pathway integrates daily experiences and stores them in long-term memory, where they are filed in many areas of the brain. Introverts are in a constant distilling process that requires lots of "innergy."

Acetylcholine also triggers the hypothalamus to send a message to the parasympathetic nervous system to conserve energy. This system slows the body down, allowing introverts to contemplate and examine the situation. If a decision is made to take action, it will require conscious thought and energy to get the body moving. This explains why many introverts can sit for long periods while they are concentrating. Acetlycholine also rewards concentration by giving Hap Hits but doesn't give the charge of glucose and oxygen (energy) to the body. The introverted process results in behavior affecting all areas of an innie's life.

The Extroverted Process

Extroverts are alert for sensory and emotional input. When they get stimuli, they can answer quickly because the pathway is rapid and responsive. Their short-term memory is on the tip of their tongue, so while the introvert is still waiting for a word, the extrovert has spit out several. Extroverts need more input to keep their feedback loop working. Their system alerts the sympathetic nervous system, which is designed to take action without too much thinking. It releases adrenaline, blood (oxygen) to muscles and glucose, thus flooding the body with energy. The release of neurotransmitters from various organs enters the feedback loop, sending components back to the brain to make more dopamine. Dopamine and adrenaline release Hap Hits from the "feel good" center. No wonder extroverts don't want to slow down.

For introverts, all that adrenaline and glucose soon leaves them feeling wiped out. It is too stimulating, consumes too much fuel, and leaves them with their fuel tank empty. Since they don't get as many Hap Hits from dopamine and adrenaline, and acetylcholine isn't increased in this feedback loop, they don't receive the same good feelings extroverts do from this side of the system.

Of Two Minds

There is a foolish corner
in the brain of the wisest man.
—ARISTOTLE

Nature has made the brain a marriage of two minds. The brain is divided into two halves, the right and left cerebral hemispheres. In some ways the two hemispheres act as if they are two separate brains. Paradoxically, they also act as a whole unit. The twin hemispheres are bound together by a bridge of fibers (called the "corpus callosum") that allow a steady stream of dialogue to pass back and forth, but each hemisphere appears to specialize in certain functions and behaviors. Research has found that some folks use both hemispheres equally (called bilateral dominance) but, as with the autonomic nervous system, most people depend on one hemisphere more often than the other. "Right-brained" and "left-brained" dominant introverts display different talents, behaviors, and limitations.

During the first two years of life, we primarily use our symbol-oriented right brains. This is why babies can learn sign language at about nine or ten months: their right-brain mind can connect a symbol with a meaning. Waving means bye-bye. Finger on the lips means hungry. (I have included in the Bibliography a great book about teaching babies sign language, entitled *Baby Signs*.) The left-brain mind becomes active around eighteen months to two years of age, when language begins to appear. Remember that this is when the Throttle-Down System also begins to function. Our "practicing stage" is slowed down so we can learn to think and speak.

The Right Brain

Each half of the mature brain has its own strengths and weaknesses, its own style of processing information and unique skills. Right-brained talents bring spontaneous, creative, and boundless gifts to the world. It is sometimes referred to as the unconscious mind. It has little language ability and cannot verbalize its thinking process. Rather, its thinking is formed in a rapid, complex, and spatial manner. Right-brained people can do several tasks at once. They are emotional and can be funny or playful.

Right-brained functions are difficult to explain because they are, by nature, nonverbal, abstract, holistic, simultaneous, and unlimited. They resemble an ever-changing, multicolored kaleidoscope in which the tumbling chips of color slide into a variety of patterns. The right-brain mind is expressed in body language, actions, free-flowing dancing, and various art forms.

Right or Left?

Introverts do not all think alike. Introverts, who are more right-brained, process information, use language, and intuit in a way that's quite unlike left-brained introverts. If, as you read this book, you find that what I am saying doesn't quite fit you, it may be because the topic is influenced by brain dominance. For example, left-brained introverts may feel more comfortable speaking in public than right-brained introverts. So, if I say introverts have difficulty finding words at times, that experience may not resonate at all with you. As you read through this section, see if you think you are more right- or left-brain dominant.

It deals with the creative aspects of human life such as rhythm, day-dreaming, images, colors, face recognition, and pattern shaping.

If you are more right-brained, you may tend to:
- Be playful in solving problems
- Respond to events with emotion
- Interpret body language easily
- Have a good sense of humor
- Process information subjectively
- Improvise
- Use metaphors and analogies when describing something
- Deal with several problems at once
- Use hands a lot in conversation
- Notice patterns and think in pictures
- See solutions as approximate and evolving
- Not realize all that you know

The Left Brain

The left brain is one of the main reasons we have been a successful species. It helps execute complicated plans. If your left-brain mind is dominant, you handle information very differently from right-brainers. Left-brained folks process one thing at a time, and if they have a series of tasks to do, they like to finish one before starting another. They are often list makers. They rely more on short-term memory, repetition, and verbal skills. You may have guessed that more men than women are left-brained. Left-brained folks tend to be tidy, methodical, and punctual. They value written and verbal information. They tend to think in concrete ways, as if they are processing data. They like to reduce information

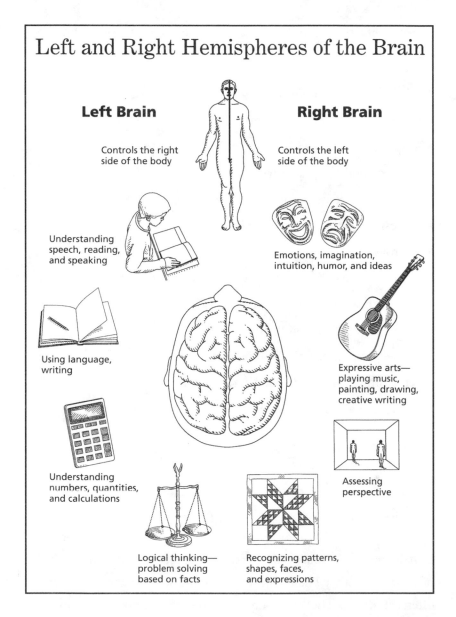

Left and Right Hemispheres of the Brain

Left Brain

Controls the right
side of the body

Understanding
speech, reading,
and speaking

Using language,
writing

Understanding
numbers, quantities,
and calculations

Logical thinking—
problem solving
based on facts

Right Brain

Controls the left
side of the body

Emotions, imagination,
intuition, humor, and ideas

Expressive arts—
playing music,
painting, drawing,
creative writing

Assessing
perspective

Recognizing patterns,
shapes, faces,
and expressions

into logical sections. In decision making they are not so influenced by emotions. If they have a sense of humor, it will be more in the witty or sarcastic department. They may appear somewhat controlled, cool, and detached.

Food for Thought

Here are a few more morsels relating to introversion and extroversion from the world of scientific research:

- Extroverts have more trouble with the law, divorce more, change jobs more, gain and lose more friends, and have more conflicts in general than introverts.

- Introverts do better on tasks that require careful attention, like air traffic controllers. Extroverts would get bored watching the screen: "Oh, another 747."

- Extroverts do better in grade school and on exams, but introverts do better in college and graduate school.

- In a study on pain, extroverts complained more about pain but seemed to have higher tolerance than introverts.

- In a test of memory tasks, the introverts performed better than the extroverts regardless of whether they received positive, negative, or no feedback. The extroverts' performance was improved by receiving positive feedback.

- Introverts tend to have more sleep problems.

- A study of 258 college students found that extroverts had higher self-esteem than introverts.

- Innie and outie middle school children discuss topics differently. Outies tend to contradict and give counterexamples while innies worked collaboratively to develop creative solutions.

- Extroverts adapt more quickly to time-zone changes than introverts.

- Extroverts prefer nonsense humor and introverts prefer humor that resolves something that is incongruent.

Left-brained introverts are closer to most people's stereotype of an introvert. They may have fewer social needs and are often focused on a career or hobby. They may use denial or obsessive thinking as a way to protect themselves from anxiety.

If you are more left-brained, you may tend to:

- Analyze pros and cons before taking action
- Be neat and tidy
- Base decisions on facts, not on sentimentality
- Give concrete examples when describing something
- Think in terms of right and wrong; good and bad
- Process experiences objectively
- Be keenly aware of time
- Proceed one step at a time
- Not pick up social cues easily
- Like to categorize
- Be idea-oriented
- Be comfortable with words and numbers
- Seek exact solutions

Play to Your Strengths

It is important for introverts to know their brain dominance to understand themselves better. I think left-brained introverts may be more comfortable living life as an introvert. They may have fewer social needs, so they may not be as conflicted over spending time alone. Often they are more verbal and logical than right-brained introverts, so they are able to succeed better at school, work, and in meetings. Many engineers, accountants, and computer jocks fit this profile. Since these individuals may be less emotional and focused on the smaller picture, they may feel okay about themselves or not even notice they are different.

Right-brained introverts have numerous talents, but many of them are difficult to translate into traditional job skills. They are creative and may seem eccentric or curious to others. The term *starving artists* was coined for these folks. Notice how many actors are on my list of well-known introverts in Chapter 2. Most are probably right-brained. Since right-brained introverts feel more emotions and see the big picture, they may feel quite sensitive about their differentness.

Educational systems are set up for left-brained learning, which requires logic, verbal ability, analytical questioning, fast responses (timed tests), and quick memorization. Children who are right-brained are often at a disadvantage and unappreciated. One of the reason's Daniel Goleman's book *Emotional Intelligence* was so popular was because he championed the strengths of right-brained people. Right-brained people often struggle with feeling misunderstood and experience bouts of depression.

Right-brained and left-brained dominance affects how we learn. It is important to realize that if you are more right-brained, you learn new material best by seeing whole patterns in images. If you can picture a new concept in your mind, you will understand it better. So illustrations or examples work best. Theories and explanations may not impress right-brained people; they learn well by doing and by asking questions as they are learning. Right-brained-dominant people respond better to metaphors and analogies than to commentary or narrative thought.

Left-brained people take in new material in sequence. They learn by repetition and understanding principles, main points, and theoretical ideas. They may need to   word or the word of an authoritative source. They may need data that supports what someone says in order to trust their information.

To sum up, in this chapter I discussed some of the ingredients that combine to make an introverted temperament. Our brains are incredible marvels. Genes create our neurotransmitters, predisposing us to take delight in the tried and true. Neurotransmitters dispatch more blood to our contemplative brain centers, so we are reflecting on our experiences as we go through our day. Our physiology inclines us to use the Throttle-Down System during stress, so we tend to pull back and appraise rather than rush into action. The last key element in determining our outlook is brain dominance: Do we process information from the world in our right brain or left brain?

By understanding the way *your* brain works, you can reduce shame and guilt. You can create the optimal environment for yourself. You can enhance your appreciation of your own unique introverted advantages.

Points to Ponder

- All humans are born with a temperament predisposition.
- Varied temperaments expand our species' chances for survival.
- Genes provide the recipes for our neurotransmitters.
- Neurotransmitters direct what parts of our brains and nervous systems we use.
- Right or left brain dominance affects how we process information and respond to the world.

PART II

Navigating the Extroverted Waters

If your ship doesn't come in, swim out to it.

—JONATHAN WINTERS

CHAPTER IV

Relationships: Face the Music and Dance

One of the oldest human needs is having someone to wonder where you are when you don't come home at night.

—MARGARET MEAD

Relationships are like dancing. One, two, three; one, two, three, oops—"That's my toe," your partner says. Then you glide, glide, glide for a while. He executes a dip, and *boom*, he drops you! He twirls and spins away, then returns and takes your hand again. So goes the choreography between couples. There will always be times when one partner is disco dancing and the other partner is doing the cha-cha.

No relationship is easy. Each has a few faux pas and more than a few stepped-on toes. Whether you are in an innie/innie relationship or an innie/outie union, there's tricky footwork to learn. Learning about some of the ways your temperament preference affects your relationship can help improve your dancing and help you glide more and bruise each other's toes less. Understanding each person's temperament reduces blame, criticism, defensiveness, and withholding, which are the major trip-ups in relationships.

Dancing into Dating

Love is the magician that pulls man
out of his own hat.
—BEN HECHT

While some introverts are perfectly happy without a committed relationship, most prefer to be intimately involved with someone. This usually means that at one time or another they have to foray into the world of dating. This is often a daunting task that many introverts approach with trepidation. Like stepping onto a floor filled with frantic jitterbugging, dating requires a huge outlay of energy. At the same time, it increases the need for processing time and cuts into recharging time. You have to plan outings, talk to an unfamiliar person, reflect about what went on, and process stirred-up emotions.

To avoid having to make a first move, introverts often find partners by being set up on dates or introduced by a friend, co-worker, or family member. Still, there are times when an introvert has to be the initiator. Think of dating like learning a new dance. It's an unfamiliar experience, and the footwork feels clumsy and awkward. But the payoff—tripping the light fantastic—is worth it.

We see many introverts married or in partnership with extroverts, and there are several good reasons for this. For one thing, there are more extroverts—three extroverts for every one introvert—and they are easier to meet. While introverts may be surfing the Internet, taking a solo bike ride, or snuggled up reading at home, extroverts are *out there* mingling—at parties, sports clubs, or professional organizations. And then there's the issue of "otherness." Carl Jung thought that as humans we are constantly seeking to be a complete person. Therefore, he believed, we are attracted to and select mates who are our opposites. Another reason introverts are drawn to extroverts is because extroverts often assume the talking and "doing" duties in the relationship, which means introverts can relax and feel less pressured.

To introverts, extroverts look as if they could leap tall buildings in a single bound. Look, up in the sky, it's SuperExtrovert, I remember thinking when I first met Mike. Boy, he really gets a lot done, all the people in his family are such busy, busy bees. Since, at the time, I was thinking something was *wrong* with me (which, as I said earlier, many introverts tend to do), I figured what they did was "right." It was a long time before I realized that it wasn't a question of right or wrong, but of differences.

Dating is a *process* that allows you to sort out your reactions to someone and his or her reactions to you. You will need to prepare yourself for dating slowly but steadily.

Gradually Gearing Up to Meet Someone New

First of all, get the word out. Tell your friends and family that you are ready to date. Give them some general guidelines about what type of person you might be interested in, such as age range, personality type (e.g., introvert or extrovert), career, interests, education, and hobbies. Don't forget a few of your top personal quality choices—sense of humor, loyalty, insightfulness, or demonstrativeness. Make a list of all of *your* nifty qualities and tape it to your bathroom mirror. Reread the list every morning. Believe it.

As you begin, if your feet get a little chilly, remember that you're on an adventure and that it will be fascinating to uncover a new person and discover his or her view of the world. Congratulate yourself for any steps you take.

Listed below are some ideas to get you started, to rev your engine, as it were. Pick and choose; they are only suggestions. There is no right way to date. Have fun.

■ Think of places that provide opportunities for short encounters—elevators, the cleaners, the dog park—where you can meet people by smiling and saying hello.

■ Ask introverted friends about dating strategies that have worked for them; how they met their spouse or partner.

■ Peruse a book or two on dating, and pick two things out of the book to try each week.

■ Practice some comments to say about yourself when you meet someone new.

■ Sign up for a group that has activities you are interested in, like the Sierra Club or a folk-dance group. Subscribe to lecture series or take a music class.

■ Volunteer for a group whose philosophy you respect, like Habitat for Humanity or the Make-a-Wish Foundation.

■ Make a list of introverted activities you might like to do on a date.

The Dating Process

Why did Mother Nature dream up dating? It is an important process to help us get to know other people in an intimate way, to learn how they react to life events. Do they withdraw if they are uncomfortable? Do they get angry easily? Do they blame others? Do they give you room to respond? Are they kind to the elderly, pets, and children? Do they need constant attention? How do they spend their leisure time? You can see how you feel over time with potential partners. Do you have good talks? Are the silences comfortable? Do you feel invigorated or bored, controlled or ignored? It's important to let the process unfold. Don't rush into selecting the first person you date as "the one." Sometimes introverts want to cut the dating process short because of the energy costs and the feelings of discomfort. Think how

Dating Strategies

With the anticipation (sometimes anxiety) leading up to it, trying to be on top of your game during it, and the stimulation of getting to know someone new, dating can be exhausting. Here are some tips to make it go smoothly.

- Make the first meeting short, e.g., have coffee or a drink. Suggest a specific start and stop time.
- Meet at a neutral location so you can leave if you want.
- Use your good observational skills to gain information about the person.
- Reveal as much personal information as the other person does, within reason.
- Take a bathroom break or two if you're feeling anxious or overexcited.
- Don't try to be extroverted!
- Don't rely on alcohol or drugs to help you loosen up.
- Don't overextend yourself; watch your energy level.
- Notice if you are getting irritable and think about why.
- Don't push yourself to have physical contact; you need time to feel comfortable.
- Look for red flags, such as how he or she handles conflict. Note whether you think he or she is too passive or too aggressive.
- Pay attention to any uncomfortable feelings you have, such as anger, fear, or boredom. Think about what messages these feelings are sending you.

good you will feel when you can finally glide through a date with less apprehension. This is where your Throttle-Down System is helpful. Go slowly. Give yourself time to think about the date and see what comes to your mind. Stick to your own pace. Give yourself processing time.

The First Date

The big rendezvous is almost here. You will probably be both nervous and excited. That's okay. Stay in a curious mode, wondering, What will tonight be like? Stay inquisitive about your date, and you will feel less jittery. Think to yourself, My body may be feeling physical excitement. It may not be fear at all. And always remember to breathe.

Pay attention to your energy level during the date. Do you feel energized around this person or depleted? Are you having a good time but your energy is dropping? If so, explain to your date that you are having fun but that your energy is plunging, so you need to end the date soon. Notice how good the person is at understanding what you are saying.

Here are some other tips to help the date go well:

- Remember to take breaks and small steps to regulate your energy outlay. Remind yourself that your date is not draining you on purpose—you feel drained after most socializing.
- Avoid criticizing an extroverted date in your mind for his or her fast-paced, reactive style.
- Ask how your date spends his or her leisure time.
- Notice if your date asks you any questions. Does he or she do most of the talking? Determine if you're out with a good listener.
- Does your date listen but not talk much about him- or herself?
- Have some fun. Dating doesn't have to be serious.

When Personality Types Collide

*The goal in marriage is not to think alike,
but to think together.*

—ROBERT DODDS

At heart we are all social animals, and although we want independence, we also long to be part of a duo. Even with the divorce rate hovering around 50 percent, most divorced people find new partners and remarry within a few years. Couples want fulfilling relationships. It's just that "fulfilling" means something different to each person. Some of the information below may help you to clarify what is fulfilling for you.

Relationships aren't easy. Even highly compatible couples misstep. Certainly temperament differences increase the possibility of getting tripped up. Misunderstandings can arise for all sorts of reasons, and it's important to realize that differences aren't fatal. Differences are neutral. In relationships, differences really boil down to specific behaviors and outlook. One person moves slow, one fast. A wife likes to sleep in; her husband wants to get up and get going. The husband doesn't want to socialize, and his wife wants the whole family to come over. These differences are neither good nor bad. It's how you *interpret* them. They can add spice to a relationship, or they can pull couples apart.

So what makes relationships flourish? John Gottman, Ph.D., a relationship researcher for over twenty-five years, says it is the way a couple handles the *conflicts of differences* that determines how long their marriage lasts and how satisfied they are. In fact, it's useful to see differences as an opportunity to strengthen the bond between a couple. Things go south quickly in relationships when partners see each other's behavior as a rejection or an attack rather than as an expression of the other person's character or personality type. "You know I hate it when you interrupt me; you just don't want to hear my opinion," an introverted husband might say to his extroverted wife. If we don't take differences personally, then new dance steps can be created to resolve conflicts. We need to learn to move in and out of our partner's space, know when to lead, when to follow, and how to adapt to ever-changing relationship footwork.

I am going to describe three relationship combinations: innie male with outie female, innie female with outie male, and innie with innie. Each combination has its challenges and strengths, and all three types can improve their relationship by interacting with good-hearted consideration.

These examples involve heterosexuals. If you are in a gay relationship, look at the three couples and find the one that best fits your relationship dynamics. I have worked with many gay couples over the years, and I have found the same strengths and challenges apply to same-sex relationships.

Innie Male with Outie Female: The Challenging Couple

The cultural environment heavily influences the course of our intimate relationships. For example, when the male is an extrovert and the female is an introvert, conflicts often arise. However, research suggests that the most serious conflicts occur if the situation is reversed— the male is the introvert and the female is the extrovert. This combination goes against our social conditioning. Introverted men can feel overwhelmed, intimidated, and unheard by extroverted women. And extroverted women may believe that the introverted man's quiet nature means he is weak, submissive, or unprotective. They can also feel lonely and understimulated by the relationship. These duos can solve their problems, but they won't be able to change each other's hardwired temperament.

Not long ago, Andrew and Brooke came to see me because their marriage was strained, and they had identified lots of trouble spots. After a few minutes, I pegged them as an innie-outie couple— Andrew being the innie and Brooke the outie.

I asked Andrew what he was most frustrated about in their relationship. He began, "I just don't see why we can't kick back, enjoy our home, and relax on—" "You just want to avoid everything," Brooke interrupted. Then she added, "You're such a wimp." Andrew looked down at the floor and clammed up. "Brooke," I said, "I'd like to hear Andrew's view of the problem; then I'd like to hear your take on it." The clock ticked loudly for several minutes before Andrew finally spoke again. "I would just like to relax more and 'do-do-do' less," he said in a low voice, not looking at Brooke. "Brooke," I said, "can you explain why relaxing is tough for you?" "It sounds like napping in a coffin to me," she said, glaring at Andrew. "I feel like I'm living inside a tornado," Andrew shot back.

The real problem for Andrew and Brooke is that underneath this fight they both feel flawed. Andrew secretly believes he should speed up; Brooke, on the other hand, is afraid to pull over at a rest stop. The shame they feel about their basic temperaments shows up in withdrawing and blaming. They don't think they are lovable for who they are.

You can see how this pattern could cause serious problems in a relationship. So how can such a couple smooth out their differences without stepping on each other's toes? Some fancy footwork and a lot of honesty are required.

Going from Slam Dancing to Soft-Shoe

Brooke and Andrew need to have an honest conversation about the disappointments they have experienced as well as their expectations and hopes they hold for their relationship. It can be painful to discuss your honest feelings of embarrassment and shame. Andrew may feel self-conscious about his anxiety and fear. Brooke may feel uncomfortable about being put off by Andrew's lack of traditional masculine traits. But only by opening up to each other and discussing their culturally based expectations for males and females can they begin to cast their own roles in *their* relationship and take the necessary steps to save it. In an equal relationship, both partners try to be attuned to each other's needs and attempt to meet them. Both people feel acknowledged and cared for. The suggestions below are jumping-off points, which you can adapt to your particular situation.

Meeting the Challenge of a New Pattern

Begin by scheduling a series of meetings to talk—without interruptions—about your relationship. Negotiate a start and stop time. Wednesday nights at eight P.M. for four weeks, starting the following week. Reward yourselves by sharing a favorite dessert or going to a movie. *Always stop on time.* It may be harder than it sounds to stick to the agreement. If you have trouble, discuss your reasons. Sometimes it may be frightening to talk about feelings and perceptions. Acknowledge that and then start again.

First Session

- Speak about how each of you sees your role in the relationship, with each partner getting about fifteen minutes.
- Discuss what the roles were in your parents' marriage.
- Talk only about your own view; let your partner talk about his or her view.
- Restate what your partner said, with each person talking for about five minutes.
- Check with your partner. Was your summation of his or her views more or less accurate?
- Restate any discrepancies.
- Thank your partner for participating.

Second Session

- Talk about what you see as the strengths and weaknesses of your roles, with each partner using about fifteen minutes. For example, the male partner may talk about how he brings his thoughts and observations to the marriage but limits communication by not discussing his feelings. The female partner may talk about how she gets a lot accomplished for the family but reduces the chances for intimacy by not slowing down.
- Rephrase what you each heard the other say; clarify any misunderstandings.
- Discuss for five minutes how you are feeling right now; stop for a moment and check your body if you aren't sure what you are feeling.

- Restate how you imagine your partner is feeling: scared, frustrated, excited, drained, etc.

Third Session

- Each partner picks two ways to change *his or her own role* in the relationship. For example, the female partner might work on needing to be right all the time, being overcritical, improving her listening skills, practicing relaxing, or letting her partner lead. The male partner might work on being more open, constantly feeling wrong, taking the lead occasionally, confronting criticism, and soothing himself when he feels overwhelmed.

- Agree to discuss in the next meeting how successful you were at improving your behavior.

- *Do not* reprimand your partner if you notice a slip back to the old behavior.

- Acknowledge how brave you are to make changes! Good for you.

Fourth Session

- Report on how you are coming along with your behavior changes.

- Talk for fifteen minutes (each) about what you like best about your partner—for example: I like the way you listen; I enjoy your telling me about the book you are reading; I like your suggestions for going to plays.

- Restate your partner's comments, clarify misunderstandings.

- For ten minutes, brainstorm about ideas for a date that would reflect both your temperaments—for example, taking a trip to the local historical society, going to the computer store and trying out new games, walking through a rose garden, visiting a new nightclub.

- Discuss what you think and feel about participating in your partner's choice. Make a date to do one of each of your ideas within the coming month.

- Write the date down on your calendars.
- Take responsibility for planning your date night (or day).
- Congratulate yourselves. This is fun but hard work, too!

Now that you've had some practice, keep talking about your relationship. Communication is a loop—do you go back and forth equally or does one person have all the airtime? (Of course that happens sometimes, but what is the pattern most of the time?) If one person is dominating, discuss ways that would help the other communicate better. For example, the male intro-vert might tell his partner he would like her to talk slower and leave breaks for him to respond. The female extrovert might talk about how she feels disconnected from him if she doesn't hear his thoughts. She can describe how she feels when she listens to him: anx-ious, scattered, frustrated, as if time's a-wasting, interested. . . .

Advantages and Challenges

The advantages to the male-innie/female-outie couple are:

- The woman may have more power than in traditional relationships.
- The man listens to her and values her opinion.
- He has less pressure to take the lead.
- Both partners have personal space, and they balance each other's activity levels.

The challenges to the male-innie/female-outie couple are:

- The man can feel overwhelmed or suffocated by the woman.
- The woman may not have emotional needs met; she may become demanding.
- She may feel ashamed of her partner; she may see him as weak, passive, or avoiding.
- His self-esteem may decline.

He can describe how he feels when he speaks: nervous, exposed, enjoyable. A wonderful exercise is to try for one day to go at the other person's pace. If you do so, notice how you feel going at your partner's pace: uncomfortable, rushed, bored, relaxed, frustrated. Set up another series of talks and pick the topics you might discuss, for example, handling conflict, or your different energy levels. Don't forget to talk about the positive aspects of your relationship. Remember, your coupling style has strengths; enjoy them.

Innie Female with Outie Male: When Opposites Attract

Life is so made that opposites sway about
a trembling center of balance.
—D. H. LAWRENCE

The most common type of mixed temperament couple is the introverted woman and the extroverted man. This combo can be tricky. Remember, the innie/outie continuum is inside all of us. If we have functioned all day from our dominant side, we may shift to our less dominant side later on, when the conditions are right. This dynamic plays out most obviously with this couple combination. The extroverted husband often gets most of his extroverted needs met at work, so by the time he comes home he wants some downtime. Plus, he feels *uncomfortable* with intimate conversations. His introverted wife, on the other hand, looks to him to fill her extroverted needs, because she's comfortable with him. She *wants* intimate conversation. From the outside, it looks as if the husband is the one who's introverted and the wife is the one who's extroverted. She wants conversation and he wants peace and quiet. No matter how people may appear to others, their basic way of refueling always reveals who is the innie and who is the outie.

Jake and Liza, who had just had their second child, came to see me because they were battling all the time and getting nowhere. Both were energetic, talkative, and creative types, with great senses of humor. Together they owned a boutique marketing company and were expanding. They were disappointed in each other and overburdened. Stress with a capital *S* had descended on their lives.

A universal human dynamic is illustrated in this example; stress or a crisis reveals our coping styles. This is why so many divorces happen when a powerful event (good or bad) occurs—a death, for example, or a wedding, a house remodel, an illness, a promotion, or a child's leaving home. If the couple can't adjust to the change (stress), the relationship begins to deteriorate.

Before the second child was born and business became more demanding, Jake and Liza had developed ways to complement each other's contrasting styles without realizing their differences in temperament. Jake is an extrovert. He handled the sales, business meetings, and schmoozing with customers. Liza is introverted. She managed the employees and coordinated Jake's schedule, working from home and going to the office a few days a week. Up until now, Liza's women friends and her creative work met her emotional needs. She didn't request much from Jake. Jake was out and about in the world, functioning in his emotional comfort zone. He had lots of freedom to meet with customers, play golf, go on business trips, and be the apple of Liza's eye.

Their past relationship fit them fine, but now it isn't working. Even with a nanny, Liza needed to reduce her time at the office and increase her hours at home. She wanted emotional support from Jake.

Jake felt trapped by the increased home and business pressures. He thought Liza didn't care about him because she didn't want to help him in the office and was focused on the children. He knew he wasn't good at organization or management, and he was afraid of taking over some of Liza's duties. Liza, torn between work and home, was exhausted. Jake was anxious and couldn't stop worrying. Emergency steps were needed.

First off, Liza and Jake shouldn't blame themselves or each other for the current state of their relationship. Changing patterns is difficult. But with challenge comes opportunity—new circumstances are giving each of them a chance to grow. Jake has the chance to improve his relationship and organizational skills and to learn to help himself when he is anxious. Liza can improve her ability to ask for help, talk about her frustrations, and stop feeling guilty.

Following are a few suggestions that worked for Jake and Liza. Remember, people change by going two steps forward and one backward and then two steps forward again.

Changing the Dance in the Middle

Recognize that each of you need to make some changes:

- Discuss your individual temperaments and how you are each affected by change. For example, the male extrovert may explain to his partner what happens when he feels trapped. The female introvert may explain how she feels deserted and left responsible for the family.

- Discuss what would help each of you make changes. For example, the woman might explain to her partner her needs for quiet time, listening, and sharing chores. The man might discuss how he can balance home and work demands.

■ Negotiate different needs without blame. Blame is fear in disguise. It is reduced by asking directly for what you want. Attempt to make your negotiations a win-win situation, with each of you getting some of what you want and each giving up some things. The man should ask to be reminded if he sounds blaming. The woman should be alert for feeling responsible for all the problems in the relationship.

■ Sit facing your partner, hold hands, and talk for three minutes each. Listen and then sum up what you heard. Check to see if it's accurate.

■ Remind yourself that each of you brings balance to the relationship: she brings relaxation; he brings activity.

■ The man should practice discussing fears and vulnerabilities; the woman should practice bringing up frustrations and disappointments about life.

■ Balance dates involving just the two of you with dates involving friends and family.

Advantages and Challenges

The advantages to the male-extrovert/female-introvert couple are:

• The female partner listens to the male.

• The male partner encourages the female to be active and social.

• She has more freedom because her partner makes few demands on her time.

• He has more personal autonomy because his partner enjoys her time alone.

The challenges to the male-extrovert/female-introvert couple are:

• The male partner often lacks intimacy skills.

• The female partner may not talk about her thoughts and feelings.

• He may blame her for all the failures in the relationship; she may accept the blame or ignore it.

• She may have trouble asking directly for what she wants.

■ Each week plan little surprises for each other—put a love note in your partner's car along with a favorite snack, leave a mint on his or her pillow, give a foot rub.

Innie with Innie:
Just Us Two Against the World

Solitude is a good place to visit
but a poor place to stay.
—JOSH BILLINGS

Many of the innie/innie couples I interviewed were very happy with their status quo. They told me how they sat and read together as the snow piled up in drifts outside. They described evenings of playing Scrabble, hiking in the woods, enjoying concerts together. Many felt less pressured than they had in their original families. I suspect that two introverts make good partners. But even if you feel very satisfied with your innie/innie relationship, sometimes too much of a good thing can begin to feel like a rut.

An innie/innie couple who came to see me for psychotherapy had been together for about seven years and were starting to feel bored. Pat said, "Every night it's the same thing: We sit at home and watch TV or read." Toni agreed. "I feel pressured to do everything with Pat. Once in a while I would like to go out with my friends."

This is one of the problems that can pop up in an innie/innie relationship: not enough outside stimulation and friendships. And no relationship does well under the grinding pressure of excessive needs and expectations.

Think of the old dance marathons of the 1930s. A man and a

woman danced and danced, learning to sleep upright in order to be the last couple standing and win a prize. Around and around they went until one of them keeled over from exhaustion. In an innie/innie relationship, one or both of the partners may start to feel numb and deadened. If you are accustomed to doing most things together, spending leisure time apart can seem scary. Even though you are a little bored, you may feel uncomfortable venturing out without your partner.

If a couple stays stuck for too long and a stressor comes along, like an illness, a problem with a child, or a loss of a job, everything may fall apart.

Advantages and Challenges

The advantages to the innie/innie couple are:

- They listen attentively to each other.
- They are patient about thinking things over.
- They understand each other's needs for privacy and quiet.
- They have fewer conflicts.

The challenges to the innie/innie couple are:

- They may lose touch with the outside world.
- They may see everything in terms of themselves.
- They may avoid discussing conflicts, differences, and separate needs.
- They may rely on each other for too many emotional needs.

Relationships that deny stagnation remind me of the award-winning children's book *Drummer Hoff*, by Barbara Emberley. It's a stirring folk verse with bright woodcut illustrations about soldiers bringing the parts to build and fire off a cannon. The weapon is assembled as the cadence and anticipation mount. Private Parriage brings the carriage; Sergeant Chowder brings the powder; Captain Bammer brings the rammer; and so on. It ends with a huge KAHBAHBLOOM, when Drummer Hoff yells, "Fire!"

Sometimes an innie/innie duo can successfully ignore their problems until an external event jolts them out of their complacency. Usually the relationship is blown to smithereens. A couple has a much better chance of surviving outside threats if they notice they are in a rut and try gracefully to climb out together before they get blown out.

Here are some suggestions that may help you take the first step:

Getting Unstuck from the Rut

- Stop to notice that your relationship is stagnating. Ask each other, Are you feeling a little stuck?

- Expand your social life by making a date with a friend or another couple once a week.

- Get out a little more. Make a date with each other once a month. Take turns arranging it.

- Flex your individual muscles—it's healthy to have separate friends and personal interests.

- Talk about how the two of you are different and why it's helpful for the relationship.

- Notice if you are blaming your partner for the lack of fun in the relationship; take turns being "the spark" (igniter).

- It's okay to have your own private thoughts. They aren't the same as destructive secrets (like affairs).

- Talk about your needs for downtime. Are they similar or different?

- Plan something unexpected to do together—go for a ride to a new destination, dine at a new restaurant, eat each other's favorite ice cream, or try bowling if you never have.

- If conflicts are scary, read Tip 2 on page 120 and practice negotiating conflicts.

■ Ask your partner if he or she has a secret wish to do something and then do some part of it. For example, if he or she always wanted to go to Nepal, check out a book about that country. If she has dreamed of going to the Cordon Bleu, sign her up for a course in French cooking at a local cooking school.

Couple Choreography

The moon is a different thing to each of us.
—FRANK BORMAN

Once you are a couple, it takes about a half second to notice that relationships take skill and constant learning. Here are five tips to improve the footwork of any innie/outie relationship. Remember all relationships are imperfect. We can continue to improve until we toddle over into the grave.

Tip 1: Try On Each Other's Specs

Remember in Chapter 1 when I described Mike and me in Las Vegas? Extroverted Mike jaunted through the hotel lobby. He saw a rainbow of dancing lights and hustling bodies; he heard laughter and the tinkling of coins; he savored the hearty aroma of the overflowing buffets at the adjacent restaurant. His whole body tingled at the novelty of gliding up to our room in the hotel's slanted elevator. He was already anticipating the "stim" of feeling the activity and excitement in the evening ahead.

As an introvert, my reality was very different. The lights flashing in my eyes blinded me. My ears rang from the coins exploding in the steel catchers. Smoke choked my airways. Bodies pressed in on me in the narrow passages. I wanted to escape. I staggered to the elevator and up to our room.

Without knowing it, couples enter into relationships wearing their own temperament spectacles. Our lenses are ground from our genes, physiology, upbringing, emotional history, social class, education, and friends. Each lens has a precise prescription, so each view is true and accurate for that particular person. But only for that person. What is very important for a healthy relationship is to realize that you are looking at life through *your spectacles.*

If we think that our view is the *right* view, then we have struggles in our relationships. Was Mike's experience of Las Vegas *wrong?* No. Was mine? No. Each was *right*—for each of *us.* Mike and I were wearing the only spectacles we have. We can only have our *own* experience.

Many introverts have grown up in cultures where fast-talking, quick-thinking, action-packed people are considered the kind of people to emulate. If you are in a relationship with an extrovert, you may think your partner behaves in the "right" way. This is something I have heard over the years from many of the introverts I have interviewed or worked with in my practice. They say to me, "I can't think of quick repartee. What's wrong with me?" Nothing. Extroverts, or even other introverts who are ashamed of their word gaps, might feel impatient with you, or even think you are withholding if you don't give snappy answers to their questions. But by now you know your brain doesn't work the same; you will always have a different perspective. This helps you to validate yourself.

Switching Specs

After we have a solid understanding of our own way of looking at things, we can begin to comprehend our partner's. What does it take to wonder what life looks like through another's viewpoint? Curiosity.

"I wonder" are powerful words. "What's it like for you?" "Tell me what you liked about it." "What is it like to have another temperament?" Relationships grow and expand through curiosity.

Mike loves county fairs. As you can imagine, considering the crowds and the multiple activities, they are not my favorite. Every few years, in the spirit of marital goodwill, I agree to go. So a while back we drove up the California coast for the last day of the Ventura Fair. I had the illusion that maybe all the fair lovers had thinned out and only a few stragglers would be left. Not so. The eager throngs packed the grounds in the glaring afternoon sun. We waited in long lines for a greasy snack and then for the overused, grimy rest room. In the science hall we watched snow crystallize and blow out over the audience. In the odiferous barn we saw a mother pig tinkle on her squealing babies.

But salvation for me was in the 4H barn, where the goat judging was going on. It was dimly lit with very few other people—just about my pace of excitement. Teenage owners led four white goats around the pen. Three of the competitors had shiny tan-and-pearl-white coats, and they held their pert little tails in the exclamation-point position. The fourth goat was grayish white, and his little nub of a tail was tucked between his legs. He appeared quiet and unassuming. He had a few embarrassing holes in his coat where it looked as if several moths had lunched. I was surprised he was even in the contest. Finally, the goat judge gave out the white, pink, red, and blue ribbons. The tail-tucked and moth-eaten goat, the one I thought was the least likely to succeed, received first prize. Turns out he won for his calm demeanor. Another victory for the introverted temperament, because, believe me, he didn't win on looks.

As we were leaving, I asked Mike, "Really, I want to understand your view of the fair. What is it you like about it?" "Well," he said, "I guess I like to see people of all ages working together on projects they love. Like the 4H kids showing the livestock they raised. The animals remind me of growing up on our farm, and it's a reminder of how I felt going to the fair as a child, the sense of anticipation." If I hadn't switched glasses with Mike, I would have left grumbling about the stinky, crowded, noisy fair. Through his point of view, it sounded pretty good. I left having a warm feeling about Mike—of how child-like he was, of how I wanted to understand him even more than I already do. This year I'm looking forward to going to the county fair. As long as we don't stay too long.

Tip 2: Try Five Easy Steps to Resolve Couple Conflict

Only a dead relationship is conflict free. No matter what combination of temperaments you and your partner have, here are five general steps to help you learn, as a couple, to resolve the issues that come between you. I am going to use Andrew and Brooke, whom I discussed earlier in the chapter, as an example of how the steps work.

Step 1: One after the other, state what you think the conflict is about.
Andrew explains his point of view this way: "I want to stay home and enjoy a quiet night, just the two of us. I am exhausted. It doesn't seem like Brooke wants to spend time with me." Brooke says, "I want to have some fun with friends this weekend. I don't see why Andrew doesn't like my friends. I feel trapped staying home, as if I wasted the whole weekend."

Step 2: State your introverted view/extroverted view.
I asked Andrew and Brooke how they thought their introverted/extroverted temperaments were affecting this conflict. Brooke said, "I see that I need to feel pepped up. I feel draggy if I stay home."

Andrew said, "I see how much energy I spend all week on my job. I am low on fuel. I need to recharge."

Step 3: Clarify the impasse.
"So the problem is that you each need something different," I said. "Andrew, you need downtime, and Brooke, you need to do some stimulating activities, like have dinner with friends. Both of you feel hurt when the other one doesn't understand what you need. You both take it personally."

Step 4: Step into the other person's shoes.
I turned to Andrew. "Can you understand that Brooke is afraid she will be drained of energy if she stays home too much? She feels energized by activities and socializing. She's not trying to get away from you." I faced Brooke. "Andrew feels very drained and overwhelmed by going out so much. He's not trying to be a party pooper."

Step 5: Negotiate and figure out ways to compromise.
It's always amazing how easily this fifth step goes if the four steps above have been followed. "How do you think you can plan your weekend to meet *both* of your needs?" I asked. Brooke said, "I feel better when I don't think Andrew is avoiding me. I could go out with my girlfriends Friday night after work, and Andrew could kick back. Maybe we could watch a video Saturday night together and then get together with friends on Sunday night?" I asked Andrew what he thought. "I guess Brooke doesn't prefer her friends to me. What you suggested sounds good, as long as we have a time limit for Sunday night, like telling our friends we'll meet them from five until nine." Brooke agreed. They were both reminded they wanted time together, and that lessened their anxiety. I could see their faces relax as they saw that they could learn to meet each other's needs.

Tip 3: Bridge the Gaps

Whether you are dating or in a committed relationship, the most important aspect of communication between introverts and extroverts is learning that because of your differences in temperament, you have different ways of expressing yourself. Often what's English to one is Greek to the other. Neither style is right or wrong; each offers advantages and disadvantages. If you understand both styles, you can "translate" and begin to work together. Let's take a look at how this works:

The Introvert's Communication Style

Introverts tend to:

- Keep energy, enthusiasm, and excitement to themselves and share only with those they know very well. Hesitate before sharing personal information with others.

- Need time to think before responding. Need time to reflect before reacting to outside events.

- Prefer communicating one-to-one.

- Need to be drawn out or invited to speak, and may prefer written to verbal communication.

- May occasionally think they told you something they didn't (they're always going over things in their head).

The Extrovert's Communication Style

Extroverts tend to:

- Share their energy, excitement, and enthusiasm with almost anyone in the vicinity.

- Respond quickly to questions and outward events.

- Share personal information easily.

- Communicate one to one or in groups with equal ease and enjoyment.

- Think out loud, interacting with others, and, in the process, reach their conclusions. In addition they often don't give others a chance to speak and don't always attach tremendous meaning to what they say.

- Prefer face-to-face, oral communication over written communication.

How to Talk to Your Introverted Partner

If you are an extrovert and you would like better communication with an introvert, try the following:

- Make a date to discuss how the two of you can "dance" better together. This gives introverts time to prepare their thoughts.

- Don't interrupt—it takes energy for introverts to start talking again. Hear your partner out, then talk about your thoughts and feelings.

- Count to five and think before you speak—an introvert will remember what you say.

- Repeat what you heard your partner saying so that you make it clear you were listening. Ask her or him if your summation is correct.

- Learn how to sit quietly sometimes in your partner's presence. Remember, he or she may have depleted energy but still wants to be with you.

- Your partner is a good listener, but be sure he or she gets a turn to talk.

- Ask what your partner's day was like. Sometimes he or she needs to be drawn out.

- Occasionally communicate in writing. Introverts can take in written words with less overstimulation. Leave a card by the phone, put a note in his or her lunch container, suitcase, briefcase, pocket, or on his or her pillow.

- Enjoy pauses. Take some deep breaths and enjoy just sitting. Experience being alone together. Share your partner's pace.

- Acknowledge how much energy it takes for your partner to talk at times; express how much you appreciate it.

- Use nonverbal communication—for example, blow kisses to your partner, wink at him or her in a crowd, hold hands, and give hugs.

How to Talk to Your Extroverted Partner

If you are an introvert and you would like to have improved communications with the extrovert in your life, here are some suggestions:

- Tell your partner you want to talk. Set a date and time to do so. Make a reminder.

- Practice short, clear sentences. That will make it easier for your extrovert partner to listen to you.

- Don't be afraid to yell or talk loud if you need to. You may feel overstimulated, but sometimes your more extroverted partner won't trust that you mean something unless the volume is up.

- Practice saying anything that pops into your mind. Don't always rehearse.

- Allow pauses. It's okay not to keep up with your extroverted partner's nonstop pace.

- Tell your partner you *know* it is difficult for him or her, that you take time to make decisions, and that you don't always say what's on your mind.

- Write down your feelings on paper and give it to your partner, if you feel strongly about an issue but have trouble talking about it.

- Don't worry if you get overstimulated during or after a disagreement. It's not a bad thing to have feelings. In any case, they will pass.

- Tell your partner how you feel about him or her. It's easy to forget this. Your partner wants to hear he or she is cared about. So leave notes and e-mails, lavish kisses, and don't forget to give compliments.

Tip 4: Take Turns Getting Your Way

No relationship goes well if one person gets his or her way all the time. Relationships flow gracefully if both partners feel they are getting some of what they want. Otherwise, resentment builds. At the same time, it's good for everyone to be disappointed at times. It builds good emotional muscles. No one goes through life without experiencing losses or disappointments. The ability to tolerate these feelings, the awareness to think about your reactions and to make choices about how you act develops an old-fashioned concept called *character*. People with character can trust themselves, and they have healthy relationships because they know they can withstand life's ups and downs.

You can both become healthier partners by giving thought to your needs and wants. Learning how to communicate and negotiate them is the hallmark of a lasting relationship.

- Let your partner know if you need downtime. Ask if he or she needs "up time."

- Think about introverted/extroverted energy differences when making plans.

- Do not criticize or idealize being an innie or an outie.

- Learn red flags indicating that your partner is underpowered (for the innie, being irritable or tired; for the outie, being antsy, bored, or shut down from lack of stimulation). Talk about ways to alert each other of low batteries.

- Let the extroverted partner be the "scout" in your relationship and introduce new adventures to the introverted partner.

- Negotiate time spent at social events; take two cars or arrange for one of you to ride home with friends.

- Balance doing things together and apart.

- Acknowledge whenever your partner does something he or she doesn't like to do.

Tip 5: Appreciate Your Differences

I have saved the best tip for last. After thirty-eight years of living with an extrovert, I have learned a valuable lesson—to appreciate our differences. Because Mike has never met a road he doesn't want to go down, I have traveled more—including dirt tracks and even a riverbed in the Hawaiian outback, which wasn't covered by car rental insurance. I'm grateful for the opportunity I've had to peek into my partner's extroverted world. He has shown me the serenity of lush golf courses and introduced me to a diverse group of people I would never have met on my own. Mike's temperament has lots to offer. So does mine. I've learned that just because my world is so different from his, it doesn't mean there's anything wrong with mine—or his.

It would be a very dull world if we were all the same. We need *all* of our strengths and limitations to flesh out life. We grow from enjoying what each of us brings to the party. One of the best ways to keep a relationship healthy is to *appreciate* each other. Sometimes introverts have a hard time saying they appreciate their partner. They aren't sure why it even needs to be said out loud. And extroverts are so busy going and doing that they may forget to be appreciative at home.

Focusing on appreciating your partner works wonders. So each night, for a week, choose from one of these topics, jot down your thoughts, and then share them with your partner.

- Share what you most appreciate about your partner.
- Describe a mannerism or quality that you find endearing or lovable.
- Describe one physical characteristic that you really like about your partner.
- Write about a fun time you had together.
- Think back on a romantic time you had together and tell how it made you feel.
- Discuss what you liked best about what your partner did today.

After you have each done this for a week, decide if you want to continue for another week. Think up your own topic sentences. If you liked the exercise but decided to stop, talk about your reasons. Sometimes we pull away from good experiences because they are overstimulating.

Mind over Chatter

There's no end to the things you might know,
Depending how far beyond Zebra you go!
—Dr. Seuss

Introversion and extroversion affect relationships in many ways. As you understand your own and your partner's temperament you can increase your awareness about the emotional impact of your different styles. You can each think about how you want to grow your relationship, instead of simply reacting reflexively. Unconscious relationships can produce distance, pain, and missed moments of intimacy. Without mindfulness we just live out repeated patterns, like hamsters on a treadmill. It is hard to change patterns but it builds emotional muscles that are yours forever. Sometimes it's even fun.

Points to Ponder

- Dating takes a lot of energy; remember that it's a process.
- Everyone looks at the world from his or her own perspective.
- Each couple combo has advantages and challenges.
- Conflicts can be settled; you can learn to talk together more easily and to appreciate each other.

CHAPTER V

Parenting: Are They Up from Their Nap Already?

Children are not things to be molded,
but are people to be unfolded.

—JESS LAIR

P arenting is a complex, twenty-four-hour-a-day job. It takes a lot of
energy and involves dealing with a lot of stress. This is particularly
true if the family consists of individuals with a variety of different temperaments. Understanding the importance of the way each person
functions—how he or she restores energy and processes information—
can improve the family's confidence and ability to work together.

When temperaments are not taken into consideration, the family
can become underpowered, crabby, and lacking in self-esteem. Everybody
ends up feeling bad.

The first thing to do is to determine the range of temperaments
under your roof. If you have been reading this book chapter by chapter,
you have figured out where you and your partner fall on the innie/outie
continuum. If not, go back to Chapter 1 and take the Self-Assessment
for Introverts test on page 30. The previous chapter on relationships

can help you to clarify which type of couple you and your partner are. This chapter will complete the family portrait by helping you determine your children's temperaments.

Is Your Child an "Innie" or an "Outie"?

With what kind of temperament were your children born? Why will it help you and them to understand their innate traits better? The more you understand your children's *nature,* the more you can *nurture* all those qualities to their advantage. In *The Challenging Child,* Stanley Greenspan, M.D., states, "Parents can make a dramatic difference in how children use their wonderfully different natural abilities." As parents we constantly shape the interplay between nature and nurture. The better you know how to read your children's physical and emotional signals, the more you can help them cope with their own temperament, and the more they will be able to use their temperament for fulfilling and valuable lives.

Read over the lists below and think about your children. They may be quite introverted or quite extroverted or somewhere in between. Notice if you think they feel pressured to be more introverted or extroverted. Remember, because of our strong cultural bias, many children feel pressured to be extroverted. We can all use our nondominant side, but by doing so we deplete our energy and end up twice as exhausted.

If your children are primarily introverts, they will probably:

■ Watch and listen before joining an activity.

■ Concentrate deeply on subjects of interest.

- Enjoy time alone in their room, energized by introspection.

- Speak after thinking things through.

- Have a strong sense of personal space and dislike people sitting too close or coming into their room without knocking.

- Be private and may need to be asked what they are thinking or feeling.

- Need validation; may have irrational self-doubts.

- Talk a lot if the topic is interesting, or if they are comfortable with the people.

If your children are primarily extroverts, they will probably:

- Be gregarious and outgoing, except during normal developmental stages.

- Be energized by interactions and activities.

- Want to tell you all about their experiences and ideas immediately, covering lots of topics.

- Think out loud. They'll walk around the house saying, "Where's my ball?" or "I'm looking for my walkie-talkie" as they hunt for these items. They need to talk in order to make decisions.

- Prefer time with others rather than time alone.

- Need lots of approval. For example, they need to hear what a good job they are doing or how much you like their gift.

- Like variety and be easily distracted.

- Often volunteer what they are thinking or feeling.

It is important to remember that few children are extreme extroverts or introverts, and that sometimes introverts act extroverted and vice versa.

See if you can find a pattern of when, and how, your child is more introverted or more extroverted. Remember, it's not about social skills; it's about how your child recharges his or her energy.

For example, my client Kara's daughter, Elizabeth, is in the middle of the continuum. One of the ways Elizabeth's introverted side shows up is that she does not want to talk *right* after she is picked up from nursery school. Kara told me how she handles her daughter's preference for quiet time. As she buckles Elizabeth into her car seat, Kara gives her one of her favorite books and puts on the audiotape that goes with it. Elizabeth loves to turn the pages of her picture book when the bell rings on the tape. Kara says, "Other days I give her a choice of music. Today we sang a Beatles medley all the way home." After a time, Elizabeth wants to talk and doesn't stop.

Understanding
Your "Innie" Child

Children are like wet cement.
Whatever falls on them makes an impression.
—HAIM GINOTT

Introverted children can be deceiving. They think and feel more than they show to the outside world. Puzzling as it sounds, they often know more than they themselves think they know. If they are not helped to understand how their mind works, they can underestimate their own powerful potential.

Introverted children learn by taking in information and then needing quiet time to process it—to integrate all of what they observed, heard, and absorbed. When they finally have their thoughts formulated, they can take action or talk about their ideas and impressions. In fact, talking can help them understand how their mind operates. Interrupting causes them to lose their place, and they have to exert extra energy and concentration to retrieve their thoughts. (Remember the long brain pathway in introverts?) If introverted children don't have time and physical space to shut out other stimulation, they can "zone out" and become unable to think.

Most activities require an outlay of energy for introverted children. If you teach them to recharge their batteries, they can thrive. Here are some of the ways introverted children can process the world and refuel themselves.

Find Private Time

Introverted children need private time built into their daily schedules. During private time they expend less energy. Private time is created by being alone or with one or two people around whom your child feels relaxed—or just stepping outside of the group. Children also need extra breaks during highly stimulating activities. In our Western culture, where extroversion is valued and many activities for children are group experiences, it is extra important for introverted children to have alone time. Being in a bad mood is often a sign they need time out. (Maybe the reason Oscar on *Sesame Street* is always so grouchy is because he needs more quiet time in his garbage can!)

When my client Bob was nine, he had a too-large birthday party—thirty kids—and too much excitement. His folks had already given him a frisky black-and-white puppy as a gift, and Bob remembers feeling crowded in when the party started. He told me, "I didn't want anyone to touch my puppy. I named him Spiderman. I wanted everyone to go home. I felt like ants were crawling under the skin of my arms. I ran up to my bedroom crying, and I stayed there for a while. My dad brought Spiderman upstairs and talked softly to me for a few minutes. I relaxed and the ants marched away." When Bob finally came back downstairs for cake and ice cream, he was like another child, a smiling host. Spiderman stayed upstairs for the remainder of the party. In subsequent years, Bob's parents threw smaller parties for him.

Introverted kids often need help learning when and how to take a break. They don't know they need one, aren't familiar with taking one, or don't want to leave the group. This is why it is so important for parents to know their child. They have to be sensitive enough

The Arrival of a New Human Bean

When a new little person enters your life, it can highlight various aspects of your temperament. Lynn, an extroverted woman who normally interacted with many people during her workday, recently had a baby boy, Aaron. She'd been home with her infant son for several weeks when she came to see me. She was really enjoying the baby, but she couldn't figure out why she felt so tired and drained. I asked her if she had much social contact during the day. She said she hadn't seen much of her friends because all of them work.

It turns out she was dragging because she was understimulated. I suggested she have short phone chats during the day or arrange to meet her pals for lunch. Also, I recommended that she take Aaron to a park with lots of other adult-child couples, stroll around the local shopping center, or go to a bustling tea shop for a cup of Earl Grey. The following week Lynn was much peppier and enjoying Aaron more.

Infants stimulate some extroverted moms. They drain others. If you require outside activity, do not feel guilty. As an extrovert, Lynn needed outside stimulation for recharging.

to notice if their son or daughter is zoning out, getting crabby, or withdrawing.

At a gathering, if you see your child glazing over, you might suggest, "It's so noisy and there are so many people in here, let's walk in the backyard for a few minutes." If you see he is getting crabby, try something like, "I'd like you to help me bring out the dessert; we'll come back in just a few minutes," or "You look a little pooped. Let's stroll down the block and see what the other houses on the street look like."

A grouchy child often objects to being told she needs a break. So he or she may need to be enticed to do something else for a few

Many introverted moms love the fascinating course of caring for an infant and enjoy cocooning with a gurgling baby (preferably one without colic!). The quieter pace of mothering allows them an opportunity for home-time solitude when they can appreciate their introverted capacities.

However, this is not true for every introverted mother. It is important to note *your* temperament temperature. Focusing twenty-four hours a day on the needs of another being can be extraordinarily taxing. Introverted moms need to find ways to take breaks and be completely alone or shift into a relaxing adult activity.

I loved being a mom, but I continued to take one or two college courses each semester when my daughters were infants. I needed brain food to balance my mothering time. If you are introverted and need time away from your infant, adjust your schedule accordingly. Don't feel guilty. Find the temperature zone you require and make the time to nurture *yourself*. Your infant and you will be better for it.

minutes. Later you can say, "I noticed you needed a little break from all the kids." Help your children notice that they felt better after they had some private time. They need to be reminded that they can *return* in five minutes feeling better and that then they will enjoy their friends even more.

Megan is a lively five-year-old. In nursery school, it was her turn to be the Student of the Week, the special child who gets celebrated at a little program. The pressure of being the center of attention agitated Megan, and she flung herself on the floor and rolled around. Her parents, who had been invited to the event, were embarrassed and shocked. When her dad handed her the award, Megan tried to yank it out of his hands. Later, when her parents and I talked about the possible reasons for this reaction, I asked if they thought she might have been overstimulated. I also asked them to talk to Megan about what happened and ask her how they could have helped her. The next week her parents were tickled to report that Megan knew that she had been overexcited. She told them, "My tummy hurt a little, and I needed to go outside for a minute." She also told her mom, "I wanted you to tell me, 'Honey, be calm. Be calm.'"

Introverted kids are often insightful if they are asked what they need—and if they are confident that what they need is okay.

Your guidance can help introverted children stay energized and happy. Talk to them about their need to take breaks. Some children actually ask for one. Pick a time when they are relaxed, and you are alone together. The more you express the idea that breaks are *good*, the more they will think so, too. You might say: "Have you noticed how some children are very peppy when they are around friends? They can play all day and never get tired, like your brother Sam. Other children enjoy their friends but need to take little breaks when they are playing. That's how you are, Cammie. You need a break to give your body energy and to take some big deep breaths. Otherwise you might start to feel tired or a little bit crabby." Ask your children if they have ever noticed when they needed some time off. Pause to let them respond. Remind them of a specific time when they were tired or overwhelmed if they can't think of one.

Give them an example of someone who takes breaks. "Have you ever noticed how Susan plays for a while and then sits and watches for a few minutes? When you start to feel a little tired, here's what you could say to your friends: "I'm going to sit down for a few minutes; I'll be right back." Or: "I need to go check on something; I'll be back in a few minutes." Ask your children if they can think of any other ways to tell friends about breaks. Praise their suggestions.

It is important to help children transition back into the play. Most introverted boys and girls need to watch for a few minutes before they enter or reenter an activity. Tell them, "It's okay to watch for a while before you go back to the group." Research shows that the best way to enter a group is to make eye contact with one person and smile at him or her, join the flow of play without drawing attention to yourself, and then ask a relevant question. For example, say: "If your friends are playing chase, see if you can catch Sam's eye, smile, and then ask him which way you should run." Praise your child's efforts to join into activities. Later, discuss what seemed to work and what didn't.

Provide a Private Space

Introverted children need their own physical space to make an actual barrier between their bodies and the outside world. There are several reasons for this. First, in order to process their thoughts and feelings, they need help to block out external stimulation enough so they can turn inward. Second, just being around people and activity drains introverts' batteries. It is very hard for extroverts to understand or imagine this. Third, introverts cannot generate new energy unless the external environment is shut out.

I had been working with an introverted ten-year-old boy, Jeffery, in psychotherapy for several months. His parents were worried because he either withdrew or suddenly blew up for no apparent reason. We were playing Sorry when, out of the clear blue sky, he said, "I hate sharing a room with Michael. I like peace and quiet." "Oh, you do?" I asked. "Sounds like you have been thinking about this." The family's house had four bedrooms, and one of them had been turned into a playroom. As a result, Jeffery was sharing with Michael, his extroverted brother. "Well, Michael could move into the playroom," Jeffery continued. "Maybe you could draw a picture of how you see his room and your room?" I suggested.

Excitedly, Jeffery hunched over the paper and drew the rooms. It was obvious he had been planning this out in his mind for some time, anticipating every objection his parents might have. He hadn't brought it up to me until he had it all mapped out. After he told me his plan, he was able to talk to his extroverted parents, with his drawing for support, about his needs for his own space. Michael moved into the playroom, and almost immediately Jeffery's sluggish energy improved and his temper outbursts abated. He had the peace and quiet his temperament needed so badly.

Introverted children show their need for physical contact in many ways. Like all children, they can enjoy being held or hugged. At other times, when they feel overstimulated, they may require distance. "He's touching my leg," they might whine in the car if they are tired. In a group, they often like to be at the back, front, or edge of the pack, rather than in the center. Instead of sharing seats on a sofa, they might like their own separate chair. Sometimes they might pull away if you touch them. Don't take it personally. Enjoy the times they want to cuddle and accept those times they feel the need to reduce outside stimulation.

I remember a time when my mother and I had been train traveling together off and on for several weeks. One day, her leg touched mine, and my skin felt singed. I yanked my leg away. She was angry with me for being so touchy. I felt bad about upsetting her, but after so much time without privacy, the lightest touch was too much.

Introverts feel drained by having their physical space intruded upon. It takes energy for them to be around people even if they are not interacting with them. This is very hard for extroverts to grasp since space is not an issue for them. Cozying up doesn't require energy.

Standing or sitting too close to introverts, or entering unannounced a room they are in, sucks up their energy. My client Kristen scratched "Don't Come In" on her bedroom door when she was about six. She was surprised and amused when her daughter Katie, at about the same age, asked Kristen how to spell "Don't Come In." Katie wrote it on a little blackboard, hung it on her doorknob, and shut the door. Later Kristen smiled at Katie and said, "I know how you feel." Giving introverts space is giving them energy.

Talk to your children about sharing physical space. "I know sometimes you feel antsy or drained if you are crowded by other people," you may say. The most important thing is to acknowledge that you understand that they may feel uncomfortable. "We will be driving to the museum with Aunt Tina and Christopher. It will take about an hour to get there. I know you sometimes feel uncomfortable sitting so close for that long. What do you think might help you?" It's amazing how often children come up with great ideas. But in case nothing is forthcoming, suggest some ideas. "Would it help if we tucked a pillow between the two of you? What do you think?" If you are on a long car ride, talk to the children about private space, stop periodically to get out and walk around, and take turns sitting in different seats. Suggest that they take a deep breath and relax if they start to feel uneasy. Help them focus on something besides their body. Give them headphones so they can listen to stories or music, provide a sticker book so they can work alone, or play a game like twenty questions. Remind them that the car ride won't last forever.

Discuss with your child the idea that all children have an invisible circle of space around them, small or large. Explain that your child usually has a large circle, which means he feels uncomfortable with people being too close. Being around other people, especially if they enter his or her personal circle, can cause your child to feel drained and tired.

To find out what size personal space circle each individual in your family has, try this exercise. Have each person stand on your driveway or sidewalk. Then have someone who is not a family member walk toward him. When the family member—say it's your son—begins to *feel* like backing up, instruct him to say "Stop." With sidewalk chalk, mark the spot where he is standing. Then draw a circle around him, using the mark as a radius. Each person in the family will probably have a different-size circle. That is his or her personal space zone. Your introverted son's will probably be large.

Explain to your child about his need for private space. Tell him that sometimes he may want to share his space circle and sometimes not. Suggest that he let his friends know he needs space by saying something like, "Could you move over just a bit, thank you." Or, "I like us to sit together on the swing, but could you move over a tiny bit? I feel scrunched. Thanks." Help your child notice when he feels crowded so he can create some room before he gets crabby. Ask him: "How did you feel when Quentin sat so close to you?" Then: "Next time you feel like that, what could you do? Could you move to another spot?" Don't forget to praise your child when you see him tolerating discomfort. "I know the car gets cramped for you sometimes, but you did so well today."

Allow Time to Reflect

Introverts need time to cogitate without the pressure to "do" something. Many introverts are called lazy because they require reflection periods. Parents get irritated and ask them, "What are you doing lolling around?" But in addition to using downtime to store energy, introverts use it to ponder. Besides storing energy, why do introverts need this pressure-free zone? Introverts absorb information from the outside world both consciously and unconsciously. Unless they can reduce outside stimulation, their inner thoughts, feelings, and impressions will never bubble up to the surface. Without processing time, their minds become clogged and overloaded. Thus, many introverts end up feeling there is nothing in their brain. The fact is there's a lot in there; it just isn't sorted and sifted.

When introverted kids feel their mind go blank, it can cause lots of confusion and embarrassment. You can help by making simple statements to explain what is going on. "Right now you don't know how you feel, but you will later." Remind them that they can count on their brain to be working even if they aren't aware of it. "I bet your mind will be munching and crunching on that assignment, and by tomorrow you will have some ideas." Point out when they have come to conclusions and solutions. "It sounds like you thought about that book, and now you can explain what you like and don't like about it."

Since extroverts like to talk about problems in order to work them out, they often get irritated at introverts for "withholding." "Spit it out," they will say. Teach your introverted boy or girl to say, "I'm still mulling it over." If your child is one of those introverts who likes to think out loud about a topic, it is best just to listen and then give him or her feedback about what you heard: "So, let me see if I got this right, Alicia. You have considered several ideas for your science project, and you have narrowed your choices down to two. Would you like to discuss them now or another time?" Reflecting back to introverted children helps them continue to problem-solve without getting overwhelmed.

Your children will be better able to use their gifts if you teach them how to be introspective. Suggest that they sit back and let their minds wander. Explain that free time allows their minds a chance to connect the pieces of information they have been gathering. The mind puts the pieces together like a puzzle to form ideas. Ask your children to notice when complete ideas, solutions, and impressions become clear. The more you as the parent appreciate this process, the more your children will. Say, "I see you have been thinking about what you saw yesterday." Ask your child, "Gary, what are your impressions of your new teacher? You can think about your answer for a while if you want." It is important to help your children trust how their minds operate.

It may be helpful to talk to your children's teacher and explain their need for reflection. The teacher may not know that people use different pathways in the brain, and that the length of the pathways determines how fast children respond. The teacher could ask students to think over a topic, saying, "We'll discuss this chapter of the book after lunch." He or she might find that many of the quieter ones contribute more when they have had a chance to reflect.

Help your children learn to tell people outside the family, "I need to think about that before I answer." Remind them that it is important to follow up with their thoughts. Don't forget to offer praise. "Emily, I really like the way you think things over." Your son or daughter has powerful advantages.

If You're an Extroverted Parent with an Introverted Child

Extroverted parents of introverted children worry a lot. They want their children to do well in life and they are afraid some of the qualities their children are exhibiting are danger signs. If the child is a boy, the parents often want him to toughen up. As one of my clients described his son, "I think Max needs to see a counselor. He's a good kid, but he's not active or assertive enough. Max takes so long to do anything, even to talk." The extroverted dad added with insight, "Max was private from the very beginning. My other son is much more outgoing." I described to Max's dad the quieter energy of introverts. I explained why Max needs uninterrupted time to answer questions. I could see the tension easing from his dad's face. As he began to see Max's behavior as normal, he began to be able to help him. For example, when his dad told him about plans in advance and let him watch before gradually joining into activities, Max was able to make transitions more smoothly. As a result, Max began to talk more, and his family began to listen.

Another client of mine, Hayley, who was on the far end of the extroverted continuum, had a four-year-old son, Ben, who was sensitive and quite introverted. She came to see me because she thought something was *very* wrong with Ben. She thought he might even be autistic. She couldn't understand why he looked dazed and cried so much. Then for ten to fifteen minutes she started describing their days together. It was like running a marathon. Go here, go there, do this, do that.

I stopped her as she listed more of the "fun" things she had planned for their upcoming family outing: miniature golf, the arcade,

---

Correcting the Introverted Child

Introverted children may be quite sensitive to anger and disapproval. As I mentioned earlier, it is best not to correct them in public. Because it's so painful, they may even shut you out and look as if they don't care. They do care. This doesn't mean you should ignore disruptive behavior.

Tell them in a matter-of-fact way what they did that you disapprove of. "I didn't like that you threw sand." Explain why. "It got in Timmy's eyes and hurt him." Tell what to do next. "I want you to apologize to Timmy. Later, let's talk it over and see how you were feeling and why you threw the sand. If you were upset about something, I'm sure we can come up with a better way to express that." Feeling angry or frustrated can be overstimulating for introverted children. They need help learning to manage their feelings, to talk them out and not act them out.

As the parent, you need to keep the shaming and blaming at a minimum. Read the section starting on page 54 in Chapter 2 about shame and blame and their antidotes. Remember, shame is felt as an attack on the child's core sense of *being*. "I yelled at my sister. I am bad, and now Mom won't love me anymore." Guilt is felt as *doing* something one shouldn't have done. "I yelled at Corey. Mom won't like it." Give your children space to talk. If they are upset, they may clam up. Check to make sure they aren't brooding over the incident. Tell them you love them. Remind them that everyone makes mistakes. Even you.

and *then* Chuck E. Cheese for lunch. I was beginning to feel queasy and exhausted myself. In my mind, I could see Ben having a meltdown. I said, "It sounds as if Ben might be a little overstimulated." "What do you mean?" she asked, pausing for the first time since she sat down. "Well, it sounds to me like you are extroverted and Ben is introverted. All of this activity is overstimulating to him. Ben zones out or cries to signal he's had way too much." "What do you mean by overstimulating?" Hayley asked. This was not a concept that resonated with her. I explained that Ben was probably feeling as if "too much" were going on, that he was tired and couldn't think. Hayley laughed. "And here I am thinking I am giving him all these great times."

Hayley, who was newly pregnant, paused for a moment and said, "I wonder what temperament this baby will have." I thought, We are making progress. I told her that was a good question. It is very important not to overwhelm your child with *your* energy level.

Another extroverted parent talked to me about his daughter, Alexa. "All she does is read in her room. I think it's a serious problem. She's avoiding life." She didn't want to do any of the activities he suggested. He felt she was angry with him. I suggested asking Alexa if he could read with her. At our next meeting, he said he was *shocked* at how Alexa lit up at his idea. Father and daughter are now reading together weekly, and their relationship has improved considerably.

Introverted children may not be as demonstrative as extroverted children. They love and value you, but they may not talk about it as much. Accept your temperament and your child's. They can't be changed. Both of you have wonderful qualities to contribute to your family and to the world.

Understanding Your "Outie" Child

There are no seven wonders of the world
in the eyes of a child. There are seven million.
—Walt Streightiff

Having people to talk to, getting feedback, thinking out loud, and being busy are all energy sources for extroverted children. Notice how different these are from energy sources that meet the needs of introverts. And remember, extroverts, like introverts, are on a continuum—some are more extroverted than others, and each is a unique individual with a unique personality. With these ideas in mind, here are some ways to help your extroverted children thrive.

Make Sure They Have People with Whom They Can Talk

Extroverted children need people. They'd have loved the old telephones with party lines where you could join in on a conversation anytime you wanted to. Allowing them to talk, share their experiences, and air their feelings as they occur gives them energy. All this chatting can sometimes be daunting for the family, so help them develop relationships outside of the family. Also, since extroverts can get caught up in the crowd, especially in the teen years, it is important to begin early to help them develop their own individual interests. Studies show that teenagers with strong interests get into less trouble. Think about what sparks their attention and encourage it. Find knowledgeable people they can talk to. If your daughter is interested in photography, for example, perhaps the owner of the local photo store could be a resource. Ask a photographer friend to take her on a photo outing or subscribe to a photography magazine in her name. Once your children feel well informed, ask them to give a little after-dinner presentation to the family about what is most fascinating to them about their interest.

Provide Feedback

Extroverted children need feedback. "Atta boy/atta girl"s are important. A few words of positive reinforcement, and they are flying high. All children need to be mirrored, to have their personality reflected back to them, but this can be especially important for extroverted children; it helps them have more understanding of their behavior. "I noticed you looked sad when Jacob couldn't play. Let's see if we can make a play date for tomorrow." Extroverted children are less self-reflective than introverted ones, and they need help to develop this capacity. It is important for them to understand that feelings are not the same as actions: they are internal states, and they can be *thought* about. I'm feeling nervous, why? Then they have a *choice* about what actions they decide to take. "I know you wanted a turn, but you waited for Sean to have one first. That was being a good friend." "What do you think would happen if you talked the whole time and your friend never got a chance to say anything?" "I know you were in a hurry, but I liked the way you waited for Kathy to come through the door first." These comments can help children to become less impulsive and develop a capacity for reflection—to learn to think before acting. When delivering feedback use the "Oreo cookie" technique. Start with a positive, add any negative, and then finish with another positive. Feedback refuels extroverted children.

Let Them Think Out Loud

Extroverts think by talking. They need another person to listen to them so they can sort out their thoughts and feelings. They may not need a response. Just a sounding board. Ask your children if they would like you just to listen or whether you should ask questions and give suggestions. (Even if you only listen, be sure to let your child know how much you like their ideas and questions.) Extroverts may talk to themselves out loud, and they may "hear" themselves better this way. Let extroverts talk about their worries and concerns and share their ideas with you; they are processing out loud. They may also ask a lot of questions. Answer as many as you want, but it's okay to set a limit. "I'll answer two more questions, and then I need to fix dinner." Hard as it is for introverts to imagine, extroverted children may study better with the TV or radio on.

Keep Them Active, but Schedule Quiet Time

Stimulation is the name of the game for extroverts; they need to have things to do, places to go, and people to see. Their attitude is: time's a wasting—let's not twiddle our thumbs and do nothing. Many extroverted children don't want to miss out on anything, which can really be exhausting for parents, even extroverted parents. Schedule quiet time even if your children don't want to slow down. "From two to three this afternoon, I want you to take a break. You can listen to music or a book on tape, or read another chapter of your book." Help them notice the benefits of private time. "You look a little more relaxed after your reading break. How does your body feel?" If your children are playing alone, daydreaming, or just kicking back, let them know you are glad they can enjoy quiet time. Review your children's activities and make sure they are not overscheduled. Even very extroverted children can do too much. They need opportunities to practice introverting.

If You're an Introverted Parent with an Extroverted Child

There never was a child so lovely
but his mother was glad to get him to sleep.
—RALPH WALDO EMERSON

For an introverted parent, extroverted children can be a joy and a curse. They are enthusiastic and excited about the world. They want to try everything. They want to sit close and tell you *all* about their day. Your individual temperaments open the door to a wonderful opportunity for your children to learn early the value of differences. Since your need for physical closeness may be much lower, give them a good hug and tell them that you love them but that you need a little more space now.

Nancy, an introverted mom I interviewed, said, "My daughter, Victoria, wanted to participate in all the school activities. She hated to miss out on anything. I couldn't keep up. I felt so guilty." Let go of feeling guilty about being you. It's important to explain to your children that you feel drained by too many activities, that you need breaks to recharge your energy in a way they may not. Help them to understand that you love being involved in their life but that you have a different pace, sort of like the tortoise and the hare. Let them know you want to hear about their other activities, but make limits. For

Correcting the Extroverted Child

Like the weather, extroverted kids show a variety of emotional patterns. Lots of highs and lows. Sometimes they are oblivious to other people's feelings. They can ignore a parent's anger. If you are angry with them, they may feel bad for a while because they like sunny approval. But unlike more introverted children, they may not give the incident a second thought. Like storm clouds that blow in and out, extroverted children may think the matter is over and done with.

Impressing upon them what you are upset about is important. Talk to them in private, and tell them the particular behavior you didn't like. Look them in the eye and sound firm. Keep your comments short and specific. "I'm upset that you took the paintbrush away from Lindsey." Explain what will happen next. "I want you to apologize to her. She is going to finish using the brush. Then it will be your turn."

Later, in a nonblaming or noncritical way, ask your children if they have thought about other ways they could have handled that situation. Help them think through their actions. Don't get into an arguing match. Many extroverted children are quite verbal and may be able to outtalk you. Stay calm and in charge. "I love you, but I didn't like what you did." Remind them we all need to think about our actions sometimes. Even Mom and Dad.

example, say you'll attend two sports events a month, which they can choose. I suggested to Nancy that she ask her daughter to tape-record her week's activities and then give a report Sunday (maybe with a toy microphone), after dinner, to the whole family. Call it Victoria's Week in Review.

One client of mine, Kevin, couldn't understand why his son Josh didn't want to stay home more. The first words out of Josh's mouth when his dad picked him up at school were, "Where are we going?" When Kevin would say, "Home," Josh would groan and slump down in his seat. "And I'd feel like a bad parent," Kevin said. "I couldn't understand why he didn't want to be with us." Don't take your children's temperament personally. They are not rejecting you; they want recharging. Remember, they are afraid of feeling drained, the same feeling you don't like. Say to your son, "I know you don't feel like going home. Let's sing all the way or take turns finding the alphabet on street signs. You start with A." If he doesn't immediately agree, you start singing or playing the game. Most kids will join in. Give your extroverted children lots of approval. They may not appreciate what's positive about themselves (and what seems obvious to you) if you don't point out those qualities.

The Team Approach: Talking to Your Child about Introversion

We worry about what a child will be tomorrow,
yet we forget that he is someone today.
—STACIA TAUSCHER

Begin when they are young to discuss with your introverted children how their bodies and minds work and how it's possible to manage them. In order to think, feel, and move, our bodies require energy. Talk with your children about how they gain their energy, their ability to feel good and full of "get up and go." Explain that some people need a lot of private time to store up energy. Others gain their energy by going out into the world. Give an example from your personal experience about how you gain energy.

Introverted Siblings Can Get Lost in the Shuffle

Most families have members all along the introvert/extrovert continuum. It is quite common, however, for a family to have one spirited extrovert who takes up a lot of airtime, leaving little space for more introspective children. If for any reason there is an imbalance in your family, it is crucial to protect introverted children from siblings who can dominate, squelch, or overshadow them.

At the dinner table make sure all the children have a turn to talk. Introverts feel uncomfortable about interrupting, so they may not join a family discussion. If they know they are going to have a turn, they can have time to prepare their thoughts. Help the facile talkers learn to wait for their slower-paced brother or sister. Don't let one sibling interrupt or talk for another. It's obvious that no child should be made fun of or humiliated for his or her communication style.

Notice if your introverted children tend to just go with the flow and, as a result, get overlooked. Ask them what they think or feel about family activities. "Was today a little busy for you?" Teach your other children to include the introvert's opinion. "Jon, I know you want to go to the park—ask Heather what she thinks about that."

Encourage the other siblings to wait if an introverted child takes longer to give his or her opinion. "Heather needs a minute to think about that, Jon. Let's see what she thinks." By respecting everyone in the family, all of your children will develop stronger interpersonal skills.

Help your children talk about how their bodies feel. Teach them to take their temperament temperature. They can begin by noticing when they need rest or activity. Reflect back to them: "I saw you had fun at Chelsea's party, but you felt tired afterward. Did you notice that, too?" Help them observe differences in other children: "After the picnic, Taylor went to sleep on the way home and Sara chatted and sang all the way. Their needs and temperaments are different."

Minds work in different ways, too. Explain to your child, "Some people think very quickly and often speak fast. Others, who are more like you, need to think over their reactions. If you have time to think, you know what you want to say. You also feel good. You feel good after focusing on your butterfly collection for hours. Other people get tired if they pay attention to something too long. They prefer being very busy."

Develop a "we're a team" approach with your children. Anticipate and prepare them for situations that might be difficult. Discuss your temperament temperature and that of others in the family so that they understand there is no stigma about being introverted or extroverted. The trick is to help them understand themselves without developing avoidance as a way to cope. At times they will feel overstimulated. You can encourage them to take deep breaths and to take breaks to calm themselves.

Don't overprotect your children or expect them to manage alone. What they need most is a sense that they can brainstorm with you. If they think you understand their strengths and limitations, they will develop into mature adults. Develop an ongoing dialogue (where you listen a lot) with your children about the ups and downs of their energy. It is very empowering for them to feel you are working together. This is the greatest support you can give them to face the natural struggles of growing up.

Gifted and Talented Children

I am always uncomfortable with the terms *gifted* and *talented* because *all* children are gifted and talented in some way. Nonetheless, I am discussing the topic because many introverted children and adults don't realize that their abilities and intelligence are valuable. Though studies show that there is a correlation between introversion and giftedness, introverted children often do not test well and may not be identified as gifted or talented. A *gifted* child is thought to have a genetic endowment that produces advanced and accelerated brain development. His or her cognitive, emotional, physical, and intuitive functioning results in high intelligence. The term *talented* refers to a child who possesses a cluster of traits that may result in an unusual level of ability. It is thought that gifted and talented boys and girls require responsive and enriched environments to develop fully their innate gifts.

Listed below are some of the early signs of giftedness:

- advanced abstract reasoning and problem-solving skills
- advanced progression through developmental milestones
- high level of curiosity
- early and extensive language development
- early recognition of caretakers (e.g., smiling)
- enjoyment and speed of learning
- excellent sense of humor
- extraordinary memory
- high activity level
- intense reactions to noise, pain, or frustration
- less need for sleep in infancy
- long attention span if interested in the topic or activity
- sensitivity and compassion
- perfectionism
- unusual alertness in infancy
- vivid imagination (e.g., imaginary companion)

Now that you have looked it over, let me add a word of caution. I believe there are three areas—activity level, verbal skills, and memory—where introverted children differ from this profile. In the first place, many introverted children do not have a high activity level. They may be rather sedentary or have bursts of activity. Second, their verbal skills may not be apparent. They may have an excellent passive vocabulary, but unless you draw them out, they may not demonstrate all the words they know.

Finally, it is good to keep in mind that introverts tend to attach to long-term memory rather than short-term memory, as extroverts do. So it may take longer for introverted children to remember something, but once they do, they seldom forget it. Extroverts remember faster but forget quicker. Look over the list to see if your child is displaying some of these qualities.

Raising a gifted or talented child can be exciting, as well as daunting. Here are a few suggestions to help you.

- Look at your child's characteristics from a positive perspective; for example, persistence and stubbornness can be seen as essentially the same trait.

- Assess your child's particular talents or interests and try to provide him or her with what he or she needs. For example, if your child loves painting, provide paints.

- Be a knowledgeable advocate; you may need to educate the educators about your child.

- Get help. Bright babies and toddlers can wear parents out. Enlist family and friends.

- Listen to your child with respect; gifted kids may ask a lot of questions and challenge existing ideas. Explanations generally result in more cooperation.

■ Teach your child how to access resources to find answers to questions you can't answer.

■ Read books about giftedness (I have included some in the Bibliography), look on the Internet for information, join a group for parents of gifted children, and talk with other parents of gifted kids.

■ Value your children's uniqueness—their opinions, ideas, and aspirations. Do not stress fitting in. Make sure they feel appreciated at home.

A Note on Shyness

Let me remind you of one common misconception I discussed for adults on page 43 in Chapter 2. Being introverted is not the same as being shy. Both introverted and extroverted children can be shy. Shyness is a state of anxiety wherein a person is afraid of rejection, ridicule, or embarrassment. Some shy children have poor social skills. They avoid social situations, whether it's with one person or twenty, because they are afraid of being rebuffed or rejected. Social activities are very painful for them. They often attack themselves for everything they do or say in social situations.

Introverted children usually have good social skills and often enjoy social situations. They may need to ease into social engagements, and they become tired if they have to deal with too many people for too long. They may feel uncomfortable because they don't like to interrupt, and this can leave them feeling left out of groups. But, in general, introverted kids enjoy social activities. Nevertheless, if an introverted child is continually pushed or criticized for being introverted, he or she can become shy, inhibited, or afraid.

If extroverted children are shamed, criticized, or humiliated, they also can develop shyness. Being shy is a very difficult problem for extroverts. One of my clients is a dramatic, fifteen-year-old,

Parent Power

Kids are always the only future the human race has.
—WILLIAM SAROYAN

We can't protect our children from every danger in the world, but we can influence how they feel about themselves. When they are young, we can teach them to value and understand their

shy extrovert. She wants to be with her friends and needs to be out and about to gain energy, but she is so anxious she can hardly sit still. In my office she rocks the glider chair so fast I think she's going to launch herself through the window. As we work to reduce her social anxiety and increase her interpersonal skills, she will be able to find sources of stimulation without so much anxiety.

Explain to your shy children the difference between shyness and introversion. Let them know you will help them learn to feel more comfortable in social situations. Although some children are born shy (with a more active fear center in the brain), most learn to be shy because of criticism, shaming, and rejection. Introverted or extroverted shy children need to learn social skills to stop that critical voice in their head and to increase their confidence.

I have included some excellent books on shyness in the Bibliography. Read a few and practice some of the suggestions. Introversion and extroversion are part of a child's temperament and cannot be changed. Shyness, on the other hand, can be improved significantly. Shy children and adults can reduce most of their fear and anxiety through learning new skills.

temperaments. (It's useful if they learn to take their own temperament temperature, as I discussed earlier in the chapter.) We can also teach them to appreciate other people's temperaments. If we use our powerful bond with our children to help them nurture their natures, they will have a solid foundation to grow into adults with character. Character is a function of the way each person uses his or her innate temperament. It is an arena we have control over.

Do our children use their gifts and their abilities constructively or destructively? The world would be a better place if every child grew up with integrity, curiosity, compassion, the ability to love and be loved, and the capacity to develop their inner strengths.

Points to Ponder

- Observe whether your children are more introverted or more extroverted.
- Think about how your children create their energy.
- Think about your and your partner's temperaments. Are you innies or outies?
- Have a family talk about your temperaments and how they affect your daily relationships. You will appreciate one another more.

CHAPTER VI

Socializing: Party Pooper or Pooped from the Party?

The room is a sea of people. The loud voices hurt my ears. I scan the room for a safe nook. My stomach tightens. My breath quickens. I feel like retreating. My husband, Mike, sees friends he wants to say hello to. He's excited. He loves parties. He threads his way through the huddled groups, smiling and nodding all the way. That's when I make a beeline for the bathroom. I stay in there, checking out the wallpaper, the hand towels, and the soap. I really appreciate a well-appointed bathroom. I begin to relax. My stomach unclenches. My breathing returns to normal. After a while, I feel prepared to leave the sanctuary of the bathroom. I locate Mike's bald spot in one of the huddled groups. I slip in beside him. He hands me a Pepsi. I chat with people. I enjoy hearing what they have to say. It's fun to laugh and talk. Every once in a while I feel that old familiar urge to retreat, so I revisit the powder room. Occasionally I'll pass another bathroom lurker. We recognize each other and smile. I know she's counting the minutes until she can leave without appearing rude. Dinner is served, then dessert. Two bites into the Peach Melba I turn to Mike and whisper: "I'd like to leave in five minutes."

This is about as good as it gets for me at parties. And, believe it or not, it has taken me years to develop even this level of coping capacity. I enjoy social gatherings—I do—as long as I know I'm leaving soon. If I know that pretty soon I can slip into my PJs and enjoy the peace and quiet of my bedroom, I can manage the uncomfortable feelings and energy expenditure that social gatherings entail. Indeed, I have found that the more I understand introversion, the easier it has been for me to handle socializing.

Many of the introverts I have had as clients or interviewed for this book find social events uncomfortable, even though they like people. In fact, many laughed in recognition when I described hiding out in the bathroom. "Oh, do you do that, too?"

My client Emily came in on a Monday morning and flung herself into the glider chair across from me. "I've got a socializing hangover," she said with a laugh. "I went to *two* events this weekend, and I had a great time, but I'm bushed. Why do I feel so pooped?"

Most introverts have good people skills and enjoy wonderful relationships with their friends and family. In fact, many have professions that put them in touch with people, just as I do. So why do social gatherings often cause them anxiety and that "draggin' your wagon" feeling?

The answer has to do with the fact that socializing in groups requires huge amounts of energy. First of all, it takes energy to gear up to go out, because introverts tend to think ahead and imagine what it will be like for them later: They will end up feeling tired, uncomfortable, or anxious. Second, most introverted people need to ease into social situations gradually in order to get acclimated to the stimulation. Noise, colors, music, new faces, familiar faces, eating, drinking, smells—everything can cause *brain overload*. Finally, just physically being around a lot of people, friend or foe, drains energy from introverts.

Snappy Repartee vs.
Substantive Conversation

To find the good life
you must become yourself.

—Dr. Bill Jackson

The type of conversation engaged in at most social gatherings is
made for extroverts, providing them with a lot of stimulation. But
it goes against an introvert's natural grain and is extremely demanding.
The chitchat often focuses on subjects like the latest news, weather, and
sports; it's often loud, competitive, and fast-paced. People usually talk
standing up; their faces are animated, and they make direct eye contact.
They speak spontaneously, interrupting each other right and left, and
ask a lot of personal questions. People who don't keep up with the chat
often look and feel awkward. They are not drawn out but rather overlooked and ignored by the group.

I recently got a call from the mother of a thirteen-year-old boy
named Cameron. "Cameron wants to talk to a therapist," she
explained. "He has diagnosed himself from the Internet, and he
thinks he has social anxiety." When Cameron came in, he talked
about his life, and in a few minutes it was apparent to me that he had
many friends—pals who sought him out for advice. "Tell me why you
think you have social anxiety," I said. "Well," he said, "I hate so many
of those normal activities—going to the beach and to concerts, the
crowd at lunch, and joking around before class. I always feel like I
don't fit into the group. I either feel ignored or put on the spot."
Cameron didn't realize it, but he understood himself very well.

Introverts can be energized by one-on-one conversations about
subjects that interest them, and they are recharged (up to a point) by a

complex discussion where each person considers the other's opinion thoughtfully. I think of this as a generative conversation because it keeps spawning new ideas. The pace of these evolving talks works better for introverts because they can sit down. (Standing seems to require more energy and increases their sense of exposure.) They can also listen more than speak, pause before they jump into the conversation, and experience fewer interruptions. They can look away (if they need to reduce stimulation) without losing contact with the other person. Smiling is less important, embarrassing personal questions are less of an issue (they can answer them or not), and they don't feel as if they are getting too much or too little attention. In one-on-one talks they are more likely to be drawn out, and if an introvert starts a comment without a preface, the other person will often ask for a connecting thought. If the dreaded brainlock occurs, it's not a problem to say, "Boy, what I was about to say flew right out of my head." When reading about what makes socializing difficult for introverts, it's not hard to understand why most people, even most introverts, confuse it with shyness.

Continuum Confusion

What is so confusing for introverts is that sometimes they enjoy socializing in noisy, overcrowded, standing-up groups, and feel energized by it. The next time they feel depleted. What gives? Since most introverts feel they *should* enjoy mingling, they wonder why they don't *always* feel invigorated. (When extroverts feel a little introvertish, they experience it as "I just need some rest." Since they feel good about mingling, they give little thought to feeling pooped. It doesn't seem as unsettling to them—or as confusing.) The fact is, we are all born with the physiological ability to extrovert or introvert. And if the conditions are right (we are not always aware of the reason), our bodies and brains may be ripe for some extroverting. Indeed, there may be times when we enjoy a good dose of chitchat or have occasional perky-partying experiences. However, if you are on the more introverted end of the continuum, the more common experience will be a need to restore after social outings.

To Go or Not to Go, That Is the Question

There is no pleasure in having nothing to do; the fun is in having lots to do and not doing it.
—MARY WILSON LITTLE

It is often a struggle for introverts to decide whether or not to go to a social gathering. We all get caught up in what we *should* do, and we forget to think about what we want to do. Obviously, there are some occasions when we have no choice—for example, certain work-related events, family gatherings, or your best friend's wedding. But there are others when we have options.

Despite what most books about shyness suggest, *you do not need to attend every function that comes along.* On the other hand, if you avoid them all, you'll end up feeling isolated. Plus, you'll think you're a social chicken, not to mention you will miss out on what could turn out to be a fun time.

As with most things in life, there's a middle road, which is usually the healthiest path. So learn to ask yourself specific questions about the upcoming social occasion to help you think through whether or not you *should* go. It's okay to be on the fence for a few days. It just means you have *two* good choices. Say to yourself, "By Wednesday, I will decide and let Hannah know." If you don't go, you may regret it. But that's all right. It doesn't mean you made the wrong decision.

If you practice giving yourself choices, you will begin to see that sometimes you *do* want to go.

Here are some of the questions you can ask yourself when you are trying to decide whether or not to attend a party:

- Is this occasion beneficial to my career or my partner's career?

- Is this event important to me—a fund-raiser for a charity I believe in or for a politician I support, or a party given by a close friend?

- Is it the type of occasion where I might be put on the spot—asked to speak into a microphone or to introduce people?

- Is this a onetime opportunity or will something like it happen again?

Boo and Hurray

I polled a number of introverts about what social gatherings they dreaded and which ones they found more enjoyable and less draining. These lists reflect personal preferences. Think about how *you* feel about the different events mentioned. The ones in the Boo category were cocktail parties, charity events, receptions, crowded events, company picnics, candle/basket/Tupperware parties, open houses, beach parties, large sports events, ear-splitting concerts, and receiving lines. Notice how many require standing up.

In the Hurray category were museum exhibits (especially with audiotape guides and benches), lectures, small guided tours, picnics, concerts, baby or bridal showers (if you're not the mom-to-be or the bride, and thus the focus isn't on you), small dinner parties, family get-togethers, movies, classes, walking with a friend, driving with a friend, and individual sports.

- Is it an activity I hate—a movie premier, a "roast," an auction, an event where there will be lots of drinking?
- Will there be a small, medium, or large crowd?
- Will I know a lot of people, some people, or no one?
- Will I hurt the feelings of someone I care about if I don't attend?
- Have I been out to too many social occasions recently, or too few?

From time to time, give yourself permission to broaden your social repertoire and stretch your socializing muscles. For example, if the occasion is important to you or your partner in terms of your careers, consider dropping in just for a short time. Talk to the people you need to see, like your boss, and then leave. It's a perfectly acceptable option to "dip in" and "duck out." You can always stay longer if you find that you are having fun.

Tactful Turndowns

The point of tact is not sharp.
—COLLEEN CARNEY

Introverts often feel guilty or embarrassed because they don't want to attend a social occasion. As a result, they may come across as curt or uncaring when they turn down the invitation, even though they care very much. Sometimes, they try to avoid saying no by neglecting to R.S.V.P. This makes matters worse.

It's helpful to learn ways of saying no tactfully, so the host or hostess doesn't feel rebuffed. The goal is to acknowledge the invitation, say whether you can attend, and make it easy for the person to invite you again next time, if that's what you'd like.

Slipping Yourself Permission

Many introverts develop social rules for themselves based on *extroverted* standards. Some I have heard over the years are: I must go to everything I am invited to. I must stay the entire time. I must talk to lots of people. I must look as if I am having fun. I must fit in. I must not be nervous.

It is helpful to let go of those rigid expectations and try to develop guidelines that are playful and flexible. For example, on colored index cards, write some "permission slips" that you can draw on in the upcoming months. Put them in a little box so you can use them again and again. Here are some possibilities.

I give myself:

• permission to drive by the party and check it out without going in

• permission to go to the party and leave after fifteen minutes, one hour, two hours, whatever

• permission to go to the party, eat one chocolate-covered strawberry, and then leave

• permission to go to the party and talk to only one person

• permission to go to the party and just people-watch (one of my favorites)

• permission to go to the party and feel nervous

• permission to go to the party and talk only to guests under the age of ten

Remember, it's okay to tell a white lie when you have to. Many introverts tend to be scrupulously honest, and this isn't always in their best interest. For example, if you declined an invitation to a party by saying, "I don't have the energy," your host or hostess would surely take it personally. Being in society, as Jane Austen pointed out to us, means that we must occasionally grease the wheels of human interaction. Otherwise, they get gummed up.

Here are some simple yet tactful ways to say no:

- "I was so delighted you thought of me. Unfortunately, I won't be able to make it." (You don't always have to give a reason.)

- "I really wish we could come to your party, but we already have an engagement that day. Thanks so much."

- "Oh dear, we can't come on that day, but we'd love to be included next time."

- "Thanks so much for the invitation. We'll just be dropping by for a few minutes since we have somewhere else to be, but we don't want to miss the chance to see you. Can we bring anything?"

Energy Conservation

Think of the fierce energy concentrated in an acorn!
You bury it in the ground,
and it explodes into a giant oak!

—GEORGE BERNARD SHAW

It's important to conserve energy *before* you go out for a night on the town. Like a dam that harnesses the flow of a river in order to utilize its power, you should store up energy to spend extroverting. Here are some tips that may help:

- Don't schedule too many social occasions in the same week.

- Take a walk, read, nap, or sit in nature before the get-together.

- Drink plenty of water and take deep breaths when you feel anxious about the party.

- Eat some protein to boost your energy before you leave home.

- Have the sitter come early so you can get ready without a hassle.

- Listen to a relaxation tape or calming music on the way to the party.
- Set aside time the following morning to recharge.

Anticipating

Worry is interest paid on trouble
before it comes due.

—WILLIAM RALPH INGE

Many introverts tend to foreshadow. They think ahead about what could go wrong, or they remember how tired they felt the last time they went out. This can add to apprehension about social occasions. If you are picturing yourself dropping shrimp sauce on your shirt or see yourself dragging home from the wedding, try to redirect your anxiety.

- Talk to your partner about your concerns; share a little humor about them.
- Remind yourself, "I will have a good time; I can handle whatever happens."
- Tell yourself, "I don't need to think about that," if you keep dwelling on something embarrassing.
- Imagine yourself at social occasions you have enjoyed.
- Anticipate meeting a friend who will be at the event.
- Remind yourself that you can regulate your energy.

Name Tagging

Most introverts hate name tags because they draw unwanted attention and increase their sense of exposure, but at some events they're expected. Here are some tips to make them more playful:

- Write each letter of your name in a different color.
- Draw a cute picture instead of or with your name.
- Attach the tag in a less noticeable place.
- Don't wear a name tag at all.

Arrival Strategies

When you go into a social occasion, you can take some pressure off yourself by realizing that you don't need to enter a party like an extrovert. You need to enter like an introvert, usually in stages, with some time to observe first. Slowly acclimate yourself to the party atmosphere—just as a deep-sea diver controls his ascent to the surface of the water, from two hundred feet, to one hundred feet, and so on—in order to reduce the social "bends." Ease into the festivities step by step.

1. Remember that you will probably feel tense (remind yourself that it's okay to feel unsettled) when you approach the door. Take two big, deep breaths, then ring the bell.

2. As soon as you enter, select a location (for example, by the fireplace, sitting on the arm of the sofa) where you can perch and look around the room.

3. Hunt down the hostess, say hello, and ask if you can help. (Giving a hand usually helps people feel included.)

4. If he or she is not too busy, ask the host or hostess for a house tour—or just walk around looking at family photos.

5. From your observation platform, pay attention to how you are feeling. Are you getting acclimated?

6. As you begin to get your sea legs, notice if there is another "percher" you could meet, a friend to talk to, or a group to join.

7. Some people like to spend the whole party with people they know; others want to practice meeting someone new. You always have choices.

Seven Guerrilla Socializing Tactics

To be prepared is half the victory.
—Cervantes

So once we have made it into the room, we are ready to mix it up a bit, but how? Most of us will make a beeline for friends—hang out with who we know. But what if we don't know anyone, or our friends are fully engaged, or we want to meet new people? Here are some tactics to make meeting people easier.

Tactic 1: The Sea Anemone

Patrick, an introvert, entered a standing-room-only crowd at a conference in Washington, D.C. He knew no one. Surrounded by a mass of businesspeople who were pressing in on him, Patrick began to feel an agitated sensation in his stomach and arms. Fortunately, he knew in advance how to react in a situation like this, so he took a deep breath—and backed out of the room. He wandered upstairs onto the balcony where a few overstuffed chairs sat empty. He settled into one of them and watched the teeming scene below. After a while, several other escapees from the crush below came up, and soon they were all sitting down and chatting at an innie pace.

This is what I call the sea anemone tactic, and it's one of my favorites for large gatherings. Sea anemones are creatures that attach themselves to rocks, their tentacles swaying with the ocean currents. Then along floats some edible tidbits, and the sea anemones' tentacles lure them in.

I always feel like this when I set up shop in some corner or viewing site at a party. I am so much more comfortable sitting down, anchored to my rock, than I am wandering around the room. Sure enough, sooner or later some folks drift by. I give a small friendly smile, and they often stop to exchange pleasantries. Some stay awhile, and some drift off. Soon another guest bobs over for chitchat.

Tactic 2: Act "As If"

When I was in graduate school studying to become a psychotherapist, I was taught to act "as if." It's a way to try on a new skill or a new role until it becomes a part of you. Pretend to know what you're doing and sure enough, you will start believing that you *can* do it. Fake it till you make it is another way to put it. At first I was irritated with my professors—were they kidding? How could I fake such an important job? Soon I realized that as an inexperienced psychotherapist, acting "as if" was all I had. It is a powerful tool, and it works.

Many introverts value being authentic, as do I, so I had to remind myself what *real* qualities were tied up in my "act." Here's what I came up with:

- First: I knew I could listen.

- Second: I knew I could reflect back what I heard.

- Third: I knew that something to say would eventually come to me, even if it was "I'd like to hear more about that next week."

- Fourth: My intention was to be helpful.

So, during therapy sessions, I would slip into my listening mode. And soon, like a kid riding a two-wheeler who doesn't realize the training wheels are off the ground, I began to feel that I could be a therapist, without the "as if" training wheels.

How does this experience translate into social life? As you enter a party or a gathering, act "as if" you're a confident *introverted* guest. Picture yourself looking poised. Remember a time when you mingled with an air of assurance. Adopt the attitude "I'm going to fake it till I make it." Smile at strangers. Look at people and be curious about them. Remind yourself that although you may feel antsy, you *look* calm.

What you project is different from what you feel. Remind yourself that you have lots of interesting things to say. Make eye contact with someone and then join their group. You can listen to what people are saying, you can comment on it, and you can add one idea. In a few minutes, move on to another group. Soon your training wheels will be up, and you will feel considerably more relaxed. The experience will not always be perfect. You may start off with that icky, jittery feeling—topped off with a dash of anxiety—and you may have some awkward moments. But overall, you'll be "good enough." And the more you act "as if" you are self-assured, the more confident you'll become. Especially since the secret trick to this technique is learning that the "as if" you is already part of you. It's you without fear!

Tactic 3: Prop Job

An introverted friend of mine has taught me a nifty trick. When she goes to parties she wears a prop—usually one of her ceramic necklaces with miniature figures on them. One is a pride of cats in frisky poses. Another has a spray of dancers circling her neck in spirited prances. They look fanciful and intriguing. People ask her about the whimsical figures. What are they? Where did she get the necklaces? A conversation has started. Other socializers are also relieved to have something to focus and comment on.

At first you may think that having a prop will draw too much attention to you, making you feel even more overstimulated. But my clients find that this isn't what happens. The job of the prop is to put the focus on the prop, not on you.

It's fun to wear a pin, an old political button, a miniature picture in a locket, a funny hat, unusual hair accessories, or a special ring or watch. I have a Winnie-the-Pooh watch (Pooh is running from bees), and I have actually had people tell me, "Well, I knew if you were wearing a Winnie-the-Pooh watch, you couldn't be all bad." I also have a collection of zany socks, and I'm always surprised by how many people notice them peeking out from under my slacks. I like to wear shoes with a subtle glitter or rhinestones on them. They usually earn a comment or two. As for ties, Mike has a collection of ties with animated characters on them. People immediately start chatting with him about their favorite cartoon characters. If you want only a few comments, choose something subtle. If chosen correctly, your prop will attract the very folks to whom you will want to talk. I like people with a sense of humor, so when I wear my Groucho glasses or my Beagle socks with floppy ears, I usually like whoever laughs at them. And people assume I'm okay because of my prop. When I work with children, I always wear my Mickey Mouse fanny pack for the first session. Kids warm up to it and to me right away.

Pets and children are great props (and, of course, they're far more than that). Another good prop is a camera. Very often it's the people who are snapping pictures at social gatherings who feel the most awkward. Many introverted people who are in the public spotlight—Tipper Gore is a good example—find that it's comforting to take pictures. They are using their introverted ability to observe from a distance—to be "out" of conversation and yet "in" the group. It's a clever way to regulate their own stimulation.

Tactic 4: A Friendly Face

As I mentioned at the beginning of the chapter, some of the elements involved in social encounters with strangers are especially problematic for introverts, including making eye contact, making small talk, figuring out when to smile, and covering embarrassing moments (such as forgetting a friend's name). Just remember, even extroverts can have awkward moments with people they don't know.

The Eyes Have It: Eye contact increases stimulation, so we introverts tend to avoid it. It's okay to look away in order to lower the level of stimulation. The secret is to know *when* to look away. Here are some suggestions:

- When people are talking to you, look straight at them.

- When you are speaking, you can look away and still seem to be "in" the conversation.

- Use eye contact for emphasis. Look intensely at someone to increase the impact of what you are saying.

- Eyes can speak volumes without words, so practice raising your eyebrows (Oh, really?), blinking (Wow!), rolling your eyes (I can't believe it!), and widening your eyes (You've got to be kidding!) to enlarge your nonverbal vocabulary.

People like to feel that a listener is reacting to what they are saying. You can show your interest without saying a word. You can smile with your eyes—not just your mouth.

Your Mona Lisa Smile: The reason human beings smile and show expression is to engage other people. Introverts are focused internally, and they often don't invite responses from outside. As a result, they tend to have still faces, inexpressive and unsmiling. Unconsciously, they know appearing more animated might bring more stimulation and distraction. But a lack of expression can be uninviting, even unnerving, to other partygoers who are desperately looking for friendly faces. At the same time, if you go to the opposite extreme and smile too often, you may feel overly aggressive to other reserved or shy people. Would you want to cozy up to a Cheshire Cat?

So learn the art of the subtle smile. Smile with your lips closed at first. After you feel more at ease with someone, you can show a little tooth. By the way, research shows that we can actually heighten our mood by smiling—it affects the chemical "mood lifters" in our brains.

Tactic 5: Small Talk

Many introverts don't realize that there's a logic to small talk that anyone can learn. Small talk is made up of four phrases: openers, sustainers, transitions, and closers.

1. Openers. Be Prepared is the Boy Scout motto, and it works for party conversations, too. Before you attend a meeting, party, or other gathering, read a magazine or newspaper, or watch a popular TV show or a movie to feed yourself conversation ingredients. Brush up on the latest political topic and prepare a comment, opinion, or question. If you want to join a group with an ongoing conversation, research shows that the best entry line is to ask a question about the topic under discussion. Don't come into the group and shift to a new topic. The group can feel threatened.

Openers are open-ended, neutral questions that invite the other people to talk with you, so write down several lines you could say about yourself or the party. Like hors d'oeuvres, these lines whet the appetite. They give others the chance to start talking. Practice them in front of a mirror or with a friend. Here are a few samples:

- "Hi, I'm Marti. How do you know the host?"
- "Hi, I love the music they're playing. Do you know the name of the piece?"
- "Hi, I'm Marti; Jim is my boss. Isn't this a beautiful home?"
- "Isn't the food delicious?"
- "I love this backyard."

2. Sustainers. Learn some comments that will keep the conversation going, sustaining it with nourishing questions. Sustainers ask folks for their opinions or comments. If the topic is the latest box office buster or popular TV shows, here are some sustaining questions:

- "Did you see that movie?"
- "What was it about?"
- "What did you like about it?"
- "What was the message of the film?"
- "What did you think of the acting?"
- "I wonder why that show is so popular; what do you think?"

3. Transitions. Introverts often feel unsteady while schmoozing. If the conversation starts to dry up or become uncomfortable or too personal, they can feel even queasier. It's good to remember you have control. Use it to steer the talk onto safer shores, before if hits the rocks and breaks up. It's often a good idea to direct the conversation back to something that was said earlier. For example:

- "You said that you were a teacher. What grade do you teach?"
- "When you mentioned your vacation, I was wondering where you went."
- "A minute ago you said you had a son. How old is he?"

Uncomfortable moments in conversations may also mean that it's time to move on. Remember, if the conversation is not only drying up but dying, don't try to resuscitate it. If you realize that the person who asked the personal question is too nosy and doesn't get the hint, stop trying to build bridges. Or if there is a general itchy feeling that either of you wants a break, take one. You can use one of the suggestions below for closers.

4. Closers. Social research has found that standing chitchat groups last an average of five to twenty minutes, thirty minutes tops. So don't be offended when others change groups. It seems to be the nature of the beast. "I hate to leave this intriguing conversation, but I see Jake over there and I need to speak to him." You can always hook up with someone again later if you really enjoyed talking with him or her. If you want, you can ask for the other person's phone number or card before you break away: "I'd love to get together with you for coffee sometime. May I call you?"

When you are ready to leave either a one-on-one conversation or a group, it's important to say something. Don't just fade away like a ghost. Departures need to be short and crisp. These lines can help you duck out of a conversation, so practice them—and don't take it personally if someone uses them on you.

- "I need to refresh my drink, excuse me."
- "I've enjoyed this conversation, but I see my boss over there and I'd like to say hello."
- "Excuse me, I promised to call and check on my kids."
- "Excuse me, I'm going to get some punch now. But I'd like to talk more later."
- "Is the bathroom over there? Thanks."
- "Oh, there's Sam. I've got to give him a quick message."

- "Excuse me, but I promised the hostess I would help out for a few minutes in the kitchen."
- "I think I'll hit the buffet now—the line seems to be thinning out."

If you are the one who is "brushed off," just say something short and sweet and let the person escape:

- "It was nice to talk to you."
- "I enjoyed meeting you."
- "I enjoyed our chat."
- "Have a good evening."

Tactic 6: Fail-safe

What if you practice these smoother schmoozing tactics, and, despite all your preparation, you max out, vapor lock, or begin to itch? What can you do for "fast aid?" Here are a few fail-safe methods for when the going gets tough. They'll help you reduce your "too much" feeling and anxiety:

- Take a few deep breaths. That always helps.
- Move away. Find a new place to sit or stand and watch.
- Take a bathroom break. Put a wet washcloth on your forehead and close your eyes for a few minutes.
- Remind yourself "it's not me." Say it over and over if you have to untie the knot in your belly. Tell yourself you will be okay.
- Ask a friend or partner to walk outside with you for a minute.
- Stroll around and hum (this seems to shift emotions).
- Let your partner know if you are tapped out and ready to leave. It helps if you work out a signal together in advance.

When you aren't in a crisis mode, watch how other folks handle needing some air. If you ask some of your friends, you may be surprised to find they have all sorts of other fast-aid break methods.

Tactic 7: Groundhog Day

Often after something icky happens at a party, we go over and over it in our heads: what we said, what others did. (Sort of like the movie *Groundhog Day*, in which Bill Murray relives the same day over and over.)

Of course, it's our own internal critic, blaming us for any possible transgression—we clammed up, we said too much, we didn't smile enough, we felt too uncomfortable. It's a painful grilling and needs to be interrupted.

I once had a client, Lori, who was a physics professor. She had an extremely harsh internal judge who criticized her every move. In therapy, Lori and I worked to lessen the judge's power. Slowly, the picture in Lori's head changed from an uptight, stern-faced, gray-haired woman in dark robes who was pounding her gavel and haranguing Lori, to a laid-back coach in a Hawaiian shirt with thongs on her tanned feet. This new, smiling, accepting "advocate" sipped a tropical iced tea with a small flowered umbrella in it and said things like, "Hey, hang loose, you did okay. Have a tea on me."

If you realize there is negative talk going on in your head after you exit a social encounter, try picturing the "judge" who is criticizing you. First tell him or her to "put a sock in it." Next, switch channels to thoughts of something pleasant, like a beach, a campfire, a snowy or rainy day. Finally, replace that critical voice with a kinder, gentler, more supportive one: "You're doing fine." If this doesn't work, then think of a kind person whom you have heard in your life, in a movie, or on TV, and let him or her encourage you. Maybe you could conjure up Glenda the Good Witch who encourages Dorothy in Oz, or the Fairy Godmother who helps Cinderella, or John Wooden (the firm but fair former UCLA basketball coach) who expected a good performance from his team, but knew everyone goofs up sometimes.

It's My Party and I'll Cry if I Want To

What if the party, shower, or meeting is at your house? You will probably be overstimulated just thinking about people traipsing through your home, and the anticipation will drain a lot of juice from your batteries. So make the occasion as easy and as user-friendly as you can. Keep it simple. Choose dishes that you can prepare ahead of time, order out, or have a potluck. It's often difficult for innies to manage cooking and guests all at once. Put a start and stop time on your invitation. If you control the guest list, stick to people you like. Make sure the number is a comfortable size for you and your home. See if you can invite at least two introverts to every extrovert.

Try to think up an activity to encourage folks to chat with one another. Here's one that I use. On the entry-hall table I set out a huge jar full of golf balls, paper clips, pretzels, dog bones, or marbles. The more diverse the objects, the better. Then I have each guest write his or her name on a slip of paper along with their estimate of how many items are in the jar. This gives guests something to chat about as they share their guesses. Later on during the party I announce the winners and give out wacky gifts.

Breaking the Ice

I like to set up some sort of game so people will be encouraged to interact. My favorite entails pinning names of famous people (or animals) on my guests' backs. (I often have my children or a friend do this.) The names can be from the movies, literature, or sports, whichever best fits my group.

The instructions are for the guests to ask one another yes and no questions, trying to determine whose name they're wearing. "Am I alive now?" "Did I win an Oscar?" "Do I have a tail?" "Is my sport a team sport?" I have always found this "famous name" game to be a great icebreaker for shy and quiet folks of all ages. The guests who can guess their own identities win silly gifts.

If it's a small gathering, I like to have group projects or a theme for activities that involves my guests: stringing popcorn, shucking corn, decorating the Christmas tree, creating banana splits, or assembling individual pizzas.

Leaving the Party: The Best Part

Never insult an alligator
until after you have crossed the river.
—CORDELL HULL

Before the party, formulate your escape plan. Have a definite departure time in mind. That way you will know your energy is protected. Discuss this with your partner in advance. You can always stay longer if you want to. (If this happens, remember and savor the moment. That nice feeling of *wanting* to stay may not come your way very often.)

Whenever possible, have your own transportation. That way, you can leave when you want, and you won't end up being trapped. While the idea of you and your partner taking separate cars may seem a bit odd, it can make sense in the long run. You can each leave when you feel ready, avoiding the resentment that can build when you have to wait to go or are dragged away too early.

And when it's time to go, don't forget to say good-bye to your hosts. Sometimes introverted people are so fried by the time they leave that they forget to say thanks.

When you are ready to run for the hills, here are some tried-and-true exit lines:

- "I'm just exhausted, so I'm going to scoot, but it's been a wonderful party."

- "I was having such a good time; sorry we have to leave."

- "I promised the sitter we'd be home at a decent hour, so we've got to go."

- "We have really enjoyed ourselves. It was great to see everyone. Thanks for inviting us."

- "It's a shame I have to be out of the house so early tomorrow. Great party. Talk to you soon."

If you feel like you can't tolerate even one more encounter, then leave without saying good-bye, but phone, e-mail, or send a thank-you note the very next day. Remember, there are lots of ways for introverts to maintain meaningful relationships and be personal without having to talk on the phone or face-to-face.

Holidays:
On Automatic Pilot?

The only gift is a portion of thyself.
—RALPH WALDO EMERSON

Holidays are high-energy times. They can be too overstimulating for introverts. Even extroverts can feel overextended. Find ways to celebrate with less hustle and bustle. Many families plan festivities year after year without ever asking themselves if that's what they really want to do, or without talking to one another about new ways to celebrate. Why? Because "that's the way we've always done it!"

Get off of the holiday automatic pilot. Give some thought to the possibility of doing something different. Ask other people in your family what would have the most meaning for them. Ask yourself the same question. If everyone likes the celebrations the way they are, then leave things that way. If they would like to try something new, then be creative.

If you have to see two sets of relatives in one day, for example, which can be too much for introverts—children as well as adults— divide up the visiting into two days. Or consider staying only two hours—instead of half a day—at each place. Alternatively, arrange for everybody to go on an outing together to some peaceful place.

Instead of having the traditional Thanksgiving around a loaded dining room table, a friend of mine and her family took a picnic into a redwood forest, lounged on pine needles, and had a feast that included turkey sandwiches. Then they lay back and listened to the wind sway the tree branches.

Maybe you'd like to start a new family tradition, like having an Easter egg hunt on a sandy beach, or serving meals at a homeless shelter. One of my clients invites a foreign college student from the local university to family holidays.

Make holidays as enriching and as simple as you can. Eliminate things you can't or don't want to do. Holiday expectations can use up your battery juices quickly, so remember always to give yourself plenty of options.

Phone Phobia

On the questionnaires I sent out to introverts asking about their experience of introversion, so many people mentioned phone phobia that I decided to include it as a separate section in this chapter.

Here's how most introverts view the phone: It's an interruption that drains energy and requires losing internal focus, which you have to gain again; it requires expending energy for "on-the-feet thinking"; it doesn't provide innies with Hap Hits. Introverts can have so many dips of energy during the day that they are not able to expend energy at the drop of a hat.

If you, too, are phone phobic, here are some suggestions:

1. Let your answering machine answer for you, and return the call only when you are ready to talk. My client Matt, a salesman, says he would be "tapped out" if he personally answered each call as it came in. So he has a phone-call-return period, and then he gives himself a reward: no phone for the rest of the day.

2. Keep phone calls short unless it's someone you want to talk with in depth. Keep breathing as you talk, and if you have a cordless or cell phone, pace while you talk. To end the conversations, say something like, "I'd love to talk longer, but I need to make a couple more calls before my next client arrives. 'Bye."

3. Don't let people make you feel guilty about not picking up the phone—*screening,* as they call it. It's your prerogative. Don't feel embarrassed about telephone tagging (you call and leave a message; the other person calls and leaves a message). I notice that people who make cracks about "tagging" are often hard to reach, but they want *you* to be available when *they* call.

4. Don't beat yourself up because you don't like the phone. It's not a character defect. It helps to understand *why* you don't like it.

5. Use e-mail as much as you can.

My Very Last Word on Socializing, I Promise

One thing everybody in the world wants and needs is friendliness.

—WILLIAM E. HOLLER

Studies have shown that introverts often have trouble multitasking in social situations. This means that they are so focused on regulating their antsy feeling and expending energy interacting with others that they often do not realize how *other* people react to *them.* For example, introverts often don't pick up on the fact that other people like them, and so the relating doesn't seem as enjoyable. In other words, they may not notice social signals that someone is responding to them in a positive way by smiling, leaning toward them, and seeking them out. (Extroverts, by contrast, generally get this right away.) The researchers describe this as a difficulty in decoding social cues. This often happens when introverts leave an event—they wonder if it was worth it, and they don't have the enjoyment of feeling secure that people liked them.

So the next time you leave a convivial gathering, just remind yourself that lots of folks enjoyed your company. In fact, I have found that most introverted people are appreciated at social gatherings—after all, those extroverts need good listeners!

Points to Ponder

- Socializing is an energy drainer.
- Conserve energy before social events.
- Plan how to enter and exit social occasions and how to start up a conversation.
- Give yourself permission to socialize as an introvert.
- Strategize carefully; by doing so you can enjoy many social events.
- Take breaks and regulate your stimulation. It's okay.

CHAPTER VII

Working: Hazards from 9 to 5

**While my work has been before me,
my reward has always been within.**

—Shaker saying

The workplace can be filled with many possible pitfalls for introverts. Most require many skills outside of their comfort zones. That's why introverts often work alone, at home, or in a job where they have flexibility. But because not all introverts can arrange a work setting that is a perfect natural niche, it is crucial for them to understand how to avoid the potential dangers of a nine-to-five schedule.

A few years ago a local company hired me to talk to two of its employees who were constantly having misunderstandings with each other. The hope was that I'd be able to help Jack (the extroverted manager) and Carl (his introverted employee) resolve their differences.

I talked to Carl first. "Jack bombards me with questions. I want to tell him stop, slow down, give me a minute. He doesn't let me think things over. He doesn't listen to my ideas. He just talks a lot and then decides to do things his way. I end up with my head pounding and my stomach in a knot. I'm starting to have trouble sleeping at night."

Then I spoke with Jack. "I'm ready to pull my hair out. Carl is so withdrawn. He hides out in his office. He clams up at meetings and contributes nothing. I don't think he's a team player."

It was obvious to me right away that the reason these two men kept butting heads was because one was an extrovert and the other was an introvert. Because neither one of them understood the other, they ended up blaming each other. It hardly made for a productive work environment.

In their book *Type Talk at Work,* Otto Kroeger and Janet Thuesen discuss the differences between introverts and extroverts on the job: "Unlike extroverts, who wear their personalities on their sleeves, introverts often keep their best to themselves. With extroverts you see what you get. With introverts, what you see is only a portion of their personality. The richest and most trusted parts of an introvert's personality are not necessarily shared with the outside world. It takes time, trust, and special circumstances for them to begin to open up."

Why Do Extroverts Get All the Good Press?

A modest man is usually admired—
if people ever hear of him.

—ED HOWE

It's easy to see why introverts, plugging away at their desks, may not appear as "on the ball" as extroverts. Jane, an introverted editor, told me, "I always see the same surprised look on people's faces when I finally open up to them. They are shocked at how much I know about my subject area. Just because I'm quiet doesn't mean I'm not informed."

Extroverts get out from behind their desks and meet and greet folks. They like to keep their ear to the company grapevine and socialize with co-workers after work or on weekends. They are often cordial and expressive. They like to talk about their accomplishments, and they don't mind being in the spotlight. In fact, they may want to be in the glare. In meetings they throw out ideas; they speak well in front of groups; and they like to chat on the phone. They like to be involved, and they can be seen darting from place to place looking busy and important. They make quick decisions, are active brainstormers, and a little "tongue foo-ing" doesn't bother them; in fact, they might think it's fun to argue. They are natural self-promoters and networkers. They are their own best press agents.

A Different Light

Extroverts are like lighthouses, focusing their beacon outward toward the world. Introverts are more like lanterns, radiating a glow inside themselves. The differences in how they focus their flame (energy) and where they direct their attention can create difficulty in almost everything they do. But as Carl's example shows, it can be especially problematic at work.

Carl, like so many introverts in the workplace, had a case of what I call Hiding Your Light under a Bushel Syndrome. Jack, like so many extroverts in the workplace, misinterpreted Carl's style (didn't see him as a team player) and failed to appreciate Carl's considerable talents and skills. And Carl, because of his introverted nature, didn't realize that Jack couldn't see his contributions. This is a common example of mutual misunderstanding. Later in the chapter, I will come back to how Carl and Jack resolved their differences.

Although your light shines differently than that of extroverts, you can influence how you are perceived in the workplace. In the first section of this chapter, Hiding Your Light under a Bushel, I will discuss how you can shine your light at meetings, blow your own horn (softly), and protect your pace. In the second section, Co-creating, I will suggest ways you can sharpen your verbal skills so those silver-tongued extroverts will hear you. And in the third section, Destressing Your Day, I will address the four most common areas of pressure for innies and how to manage them. The final section, Business with Bosses, is a word about innie bosses. Some of these topics pertain not only to work but also to other areas of your life.

Keep in mind that it is important to let your colleagues and bosses know exactly how valuable you are.

Hiding Your Light under a Bushel

Never desert your own line of talent.
Be what nature intended you for, and you will succeed.
—SYDNEY SMITH

Introverts are often surprised when they are not valued for their considerable contributions. And if they have had the experience of being unseen or overlooked repeatedly, they may resent it. Still, they are puzzled about why it happens. The work environment, like the social arena, requires abilities that go against the natural grain of introverts. Their brain physiology predisposes them to act in ways that can contribute to their being ignored. Let's look at three of the biggest sources of difficulty—reluctance to speak up in meetings, failing to blow their

What Every Extroverted Employee Should Know About Introverts

When extroverts (the majority) tangle with introverts (the minority) in the workplace, both sides need to be educated about what the other is like.

Introverts

• like quiet for concentration

• care about their work and workplace

• may have trouble communicating

• may know more than they reveal

• may seem quiet and aloof

• need to be asked for their opinions and ideas (won't simply supply them)

• like to work on long complex problems, and have good attention to detail

• need to understand exactly why they are doing something

• dislike intrusions and interruptions

• need to think and reflect before speaking and acting

• work alone contentedly

• may be reluctant to delegate

• prefer to stay in office or cubicle rather than socialize

• do not like to draw attention to themselves

• work well with little supervision

• may have trouble remembering names and faces

own horn, and working at a slow pace—and see why each of these areas are problems and how they can be ameliorated.

Why don't innies speak up in meetings? One reason is that when innies are in large groups, they usually find it hard to both absorb all

What Every Introverted Employee Should Know About Extroverts

Just as extroverts need to be educated about introverts, introverts would do well to remember the following about extroverts:

Extroverts

- network well and socialize with co-workers
- keep track of the company grapevine
- respond quickly to requests and spring into action without much advance thinking
- enjoy phone calls and see interruptions as a welcome diversion
- become impatient and bored when the work is slow or repetitive
- develop ideas through interaction and discussion
- are good at marketing themselves
- like to physically move around a lot, prefer to be out and about
- speak while they are thinking
- have excellent verbal skills, enjoy verbal jousting, ask many questions
- like to be part of the majority opinion and feel isolated without management support
- appreciate and enjoy attention
- are attracted to other extroverts

the new information *and* formulate an opinion about it. They need time away from the meeting to sift and sort the data. Next, they need to retrieve and then add their own thoughts and feelings. In privacy they can blend the components together and condense them into original ideas and suggestions. But it takes time. (Remember that long neural pathway in their brains?) It's like making wine or baking bread. It isn't a process that can be rushed.

The second reason is that innies must expend extra energy to attend to what is being said in the meeting. For them, focusing on the outside world is like driving an SUV: it's a gas guzzler. There is little left over for speaking. Drawing attention to themselves by speaking up truly depletes them. If they do speak, it may be in a low voice, without eye contact, and in a halting way. Co-workers may not pay attention or may not think they sound knowledgeable.

Third, speaking up often increases the tension innies may feel from being in a group situation. This makes it hard to be articulate. Introverts don't usually talk easily unless they are relaxed and comfortable. If the group has conflict or becomes overstimulating for some other reason, they can become even more "brainlocked": they search for words they can't find. After this has happened a few times, they anticipate that awful anxious feeling and become reluctant to speak up.

Fourth, introverts often do so much thinking ahead of time that when they add a comment in a meeting it can be out of sync with what's happening at the moment. Or, because of their different thinking style, they may state the middle of their idea or just the final thought. After they realize that what they have said doesn't fit with the timing of the group or is a little confusing to people, they often conclude that they don't express themselves well and may stop talking altogether.

How to Let Co-workers Know You Are Participating at Meetings

- Relax before meetings by deep breathing for five minutes in a quiet, private place.
- Try not to schedule too many meetings the same day; take breaks between them.
- Say hello to and smile at others in the room as you enter; say good-bye as you leave.

- Find a strategic location to sit (near the door for a quick break) when you arrive.

- Take notes. This helps you focus on your thoughts and reduce overload from the outside.

- Use nonverbal signals like nods, eye contact, and smiles to let others know you are paying attention.

- Say *something*—ask a question, restate what someone else said.

- Get people's attention by giving an opening phrase in a firm voice: "I'd like to add something . . ." or "My thought is . . ."

- Give your thought a beginning, middle, and end.

- Say, "I want to add something to what you mentioned a few minutes ago, Stan," if you know your thought is out of sync.

- Let people know you will continue to think about the topic: "I'll give this some thought and let you know my reactions."

- Thank presenters, speakers, or department heads at the end of meetings.

- Congratulate yourself if you speak, no matter what happens.

- E-mail, jot a note, or send a memo with your comments the next day. Ask for feedback about your ideas: "What do you think?"

If I Tell You, I'll Have to Kill You

If you don't place your foot on the rope,
you'll never cross that chasm.
—LIZ SMITH

My client Samantha is quite reticent, and I usually need to ask her, "Can you say more about that?" One day I said to her playfully, "Are you working for the CIA today, and you can't disclose anything personal to me?"

She looked at me with a twinkle in her eye and said, "If I tell ya, I'll have to kill ya." We laughed; we both understood how exposed and overstimulated she felt most of the time—even with her own therapist. Imagine how difficult it must be to reveal any part of herself to a co-worker.

Why don't innies disclose more or promote themselves? As I mentioned in an earlier chapter, introverts are territorial. They like their own protected space. One way they keep it private is by guarding what they show the world, thereby reducing outgoing energy and limiting what the world directs toward them.

Another reason introverts may not share their knowledge is because often *they* don't realize all they know. They take their rich emotional, intellectual, and imaginative life for granted. Unless a particular topic happens to come up with a friend, innies may not realize that they are a wealth of information on, for instance, sailing. Or they may know they are interested in an arcane subject, like how pandas breed, but they think no one else will be.

At the same time, introverts often feel they don't have to let other people in on what they are up to—at work, in particular—because, if they were the boss, they would notice how much time and effort they were putting in. Innies don't realize that extroverted people don't pay attention to the same behaviors in the same way they do. Extroverts need to be told in more detail what introverts are doing at work because otherwise they may not think anything is happening.

The last reason innies don't expose their internal selves is because they aren't looking for outside approval. Though they want to be appreciated for their achievements, getting public attention can be painful and/or uncomfortable—like hearing fingernails scratch on a blackboard: squirmy and shrill.

All of these factors can add up to innies appearing remote, uncooperative, or, in the worst-case scenario, expendable.

How to Blow Your Own Horn Without Feeling Overexposed

- Remind yourself that if you share personal information with a colleague, you always have the right to end a chat or dodge a personal question.
- Let your boss know what type of work, projects, and tasks are interesting to you.
- Initiate a meeting yourself—selecting time, place, length, agenda, and participants—if you are working on a group project.
- Write a short article for the company newsletter about an interest of yours.
- Tell your boss about one of your successes: "I licked that last problem, I'll get the report to you tomorrow."
- Share personal information with colleagues in an easy, relaxed way. For example, chat about your hobby while waiting to use the copier or fax machine.
- Learn to accept a compliment: "Thank you," or "I appreciate your telling me that." This encourages folks to acknowledge you and feel good about it.
- Give other workers compliments and acknowledgment.
- Volunteer to help at the company picnic or to collect money for flowers for an ill co-worker; others will see you as a team player.

Measure Twice, Cut Once

Introverts generally move at a slower pace than extroverts. This is another reason they can appear aloof or uninterested. They need to expend energy reserves in small amounts, measuring out their energy in predictable increments. Otherwise, their tank will end up on empty, and they will feel exhausted and burned out. They want time to think things through and to keep assessing the work as it unfolds. In an intense environment, extroverts may assume that because introverts are slower-paced they aren't as sharp, involved, or competent.

Because introverts tend to speak slowly, with long pauses, they can appear hesitant and uncertain of their opinion. Actually, they give deep thought to their ideas. And since they value meaning, they want to be precise and select just the right words to express them. But this can drive extroverts nuts. Spit it out, they think.

In addition, introverts are willing to consider the value in the other person's opinion. But what is actually openness can be misread as a lack of conviction in their own opinion. As I mentioned earlier, innies often don't bother to tell other people about their thinking process. Predictably, this leads to lots of misunderstandings.

How to Let Co-workers Know That Although Your Pace Is Slow, You Usually Win the Race

- Have a sense of humor about your pacing.

- Do tough assignments early in the day; don't let them hang over you, wasting energy.

- Don't get flustered if something unexpected comes up. Take a few deep breaths before you proceed and remind yourself that you can go back to working at your own speed after the crisis is over.

- Express your emotional reactions occasionally: "Erin, I was excited to see your ideas; they're great."

- Tell colleagues that when you are silent, you are reflecting. "That's a good point; I'm giving it some thought."

> ### Travel Time
>
> Use your commuting time to nourish yourself with positive thoughts:
>
> - Remind yourself of what you accomplished that day.
> - Congratulate yourself for any healthy habits you practiced.
> - Remember pleasant conversations and compliments you received.
> - Recall any new ideas you came up with.

- Don't let yourself be insulted if the group walks ahead of you. Ask them to save you a seat.

- Prepare a few comments (write them down) when you know a specific topic will come up so you can make a few quick remarks.

- Let people know you are concerned with *their* project: "I've been thinking about your assignment, Bill, and I had a couple of ideas. If you like, I could e-mail them to you."

- Negotiate deadlines by explaining to your boss why you need the time.

- Ask others for feedback about your contributions.

Why You Should Shine Your Light

You are an excellent employee, and it is important that you not forget your own contributions. Remind yourself every day of what you bring to the party: concentration, loyalty, thoughtfulness, persistence, tough-mindedness, creativity, originality, foresight, and a wide range of knowledge, to name just a few introverted advantages. Introverts are often the employees who go about their day quietly improving the workplace. They have the ability to both make difficult decisions and give co-workers space. They develop lasting one-on-one relationships and work well without close supervision. Innies tend to be considerate and want cooperation. They are good listeners and good teachers. Every day shine a little positive light in your own direction.

Co-creating

One man interacting creatively with others
can move the world.

—JOHN GARDNER

Talking makes the "work go round." Different communication styles make for a rich and innovative work environment. I will now discuss five areas in which co-creating allows us to blend our styles to produce results no individual could achieve alone. Successful companies grow and sustain themselves when employees have mastered nonverbal communication; have strong conflict resolution skills; and have the ability to argue, brainstorm, and ask directly for what they want. Enhancing communication skills in these areas creates a workplace culture in which everyone can thrive.

Dialoguing Dilemmas

All workplaces are strengthened or weakened by the ways in which people communicate with one another. Nothing brings into sharp focus the differences between introverts and extroverts faster than their communication styles, nor, as we have said, presents a greater potential for misunderstanding.

Every form of communication requires energy. Verbal communication involves how we speak, what we pay attention to, what we hear, and how we respond. As we have seen, speaking is often problematic for introverts, since it requires a full tank of fuel. Introverts need to

Bridging Innie/Outie Communication Gaps

Best bets for communicating with innies:

- Talk about one topic at a time.

- Ask, then listen.

- Give each person adequate time for a response.

- Don't finish anyone's sentences.

- Communicate in writing, if possible.

Best bets for communicating with outies:

- Communicate orally.

- Let them talk and think out loud.

- Include a variety of topics.

- Expect immediate action.

- Keep the conversation moving.

have good reserves before they speak, because the actual talking and searching for words to respond to another person's remarks quickly deplete their tank.

In fact, studies show that more than half of what we reveal about ourselves—whether we are friendly or unfriendly, cooperative or aloof, for example—is not conveyed by our words. It is conveyed by our body language: smiling, frowning, sighing, touching, drumming our fingers, making eye contact, etc. Communication with your colleagues in writing (or by e-mail) is another way to express your ideas and let yourself be known. Because these metacommunications, as they are called, burn less fuel, they are the best ways for introverts to improve their communications at work. You can strut your stuff, but in a stealth mode. You can let co-workers know more about you and reserve most of your "innergy" for only the most necessary conversations.

How to Talk Less and Communicate More

- Smile when you greet a co-worker or boss.

- Nod and keep eye contact with the speaker in meetings and groups.

- Lean toward the speaker to show interest in what he or she is saying.

- Acknowledge physical space differences. For example, you might say, "Let's keep the chair empty between us so we can both spread out a little."

- Say hello and good-bye to fellow employees (seems so obvious, but sometimes we forget).

- Send thank-you notes, e-mail, or electronic cards to co-workers to congratulate them on an accomplishment or to tell them you appreciate something they did.

- Copy an article you think would interest a colleague or boss, and give it to the person with a note from you.

- Give out birthday cards or holiday cards if this is appropriate in your work setting.

- Put your name on *everything* you write or produce.

How to Resolve Conflicts Productively

Conflicts arise anytime there are opposing needs. While some people (usually extroverts) thrive on seeing the sparks fly, other people (usually introverts) are conflict-adverse. They'll do anything rather than face a fight. Conflicts use up their energy, and they go out of their way to avoid them. But ignoring them is generally a mistake. For one thing, the conflict doesn't disappear. For another, innies feel the unresolved stress in their bodies—literally. They experience headaches, stomachaches, and a general feeling of malaise. Since conflicts can easily escalate, it is always a good idea to learn to deal with them early on. You will end up feeling more confident.

Practice these steps so you can take them when needed:

Steps to Resolving Conflicts

1. Define and agree on the problem.

2. Understand how your introversion and the other person's extroversion affects the problem.

3. Try to see it from your co-worker's perspective.

4. Problem solve with an innie/outie perspective in mind.

So how did the two fellows I mentioned at the beginning of the chapter, Carl and Jack, resolve their disagreement? What steps could they take to bridge their difficult communication gaps? Following the plan above, I recommended that Jack and Carl first define the contentious areas and agree on what they were disagreeing about. Jack and Carl explained that they always misunderstood each other. Second, we discussed their different, introvert/extrovert styles—not right or wrong but *different*—and how these affected their communication. Third, I suggested that they step into each other's shoes. Did Carl realize how frustrating it was for Jack to want his opinion and think that Carl withheld it? Did Jack understand how much pressure Carl felt in meetings and how this made it hard for him to speak? Fourth, I asked them to problem-solve without taking each other's behavior personally.

The result was that Carl saw he needed to be as far from the hectic pace of the office as possible. So he asked for and received from Jack a work space away from the action. Jack, understanding that Carl does not like coming up with quick answers, agreed to give Carl the agenda for the meetings a day before. This way Carl could develop his (good) ideas without pressure and with plenty of time to weigh his thoughts.

Jack decided to give Carl some long, boring projects that he himself hated and never thought anyone else would like. Carl realized he needed to let Jack know more about his talents, which would secure him a solid place on the company team.

Sometimes it's not possible to resolve problems directly with co-workers. Danielle, an introverted patient of mine, found herself in a similar situation. It started when she was asked to share a cubicle with a very talkative, extroverted co-worker, Ina. Spending all day with Ina—who chatted endlessly to her, to herself, to people on the phone, to anyone who happened by —made Danielle a nervous wreck. What's more, it was interfering with her ability to concentrate on her work. But when she talked to her boss about moving into a different cubicle, he said no. The reason? He was hoping Danielle's quiet demeanor and good work habits would rub off on Ina. Danielle didn't know what to do. She didn't want to lock horns with Ina, especially since she was stuck in a small cubicle with her. "I feel helpless," she told me.

Danielle had to find solutions on her own. She knew

Presenting Yourself

At some point, almost all of us, like it or not, find ourselves having to address a group. Here are some tips to help make the best of it:

- Accept speaker's anxiety— it happens to everyone.
- Analyze your audience, and direct your talk to them.
- Know your topic.
- Practice until you feel comfortable.
- In the week before your presentation, visualize yourself feeling confident. Visualize an attentive audience.
- Find a few friendly faces, when presenting, and look at them.
- Speak a bit louder than you normally do.
- Use your natural humor.
- Remember that every presentation doesn't need to be perfect.
- Congratulate yourself when it's over!

Ina couldn't change her "Chatty Cathy" personality, especially since the boss had already talked to Ina about it. Danielle and I brainstormed and came up with several ways she could improve the situation without quitting or going nutty.

Danielle told Ina she worked better when she had quiet, "park-like" surroundings, so she separated the cubicle down the middle with a row of leafy green plants. It looked outdoorsy and was not so obvious as a rejection of Ina. Danielle took headphones to work and played soft music so she wouldn't hear Ina talking to herself. We decided she would talk to Ina occasionally, but only if Ina spoke to her directly. If she talked into the air, Danielle wouldn't answer. If Danielle needed to concentrate, she could use earplugs or ask Ina if she would refrain from talking for a specified period of time. Danielle now feels less drained, and she and Ina are getting along fine.

Instead of avoiding conflicts, try to resolve them creatively. You may be surprised at how much you can improve both your work life and your work-based relationships.

Verbal Jousting

Researchers have found that introverts and extroverts do not argue in the same way. Extroverts often argue in a win-lose style. They emphasize being right. Sometimes this leaves the other person (often the introvert) feeling wrong. Many introverts argue in a win-win style. They want each person's ideas to be heard. In general, introverts tend to question more and criticize less. They are less invested in their own perspective, and they tend to consider all points of view valid.

It can be quite an energy drain to verbally joust with extroverts at work. Remember not to take the extrovert's more aggressive style personally. Here are some additional tips to help you sharpen your skills.

- Stay calm and breathe.

- Think ahead about possible objections to your arguments. State them, as well as your response to them, in your presentation.

- Include the possible objections before others raise them.

- Listen carefully if someone raises an unanticipated objection. Restate the objection, and ask if you have given an accurate summation. (This will give you time to think.)

- Compliment the person in a general way, if the objection is valid: "You're right. We need to figure out a way to address that angle."

- Ask "How do you think we can come to a workable solution?" if objections continue.

- Remember you have valuable ideas and the right to disagree.

Brain Flashes

Coming up with a slew of ideas is the goal of brainstorming. Not good ideas or bad ideas, just *lots* of ideas. Your bolts of lightning can knock things out of the box, lead you to innovation, and help you remain competitive in today's changing marketplace. Extroverts brainstorm naturally because they get energized by letting the juices flow and have no difficulty talking and thinking at the same time. On the other hand, in order to be free and frivolous, introverts need to feel safe and accepted. Since their ideas tend to be more "out of the box," they need assurance that they won't be criticized. It may be helpful for them just to listen while others generate the flashes of lightning and then bring back their ideas the next day. This gives their nighttime munching (reflective) minds time to digest and generate something new-fashioned.

If you are in charge of brainstorming, here are some steps you can take to ensure a productive environment:

Initial Session

- Explain that a problem or concept will be tossed into the ring and that anyone can throw out any idea or association.
- Explain that some people will just listen and return their input the next day.
- Write down all the ideas and associations.
- Make it clear that all ideas are okay. None is right or wrong.
- Say absolutely no criticism is allowed!
- Say you will accept follow-up e-mails.

Second Session

- Group the ideas and associations into themes.
- Prioritize the themes according to your company's goals.
- Discuss the results.
- Choose the top three solutions.
- Select alternatives.

Ask for What You Want

If you are an innie employee, there are times when you need to ask your boss for what you want. Many introverts have trouble doing this. Asking for something not only puts them in the spotlight (which they are naturally averse to) but is also an energy drain. Many fear they will go blank and forget what they want to say. Or they are afraid they will not be able to think on their feet in a meeting. If this is a problem for you, try one of the following strategies:

1. Write out what you want to ask for. Be specific.

2. Anticipate your boss's possible objections, and write them down. Jot down your rebuttals.

3. Practice your talk in front of your mirror or with a partner or friend. (Introverts generally do better if they rehearse before they talk about something anxiety-producing.)

4. Congratulate yourself for asking for what you want, no matter the outcome. If you don't succeed, remember you can always come back and talk about the request again. See if you can rethink your approach and come up with more ways to counter your boss's concerns.

Destressing Your Day

I have found that there are four elements of the workplace that are especially problematic for innies. The first is the dreaded deadline. Following are strategies for handling deadlines without losing your cool. The second is interruptions. With just a few tips you can manage those extroverts popping in and asking you "just one quick question." Third, if you worry about remembering names and faces, there are some techniques to plant them firmly in your memory. And finally, as an innie, you will occasionally feel overwhelmed at work—so I have included a five-step plan to reduce that awful "fried" feeling when it attacks you.

Five Strategies to Handle Deadlines

As I discussed earlier, innies often have trouble with deadlines. They worry about generating enough energy to complete the project *and* think about what they are doing without feeling overwhelmed. They may need to explain to their boss why they need extra time for completing work. Sudden deadlines are the most problematic. These can feel like "sudden death" (a term from the sports world, used when teams are tied and one side must score first in order to win). If you work with an innie boss, deadlines may be an easier subject to discuss. Try to get him or her to be flexible. Say you realize deadlines can't always be roomy, but that the more advance warning you have, the better your work will be.

Whenever the deadline is, start by breaking the task down into bite-size pieces. This is the most useful approach for introverts. It helps you decrease feelings of anxiety, fuzzy headedness, and helplessness.

1. Write your deadline down on your calendar. Then divide your task into small sections. Figure out what you need to do by when to complete the project on time.

2. Write on your calendar what you need to accomplish each day. Set aside specific times for the project in your peak energy hours. (For example, I write from six A.M. to ten A.M. every morning except Sunday.)

3. Leave room in the schedule for unexpected work and interruptions.

4. Don't criticize yourself if you don't accomplish everything you planned on any given day. Just redivide the work into larger sections over the next few days and keep at it.

5. Always give yourself a reward for what you do—buy a new book, see a movie, eat a cookie, play a video game.

How to Avoid "Just a Quick Question" and Other Interruptions

Unless an introvert is expecting the interruption or his or her energy tank is full to the brim, interruptions are very disruptive for introverts. They feel annoyed, often without knowing why. Extroverts, on the other hand, move easily from one thing to another. They thrive on unexpected breaks in their schedules. And they simply cannot understand why you don't love it when they pop by your desk, hold up their finger, and say, "Just a quick question."

There are physiological reasons why interruptions are difficult for many introverts. First, you may be deep in thought, and it is hard to "come up" out of concentrating to interact on another topic—a process that extroverts often experience as unresponsiveness. It may take a minute or two for you to break concentration, so you may feel confused or may not even immediately register what the quick-talking extrovert is saying to you. You have to grasp the new topic. It takes energy to switch gears. After the interruption, you use more energy to regain your previous "place" and concentration. Sometimes you can't find your exact "place" for days.

I have clients who are a couple and who are partners in a law firm. Zoë is introverted, and Ethan is extroverted. If she is writing a brief, she gets anxious and irritated when someone—even Ethan—opens her closed door. Ethan likes to drop into her office and ask her this and that and feels angry at her remoteness. I explained to them why each views the interruption in different ways. After I explained why, Ethan said, "It sounds strange to me; I feel energized by quick chats." Zoë became animated and said to him, "You don't understand how exciting it is for me to realize there's a reason interruptions irritated me so. I have never understood why I hated them."

Here are some strategies that may help you to reduce or deflect intrusions and interruptions:

- Put a clock sign on your door giving the time when you will next be available.

- Create your own "Do Not Disturb" sign. Try to infuse it with humor. For example, add a cartoon or an image, like the statue *The Thinker.*

- Cover the chairs in your office with papers, or go a step further and remove the extra chairs from your office.

- Say, "I can't see you now, but I'll be free at ten o'clock. Can you come back then?"

- Cut a meeting short by standing up and gradually moving toward the door. Say, "Sorry, I have a deadline, and I need to get back to work."

- Set a time limit for every conversation: "Let's talk Thursday for fifteen minutes. Is that enough time?"

- Head off unexpected visitors by walking to the door of your cubicle or office and say that you were just on your way to another meeting or to the rest room: "We can chat on the way."

- Keep nodding but stop talking and occasionally look away or at your watch if you need to make a getaway.

- Find a hideout to think—the bathroom or a quiet corner in the employees' lounge or dining room—when all else fails.

Four Memory Joggers

When I was younger, I could remember anything, whether it happened or not.

—MARK TWAIN

Marta told me how embarrassed she was when she was introduced to a new customer and then only a few minutes later couldn't remember the person's name. "I felt like sliding under the table," she said.

Studies show that many introverts have trouble with face and name recognition. In fact, some researchers theorize that the difficulty of recognizing familiar names and faces adds to introverts' anxiety about social and work encounters. If either of these problems applies to you, here are some techniques that may help to implant a name or face in your memory:

1. Look for an unusual feature—a scar or mole, lip shape, comb-over hair, glasses, or hair color.

2. Translate the person's name into a vivid image. For example, "Karla" reminds me of a red sports car. "Glenda" reminds me of a mossy glen in England.

3. Repeat the name as you say hello: "Hi, Karla."

4. Look back at the person a few times as you move around the room. In your mind, put together the name with the associations you have made.

If you do forget a name or face, give yourself a break. Everybody draws a blank now and then.

A Five-Step Plan to Reduce "Overwhelm"

When we are overstimulated and overwhelmed, we can't think, we can't be creative, and we aren't very productive. It is vital to learn ways to calm yourself down.

Step 1:
Figure out what's going on in your body.

The first step toward relaxing—reducing "overwhelm"—is to try to tease apart your "mind" from your "body." I know this is easier said than done, but you *can* learn to do it. As a psychotherapist, if one of my clients comes in feeling overwhelmed, I always start out by asking the person (let's call her Cassandra) to get comfortable in the glider chair. Then I ask her to describe how she is feeling physically: "Tell me what's happening in your body, Cassandra." If she has trouble answering the question, I ask, "How do your arms feel? Are your hands tingling or numb? Are they tense? Do they feel heavy? Wiggle your shoulders, do they feel constricted?" Usually these questions prime the pump, and the client begins to describe anxiety (tingling, tension, an urge to move) or depression (heavy, tired, logy, sluggish) in her body. The more you can articulate to yourself or someone else what is happening in your body, the more you can learn how to help yourself.

Step 2:
Breathe and have a drink of water.

The second step is to take in some oxygen. Pay attention to breathing. Most people hold their breath when they are in an overstimulated condition. So take a tummy breath and blow it out. After your breathing becomes deeper, tense the muscles of your body and hold for one minute. Notice the difference between feeling more relaxed and feeling tense. Drink a glass of ice water. Studies show that even mild dehydration affects concentration, thinking, metabolism, and the flow of neurotransmitters. In his book *High Energy Living,* Dr. Robert Cooper says that water "stimulates increased energy production throughout your body and increases alertness in your brain and senses."

Step 3:
Notice what you're saying to yourself in your head.

The third step to reduce feeling overwhelmed is to notice what is going on in your mind. When we feel certain bodily sensations, we assign *meanings* to them. We don't even know this is happening. We start this process when we are children, so by the time we are adults, it is on automatic pilot. It goes like this: Your tummy tightens. Your unconscious response is one of fear. Fear means danger. Danger means something bad is going to happen. What happens next is usually conscious. A voice in your head says, I can't do it, I'm going to fail. This voice heightens your original fear, and you feel paralyzed. Remember in Chapter 3 when I talked about how introverts have a mechanism in their brain that reduces stimulation when they are overwhelmed? Clients will say to me in a panicked voice, "I can't think. I won't be able to answer questions at my presentation."

Pay attention to the voice in your head, and listen to what it is saying. Learn to change it into a calming voice that can reduce your fears. "I am just feeling anxious, but it will be okay." "I am feeling tense. It doesn't mean something bad will happen. I will be okay."

Step 4:
Remember when . . . ?

Step four is to remember other stressful situations you have handled. When we are overwhelmed, we can forget what we know. I asked one of my patients, Allie, who was fearful about a lecture she was going to give, about other presentations during which she was able to handle questions. "Oh yes," she said, "I remember. I have done that, haven't I?" "What can you do if your mind goes blank?" I asked her. She replied, "I can say, let me think about that, or I can ask if other people have encountered that problem. What did they do about it? I don't have to answer everything myself." "And remember," I said, "you can always say, I'll have a good answer for you on my way home in the car, but nothing is coming to me now." Remind yourself: You can learn to manage the overwhelmed feelings in your mind and body. You have done it before, you can do it again.

Step 5:
Understand the "up" side of feeling overwhelmed.

Feeling overwhelmed is part of being introverted. Do not criticize yourself. It's one of the priceless qualities about you. Remember, it means that you take in lots of information and that your brain is very active.

Business with Bosses

It may surprise you to learn that many introverts are bosses. They often display excellent leadership qualities: integrity; good judgment; the ability to make tough decisions; a sense of humor; intellectual curiosity; and the ability to look to the past, present, and future. Although in many ways it can be easier to work for an introverted boss, it can also be problematic. Introverted bosses may forget to communicate expectations, may fail to delegate, and may not realize the importance of praise and rewarding good work.

Earlier in my career, I worked for an introverted boss for more than a year. It was lucky for me that I didn't need much supervision because I saw Trisha, in living person, about twice—mostly she communicated in writing. She jotted comments on the training materials I developed and sent me notes on the evaluations my students gave me. That was it. For extroverts this management style would be horrific. They would want more collaboration, more feedback on their work, and more meetings. I don't recall one staff meeting the whole year.

Whether you're an extrovert or introvert, you work better with these bosses if you learn to keep them up to date on what's happening by dropping them e-mails, notes, and memos. If you would like more feedback, ask for it. Innie bosses may not think you need it. Because they are not motivated so much by outside forces, they may not realize that many employees need to be encouraged and empowered.

Studies show that introverts in management positions do not empower employees as effortlessly as extroverts. If you are an introverted boss, note the points below and keep in mind that extroverts are motivated by different factors than introverts are.

Communicate Your Expectations

■ Discuss expectations and put them in writing.

■ Ask your employees for feedback.

■ Give them feedback on what you see as their strengths, as well as the areas you feel they need to improve.

Sign Language

One of my introverted clients, Anna, recently started a new job. She told me, "Marti, you won't believe it, my new boss is very introverted and has a very hectic position at the agency with loads of interruptions. She has a big sign taped to her desk, Be Here Now, to help her focus. She wears signs around her neck on orange ribbons to let people know what sort of mood she's in—if she wants to chitchat with her co-workers or if she just wants to stick to work." I asked Anna to bring me a list of the signs. We laughed as we looked at the selection. "Your boss really understands herself. She'll be a great role model for you," I said. Here is a list of the signs she wears around the office:

• Do Not Disturb

• Come On In, I'm Ready for Questions

• On Break; Prefer Not to Talk about Work

• Do Not Disturb; Trying to Meet a Deadline

• Sorry, I'm in a Bad Mood

Delegate

- Delegate authority by giving your employees increasing responsibility.
- Let your employees know how you rely on them.
- Ask for suggestions, ideas, and solutions; implement some.
- Stand behind your staff; encourage good intentions.

Keep Those Motors Humming

According to most studies, one of the most effective ways to motivate employees is to recognize them. This is more complicated than just giving raises and promotions. It means finding rewards that match their personality. Introverts are not motivated by the same incentives as extroverts. Extroverts are motivated by external reinforcements like praise, opportunities for rewards, public acclaim (like being "employee of the month"), and competitive contests. Introverts, by contrast, like to stay out of the limelight. They find being the object of public attention a punishment rather than a pleasure. This doesn't mean they don't respond to validation and feedback. They do, as long as it isn't too overstimulating. I recommend reading *1001 Ways to Reward Employees* by Bob Nelson, in which he discusses the main aspects of recognizing employees:

- Find out what each person finds motivating.
- Think up personal motivators; it can be fun and rewarding for everyone involved.
- Match the reward to the person.
- Match the reward to the achievement.
- Be timely and be specific.

Enjoy Your Work

**The more I want to get something done,
the less I call it work.**

—RICHARD BACH

This chapter has focused on many of the pitfalls the nine-to-five world presents for introverts. But despite all of the hazards, introverts enjoy their work, and work is often an important part of their lives. In fact, a recent study by the Oxford Happiness Project revealed that happy introverts enjoy their work more than happy extroverts. If introverts can learn to interact without feeling washed out at the end of the day, they can use their "innergy" to bring their company incredible advantages.

So don't forget to "strut your stuff" in a way that is comfortable for you. After all, you deserve recognition and appreciation for your valuable contributions. No organization can get along without introverts. Extroverts need us even if they don't always know it. You can enlighten them.

Points to Ponder

- It takes some effort to get acknowledged at work.
- Every day, in some small way, do some subtle self-promotion.
- Protect yourself from energy drainers.
- Learn the steps to calm yourself if you feel "fried."
- Remember, your employer is lucky to have you as an employee.

PART III # Creating the "Just Right" Life

Great ideas need landing gear
as well as wings.

—C. D. JACKSON

CHAPTER VIII

Three P's: Personal Pacing, Priorities, and Parameters

My strength lies solely in my tenacity.

—Louis Pasteur

In Chapter 3, I talked about the physiological factors underlying our introverted temperament. Because of the way we are put together, we require a particular kind of care and feeding. We need to harness our energy, get the right rhythm, and implement our objectives while protecting our internal resources. In this chapter, I talk about the three P's—personal pacing, priorities, and parameters— three concepts that can help you cope with your introversion. Personal pacing is learning to set your own tempo, the rate that allows you to accomplish what you want without feeling overwhelmed or drained. Personal priorities allow you to think about what goals have the most meaning to you so you can direct your energy toward fulfilling them. Personal parameters help you create boundaries to keep your stimulation in the "just enough" range—neither too much nor too little. When you learn to use these suggestions, you will find that you can achieve a more satisfying and fulfilling life.

Personal Pacing

People seldom see the halting and painful steps
by which the most insignificant success is achieved.

—ANNIE SULLIVAN

Remember the characters in the classic fable "The Tortoise and the Hare"? The hare was so confident he could beat the tortoise in the race that he stopped by the side of the road and took a little nap. The tortoise, trudging along, slow and steady, crossed the finish line as the hare was scrambling to catch up.

Several of the introverts I interviewed for this book referred to themselves as a turtle or a tortoise. They have always been aware that they are rather slow-paced. Because of our physiology, introverts may eat slower, think slower, work slower, and walk and talk slower than more extroverted people. Although some of us may have tried to be hares our whole lives, we may not be aware of how much better we would feel if we slowed down.

Take me, for instance. I move slowly. My best friend, Val, a hare, often strides ahead of me when we are walking. I can't go any faster. I arrive at our destination a few minutes after she does. Usually she has already scoped things out and gives me tips. I used to try to keep up with people, but now I don't, and it turns out all right.

I eat slowly, too. I have learned to be prepared for waiters to try to snatch my plate. If they get near me, I am ready to fight them off. "I haven't finished yet," springs from my lips, and they back away. I talk slowly, and my clients are used to waiting for me finally to eke out my words. I may plod along in life, but I get quite a bit done. It's all about pacing. Introverts are like Timex watches—they can "take a licking and keep on ticking."

Pacing means establishing your own tempo and then proceeding. When you do this, you balance your energy supplies with the demands on your system so you won't end up underfueled. Pacing is also breaking activities up into smaller measures. Since you'll never sprint through life, it's important to know your own ebbs and flows—when and how you work best, how much time to allot to projects, and so on. Your rhythm may be different from other people's. It is something that's very important to accept about your introverted self.

If you don't pace yourself, you can end up feeling stressed and overwhelmed, unable to do anything. It gets worse if you procrastinate. A "major stall" may set in. Then anxiety or depression can descend on you. Anxiety whips you up into a frenzy, and you become forgetful, lose your concentration and your ability to think. Or depression drags you down into exhaustion and listlessness.

The rewarding part about setting your personal pacing is that it allows you to get a lot done without wearing yourself to a frazzle. Plan what you *can* do out of what you must do, and then set your pace. Keep working until you're finished. If

---

Adjusting to Change

Researchers have found that introverts (tortoises) often adjust better than extroverts (hares, racehorses) to life changes such as aging, retirement, illness, or injury. Racehorses are used to galloping along, amassing lots of trophies for their winning style. As a result, they often have trouble handling a slower pace. Tortoises, on the other hand, are used to measuring out their energy, and they find it easier to adapt.

---

you develop a proper tempo for your life, you will be able to avoid stalls as well as a bushelful of depression and anxiety. It will be useful in all areas of your life.

Here are several tactics to help you figure out your personal pacing:

1. Notice your ebbs and flows. Use the time when your energy is the highest to do the most important or difficult jobs. When your energy dips, get those simpler tasks finished.

2. Be realistic about your goals. We live in a culture that tells us we can each have it all, which only adds pressure to introverts. Focus on what you can reasonably achieve and enjoy, which certainly isn't everything.

3. Choose how you spend your energy. Remember that you have only so much to go around.

4. Break projects into bite-size pieces.

Peaks and Valleys

It is important for you to notice your body's rhythms, when your energy crests and falls. Ask yourself these questions:

- Do I feel peppy or tired in the morning?
- Am I tense or relaxed by late afternoon?
- Do I come alive or bottom out in the evening?
- When do I like to exercise and/or do physical tasks?
- When do I concentrate best—morning, afternoon, or midnight?
- When does my brain seem the most frazzled and/or full of static electricity?
- What time of day do I most enjoy being with people?

If the answers to these questions aren't immediately obvious to you, keep a journal and monitor your energy levels for a week or two. Each day, jot down how you feel when you wake up. Make notes about your ups and downs (add fun stickers to represent your moods). Are you shining or sleepwalking in the morning? At ten A.M. are you slumping or hitting your stride? By noon are you fuzzy-headed, raring to go, or just waking up? By late afternoon are you groggy or feeling full of vim and vigor? After dinner do you feel like playing a game with the kids or are you ready to hit the sheets?

Now that you have an idea about your energy rhythms, try to set up your day so that you use your peaks for your most important work and your valleys for less taxing activities. Although we have certain rhythms, energy is always in flux, so keep assessing, and adjust when necessary.

Jill, an artist and psychotherapist I interviewed for this book, has her personal pacing down to a science. She has paid attention to her energy patterns for years and has learned that she works better by seeing her clients in three jam-packed days, Monday through Wednesday. That gives her four days to play and paint in her exquisite English garden. She also knows exactly how many social engagements she can attend before she gets a social hangover. Another woman I interviewed, Courtney, told me, "We are going out to a movie on the weekend, so I only have room for one other engagement this week. Two outside activities are as much excitement as I can take." Courtney is also a master of her own peaks and valleys.

Limited Edition

What really matters is what you do
with what you have.

—SHIRLEY LORD

We grow up in a society that promotes "having it all," "doing it all," without limitations. But the fact is, we all have limitations—introverts in particular. We do not have boundless energy. Our

A Slower Tempo

I sometimes think introverts were made for an earlier time in history. I have a shoebox crammed full of the flowery, romantic letters my paternal grandparents wrote to each other during their three-year engagement from 1896 to 1899.

My grandfather was a bridge contractor who traveled all over the Midwest building arrowback bridges. When he was separated from his fiancée, he would send off a letter in the evening post about his day—his business meetings and what he saw from train windows. She would write, on thin vanilla paper with beautiful blue-inked script, about the music she played, the friends she had tea with, and the gardens she rested in. Life had a slower tempo.

A calling card evocative of my grandmother's turn-of-the-century life fell out of one of the letters: *I Will Be Receiving from 2 to 4 on Sunday Afternoon.*

Social etiquette in this gracious era helped to measure the pace for people. A time for visiting, then a time when they were not receiving. It was perfect for introverts.

energy is limited, and we need to think carefully about how we spend it. This can be a hard pill to swallow. However, it can also make our life more precious. When we make conscious choices, it allows us to really appreciate what we *can* do.

Many of the people I interviewed for this book had come to terms with the fact that they will not have as many friends, be able to work as much, or do as many things as extroverts do. But their friendships are deeper, they do meaningful work, and they enjoy the smaller, quieter, more precious moments of life. The more you are able to appreciate the advantages of being an introvert, the more you will be able to accept the fact that you have limitations. This does not mean something is wrong with you. Having limitations is not the problem. It is the *meaning* we give limitations that causes us so much pain. See if you can put a positive spin on your inborn traits. Say to yourself, "I have low energy, but it's part of my nature, and I still get the things done that are important to me." Don't let yourself be boxed in by things you can't change—once you accept this fact, it can be very freeing. And remember, every human has limitations, even frisky extroverts.

One of the quickest ways to accept the absence of something we wish we had—but don't—is to acknowledge disappointment. Many people want to skip over this step. It's called denial. But if you pretend you don't mind not having an energetic body or the ability to spit out snappy repartee, you may be secretly mad—critical of yourself—or feel that you have a serious flaw. And you may keep expecting yourself to be different. We are given feelings to help guide us through life. It is disappointing not to be a giant ball of energy. If you let yourself feel the loss, the sadness will pass. In its place will be appreciation for the efficient energy you *do* possess.

Trade-offs

Even the most energized extrovert can't do it all. Trade-offs are important to everyone. We all have to make exchanges or compromises. Innies especially must make adjustments because their limited energy requires them to pare down their activities. If you learn to make trade-offs with ease, it will help you feel in control of your life and allow you to keep things humming along in balance. It eliminates any tendency to feel as if you are a victim. "I can't" turns into "I can do this but I'll have to pass on that." You can select some of the tasty dishes of life—little bits of this and little bits of that—without feeling deprived.

If I am going to have a very social weekend, for example, I schedule nothing extra during the week. The following week, if I have two lunches on my calendar, I won't stick in any other social engagements. I think of them like calories. If I am going to a fancy dinner next weekend, I will cut down during the week and save some for the big occasion. If I have my grandson's birthday party on Saturday, and I am also invited to lunch with my girlfriends on Sunday, I will consider compromising. I might arrange to meet my friends just for dessert or pass on seeing them altogether. Alternatively, I might decide to go to the birthday party a bit late and be more of an observer than a participant. Or I might volunteer to take the photos. Trade-offs put you in the driver's seat of your own life; you can go as fast or as slow as you want.

Bird by Bird

You get your intuition back when you make space for it, when you stop the chattering of the rational mind.
—ANNE LAMOTT

In *Bird by Bird,* an amusing step-by-step guide to writing, author Anne Lamott recalls a time in childhood when her brother was working on a report on birds. He'd had three months to write it, had procrastinated, and now it was due the next day. "He was at the kitchen table close to tears, surrounded by binder paper and pencils and unopened books on birds, immobilized by the hugeness of the task ahead. Then my father sat down beside him, put his arm around my brother's shoulder, and said, 'Bird by bird, Buddy. Just take it bird by bird.'"

I remember how empowering this quote was to me when I read it in 1994. I thought to myself, If I write one page a day, by the end of the year, I could have a book. Page by page. Bird by bird. It seemed quite possible.

Almost anything can be done by breaking it down into itsy-bitsy, teeny-weeny steps. Sark is a whimsical writer of books for creative readers. In her book *A Creative Companion: How to Free Your Creative Spirit*, she explains, "Micro-movements are tiny, tiny, steps that move us forward in some way." (She also must be an introvert because she advocates taking lots of naps.) The greatest thing about small steps is that they immediately reduce overwhelm. They get us going. When innies are faced with a daunting task, they immediately imagine how much energy it will consume. A step-by-step approach instantly reduces the fear that they won't have enough stamina. Micromovements give us the encouragement we need so that we don't shut down or begin to get that glazed look I mentioned in Chapter 1. And the funniest darn thing—once you take a couple of little steps, you may actually *want* to do more.

One of my introverted clients, Dru, was ready to start dating again after several years of trying to understand why she picked men who were always unavailable. She felt overwhelmed and terrified about the prospect of meeting new partners. We talked about a bird-by-bird strategy. The first week after she made her decision, Dru picked up *L.A. Weekly*, a newspaper that lists all the "goings-on" in Los Angeles, including the singles activities. She circled a few that interested her. The next week she went to a bookstore and looked at dating guides. *Dating for Dummies* caught her eye, and she bought it. During week three, Dru signed up to go hiking with the Sierra Club for Singles. We agreed she could initiate a conversation with someone if she wanted—or she could just hike. Talking to another hiker might occur on week four. Job hunting, house hunting, doing a repair job, having a party, decorating—virtually any activity can be broken down into small *doable* steps.

Suppose you had to research information about refinancing your home—a task most of us wouldn't be too fond of. Let me show you how you can break it down into manageable segments. Once you get the idea, you can modify the approach to your own personal situation. What could be the first itsy-bitsy step you could take to get started?

Think small.

- Write the name of the project, "Refinancing," on a file folder.

- Just think about where you could go for information: library, Internet, or loan broker.

- Call a friend who has recently been through a refinancing to get his/her recommendations.

- Set a generous but realistic deadline for when you want to have the task accomplished.

The key is to keep inching forward and reminding yourself you can do it. Decide, for example, to make one phone call a day on the project for five days. Making teeny-tiny microsteps is the way introverts work best.

Here's another example. My house needs to be tidy since I both live and work there. My office is upstairs, so every time I go upstairs or downstairs, I take something with me. I carry my heart necklace upstairs to the counter in the hall. Later, if I go into my bedroom, I carry it there. That night or the next morning, I put it in the jewelry box. That way the house stays pretty neat, and I don't feel overwhelmed by the task. I do *everything* in stages. I know my own beat.

Now here is the best part. Pamper yourself. After you have completed a predetermined number of steps of your task, take a soak with bubbles, listen to music and light candles, or watch a football game. After a few more steps, watch your favorite old movie (anything with Cary Grant is my cup of tea). A moist cookie is great after accomplishing twenty tiny steps. After you have finished the whole project, buy yourself a book you've been wanting. As I have said throughout this book, it is important to find your own rhythm. Use the micro-stepping strategy and set the pace that works best for you.

Personal Priorities

Anything you may hold firmly in your
imagination can be yours.
—WILLIAM JAMES

As you learn to appreciate your temperament and are able to pace yourself, then you are ready for the next step—setting priorities. In James Fadiman's book *Unlimit Your Life*, he says, "Let's start at the beginning. To set goals means to set a course for your life." This is a crucial task for introverts because we need to harness our energy and direct it toward what has the most meaning and value to us. Established priorities help us achieve our objectives—from the smallest daily decisions all the way up to major life choices like picking a career, choosing a partner, or deciding how many children to have.

What Does It Mean to You?

Most introverts care about meaning. Think about the different areas of your life and what is important to you. Meaning is what gets your juices going, what makes you feel like hopping out of bed in the morning. It might be X, or it might be Y. One of my clients, Pam, works in the movie industry, and in between film jobs she took an interim position as an administrative assistant. She said, "I had to find some purpose. I couldn't just go to my new office and type letters all day. I began to imagine how the whole place could flow better. I told my boss my ideas, and he gave me the responsibility to reconfigure the department. Now I feel better, because after I leave there everything will be more productive." Meaning for Pam is making the organization function better. It changed what she described to me as a "gray" experience into a "rainbow" experience.

Meaning, to me, is helping people continue what seems to be the purpose of life—growing. All of my occupations—nursery school teacher, librarian, trainer, psychotherapist, and writer—embody that purpose: helping people grow.

One of the quickest ways to find out what has meaning to you is to think about your own death. Try jotting down the main points you would like included in your obituary. Imagine your life as if you were a newspaper reporter. What stands out? What are you proudest of? What do you care most about? What moments in your life have the most meaning to you?

Now, make a list of some of the things you haven't yet learned, experienced, or completed. Write down what you would like to accomplish before the end of your life. Anything is okay; don't limit yourself. Jot down any idea that occurs to you. You can always change it in a month or in a year. This list won't be carved on your gravestone. Keep in mind this is *your* list—what you want for yourself—not what others expect of you.

Here are some examples my clients have thought of: Finally feel comfortable in my own skin. Feel as if I followed my own path and learned to know myself well. Paint. Write in a journal every few days. Buy a jewelry-making kit. Learn to play the piano. Take a sailing class. Travel to England. Take a trip in a paddlewheel boat down the Mississippi. Let go of some of my anxiety and fear. Support myself with less criticism. Feel more at ease about financial matters. Work for a charity. Develop new relationships. Eat better and take better physical care of myself.

Writing goals down may seem like a daunting task. Fears may pop up: Suppose I don't achieve them, or they aren't the right ones, or I can't think of any. You may decide it would be better to take the ostrich-head-in-the-sand approach. Bury the whole subject and blindly hope you will achieve everything you want. But when you do this, it usually means one thing: You aren't leading your own life. Head-burying is like running alongside your car while someone else is driving.

Determine what you truly want

1. The first step to understanding what your life is about is to write down your goals in the following areas (it's okay to do a few at a time as they occur to you):
     - Your health
     - Your renewing time
     - Your family life
     - Your personal growth
     - Your marriage or partnership
     - Your career
     - Your friendships
     - Your creativity
     - Your social life
     - Your spiritual self
     - Your hobbies and play
     - Your _____
     - Your _____

2. From your goals, determine your overall priorities.

3. Write down some steps that you can take toward achieving your priorities.

4. Make a list of four steps you can take this week. Remember to keep them small, one baby step after the other.

5. Ask yourself what barriers are keeping you from achieving your goals.

6. How can you overcome those barriers?

7. Reevaluate your priorities. Do you still want everything on your list, or should you adapt them a bit?

8. Reward yourself for any progress you've made.

One of the advantages introverts have is that we usually know ourselves pretty well. By thinking about what has meaning to us and giving thought to what gets in our way, we can focus our energy on what we truly want.

Here is an example of how I followed the eight steps:

1. What are my goals regarding my health?
To maintain my health so I feel as energetic as possible; keep my energy flowing by getting enough sleep, eating nutritious food, and consistently stretching and exercising.

2. What is my overall priority?
Give my health more attention by eating well, exercising regularly, and sleeping more.

3. What steps toward my priorities can I take in order to achieve my goal?
- Walk four times a week.
- Avoid my favorite doughnuts.
- Sleep at least seven hours a night.
- Make time for yoga by next month.

4. Inching toward health this week:

- Walk once this week.

- Eat healthfully for two dinners even if it kills me.

- Turn off TV one night at ten P.M.

- Watch three yoga tapes and select one I like.

5. Possible barriers:

- No time to exercise.

- Hate grocery shopping, so no healthy food for dinner.

- Like to relax watching late-night TV.

- Don't want to make decision on when to fit yoga in schedule.

6. Possible solutions for next week:

- Write exercise times in calendar with fun stickers (so I'll notice them).

- Make shopping date with Mike. Sing oldies on the way to the store. Buy magazine as a reward.

- Turn off TV at eleven P.M. Turn on music and light candle.

- Get out yoga tape and do once. Notice how I feel.

7. Reevaluate priorities:

- Start walking by listening to books on tape (it's easier).

- Hate shopping, better with Mike; love having food available.

- Feel more rested when I sleep more.

- Enjoy yoga, but not sure I want it as a priority right now. Do it once more and check in with myself.

8. Rewards:

- Bought a book I have been wanting after doing yoga tape twice.

- Complimented myself on taking steps toward my goals.

- Bought myself a low-fat yogurt frappe after my fourth walk around the lake in one week.

- After three weeks of taking small steps, treated myself to a massage.

Okay, you've got the idea. Pick a section of your life and set your goals, priorities, barriers, and solutions; then reevaluate your priorities after a week or two. You may want to tackle only one section, two or three, or add one I didn't include, like finances. You may want to do a Scarlett O'Hara and think about it tomorrow. Whatever you choose, just keep in mind how powerful this approach can be.

Inch by Inch to
Yard by Yard

Lord, give me the determination
and tenacity of a weed.
—Mrs. Leon R. Walters

Remember, this is always an ongoing process. It's okay if you slip up. Just start over again. Reevaluating is very important. Keep thinking about what is important to you and what has meaning for you. See how you feel after you make some progress. If you are not doing something on your list, consider whether you really want to do it. Is it something you think you should do, or something someone *else* thinks you should do? (Remember, one of the great things about finally being a grown-up is being able to make choices.) Is it something you are afraid of? (If it is, take a micro-mini step toward the priority and see how you feel.) Do you want to do it even if you are afraid? Do you want to try it later? Could something other than fears be stopping you?

Carol, another one of my clients, said she uses the inch-by-inch approach not only for setting long-range goals but for short-term goals, too. "I know I need to balance conserving and spending my energy every weekend," she told me. "I really need to use the time wisely, so I set goals and priorities on Friday night. I think about how I am feeling, what events I have for the weekend, and what my family has planned." Carol continued, "I think to myself, on Monday when I look back over the weekend, what will I feel good about doing? This always helps me to put things into perspective.

"Then I decide on my weekend goals. I always try to include activities from several categories. For instance, I might select one activity each from the play, health, family, and renewing category. Then I jot down what I want to do, in case I get overtired and can't remember what I wanted out of the weekend. My notes might look something like this: My daughter Beth and I could polish each other's fingernails and toenails; Beth could choose a video for us to watch together; the entire family could prepare dinner and clean up together Saturday night. I check with my husband, and we negotiate any huge differences in our agendas—we can always shift some of our activities to the next weekend. As long as I get some restoring time and some Beth time this weekend, I will feel okay." Remember, developing your goals and priorities harnesses your energy for what will give you the most fulfillment in life.

Personal Parameters

One of the secrets of life is to make stepping stones
out of stumbling blocks.

—JACK PENN

N ow that you have your pace just right and know what you want to accomplish, it's time to make sure you have adequate borders. Setting parameters means putting boundaries around yourself—saying, "Sorry, I can't talk right now; I'll call you back," if you don't want to talk on the phone. Or, "I'm tied up next week, but I'd love to get together the following week," if you already have too many engagements.

We introverts often feel guilty that we can't do more than our time or energy allows, so we capitulate to whatever demand is made upon us, setting no parameters at all. Or we are unable to accurately evaluate our energy supply and set boundaries that are either too firm or too wishy-washy. We need to regulate the outside world so that it does not invade and overstimulate us but at the same time we can participate in it. Many people won't understand our need for personal time and space. It's tough to disappoint a friend or say no to a boss who wants the project done immediately or refuse your child's teacher's call for volunteers for a class trip. What usually helps is making some other proposal. Tell the person

---

Protect Yourself

W hy we need to create personal borders around ourselves and erect stop signs:

- to protect ourselves
- to reduce stimulation
- to give us space to conserve our energy and to fulfill our responsibilities and accomplish our goals
- to generate the energy to go out into the extroverted world

what you *can't* do and then what you *can* do. Say to your friend, "I can't have lunch today, but how about coffee the following week?" Suggest to your boss, "I can complete the first part of the report this afternoon, and you can have a few days to review it. Then I can deliver the second part the day after tomorrow." If you can, offer a substitute (a grandparent or a friend or relative) to fill in for you at your child's school, if that helps. "I can't go on the field trip to the planetarium, but Jonah's grandfather would love to go."

Mushy Parameters

To be alive at all involves some risk.
—HAROLD MACMILLAN

Humans are born hardwired to connect with their parents, so they usually adapt to whatever family situation in which they find themselves. Introverts who are raised in a home where everyone else is extroverted, or one in which the parents are introverted but feel as if they shouldn't be, the child can feel lots of pressure to be "outgoing." The introverted child may be criticized or shamed or made to feel guilty for needing or enjoying solitude. Cara, a teacher, told me, "My mother would walk into my room, take the book I was reading out of my hands, and make me come out and be with the family. I never could rest by myself. I wondered why I was so tired and overwhelmed so much of the time. I needed seclusion, but my family thought I was avoiding or withdrawing." Cara, like many innies, was influenced by her parents into concluding she *shouldn't* want to be alone, she *should* want to be around people. She didn't understand or connect her low energy to her lack of private time.

Children who don't feel accepted go one of two ways. They decide to ignore their own feelings and let others influence them too much, constantly molding and reshaping themselves to other people's wants and needs, like the shape-shifter character on the television show *Deep Space Nine*. Or they decide to pretend their family didn't influence them at all. Since adults learned these coping mechanisms as young children, they are not aware of them—they are just unconscious reactions.

Right-brained introverts, whom I discussed in Chapter 3, require large amounts of protected sifting and sorting time because they take in so much unconscious information. Without private time they end up feeling confused and fragmented. Left-brained introverts also need replenishing time, but they don't become as fuzzy-headed if they don't get it. They may, however, become quite withdrawn.

If you were not allowed your own quiet place, either physically or emotionally, then when you are overstimulated, you may:

- feel chaotic or lacking in focus
- feel stuck; lack motivation
- feel overwhelmed, fuzzy-brained, or full of static
- feel victimized
- feel invisible but appear wishy-washy
- be self-critical and hear harsh internal voices
- have a sense of being out of control—on an emotional roller coaster
- have a knot in your gut and feel nervous

When you experience any of these red flags, *stop* and put on your thinking cap. Ask yourself if you need to set some limits. Are you feeling confused and unsure? The underlying fear of people with mushy parameters is that they will be abandoned if they don't do what others want. Often they feel as if they should do *more* for others, when they really need to let go and do *less*. Sometimes they think others are requiring so much from them, they feel like victims.

Take a peek at your own behavior. Are you forgetting your own needs? Are you attempting to do more than you can? Are you doing something for another person automatically without checking in with yourself to see if that's really what you can or want to do? Begin to puzzle out what boundaries you need to set. Later in the chapter I'll discuss some tips for creating personal parameters. Setting boundaries is a powerful way to take back your own life.

Rigid Parameters

Some introverts were raised in a family in which they felt either completely trampled on or disregarded by their parents. In this type of home—which is often alcoholic, neglectful, or abusive—the children decide to wall themselves off, as if they were constructing a moat around themselves. A client who is in his forties and never married told me, "When I did something my mother didn't like, she would not speak to me for several days. In the mornings I'd go out in the backyard and climb my favorite walnut tree. I would stay there until it was dark." As they grow up, people like this learn to protect themselves by making their boundaries inflexible—often avoiding or withdrawing from others, which limits their ability to interact with the world around them.

Left-brained introverts (mentioned in Chapter 3) often develop rigid parameters, too. They value thinking over feelings and interpersonal relationships. They're like Mr. Spock on *Star Trek,* who overcontrolled his feelings and always relied on his logical thinking. Such individuals use a detached style to manage their lives, not shape-shifting to anyone. But this leaves them missing something important: the glue of human connection—feelings. Some of the other consequences of having rigid parameters are:

- feeling relationships as demanding or invading
- feeling helpless and hopeless
- feeling trapped and unable to see choices
- being unable to grow emotionally
- being controlling, thought of by others as having an "anal personality"
- appearing self-absorbed and critical
- pushing people away

If you tend to have more rigid boundaries, you may feel lonely or angry with others in your life. You may think *they* are causing the problem. It may be difficult for you to connect the loneliness you feel with the parameters you set. You may not realize you are so walled off.

Give some thought to how you interact with your friends, family, and co-workers. Ask someone you trust if he or she feels you tend to be aloof and critical. Think whether in your childhood you needed to withdraw to feel safe. If you decide that the traits listed above describe you, don't despair. There are ways to reduce your fears about being invaded or disregarded by other people. You can develop strategies to protect yourself without retreating. As you learn to interact more with people, you will find greater richness and less isolation in your life. You will find your sense of yourself stronger, more motivated, and clearer about where and how you want to spend your energy. It will be worth it.

Tips on Creating Personal Parameters

Setting parameters is not hard; it just takes practice. The challenging part is learning to reset your awareness meter on high so that you can set the appropriate boundaries—not too rigid, not too relaxed. Below are some tips to help you create new parameters for yourself.

Tip 1:
Maybe Maybe

Instead of responding to the world with mushy (too flexible) or rigid (too inflexible) parameters, we function best with a protective layer that can transform itself from permeable to impermeable as the situation demands. The skin on our bodies is like that—our pores keep some things out and let others in.

One way to develop more flexible parameters is by expanding our assumptions. Susan Patron is a children's librarian and the author of numerous books, one of which is the charming children's book *Maybe Yes, Maybe No, Maybe Maybe.* An introvert, she understands the "maybe maybes" of life. I have heard her speak about her need to get away to the small cabin she and her husband have in the desert, where she can think about what she wants to do. In her book, Susan gives the oldest sister the job of expanding every situation to fresh possibilities by saying, "Maybe." Maybe means that the world is not black and white—it's shades of gray.

Introverts often feel as if they should make decisions the way extroverts would, without letting themselves wonder how they feel, and deciding what to do based on their own thoughts and impulses. But maybes broaden the world and open decision making to lots of prospects, views, and options. Another valuable benefit of saying maybe is that it grants introverts the time to "noodle" out their responses to something. It is hard for all introverts to make instant decisions. We generally can't (because we're too overwhelmed) or shouldn't (because we need to think things through owing to our long brain pathway). What might seem obvious to extroverts—where to get a quick bite to eat, for example—can seem like a monumental decision to a tired introvert with a fuzzy head. Introverts need the roominess of maybes.

I remember when I was in my teens, a friend and I were talking on the phone about scheduling, and she said, "Let me think about that and I'll call you back." I felt so surprised. Wow, it was okay to think about something and come back to it. It was striking for me because I often didn't have a clear idea about what I wanted to do. I felt scattered and pressured and had trouble thinking when I was around other people. Sometimes I would make several social engagements on the same day. My all-time record was scheduling three dinners on the same evening.

It was easier to make plans when I was away from people and I felt less stimulation. I would let myself have time to think about what fit for me.

It is very powerful to say yes. If you want to do something, say yes. It is also very powerful to say no. If you do not want to do something, say no. If you want to think about a response, say maybe.

Tip 2:
"Reply Hazy, Try Again"
(The Magic 8-Ball Answer)

Remember those grapefruit-size black Magic 8-Balls from junior high? I have one in my office. You ask it a question. Then you turn it over, and a little triangle answer floats into the viewing circle on the bottom of the ball. If it's feeling extroverted, the answer is "Yes," "No," or "Without a doubt." Sometimes it responds in a more introverted way: "Cannot predict now. Concentrate and ask again." Or "Better not tell you now."

One day it hit me that my word-retrieval process was like the Magic 8-Ball's. I felt as if I were waiting for the triangle with the answer to float up. And the more anxious I became that no words would come into my mind, the longer I would have to wait. I have since learned how important it is to be patient. I can almost feel words actually drifting up into my consciousness before they pop out. My brain needs time to snag some words and connect them to the information it is digesting. Now I can relax. Practice this pausing and waiting, and words will appear. Learn to trust your brain. Then you can set your parameters.

Tip 3:
Getting the Night Munchies

Most introverts take in lots of information and process it on many different levels before coming up with an idea or making a decision. Often, they like to wait until the next morning before committing themselves to something. Now we know why this is so. The main neurotransmitter introverts use, acetylcholine, is also the neurotransmitter that helps them store information in their long-term memory during REM (dream state) sleep. Since introverts use their long-term memory more often than extroverts, they need to sleep on decisions in order to benefit from the way they process information.

I heard the film director Mike Nichols being interviewed, and he talked about this unconscious process. He

Give Yourself Time and Space

- Let yourself think of options—there are almost always more than two.

- Tell people, "That sounds good, let me think for a minute," or "I don't know yet," or "My concern is . . ."

- Feel comfortable having mixed feelings—it's a sign of mental health.

- Let yourself sleep on decisions; introverted brains munch on things in the night.

- Let the answer float up from your Magic 8-Ball.

- Don't be pressured by extroverts to answer quickly.

- Trust your brain.

said he has learned to sleep on ideas, and he refers to it as "a good kind of lazy."

We are often pressured by extroverts to answer quickly. Don't fall into that trap. Practice sleeping on ideas, projects, or anything that involves complex thinking. If I have to make a decision, I remind myself that the pros and cons will be clearer in the morning. Sometimes I imagine I will wake up from the loud crunching sound caused by my brain's working on an especially challenging question.

Tip 4: Try Yes

As I discussed earlier, rigid parameters are usually developed early in life in response to feeling like it's not okay to be who you are, an introvert. It was not okay to take a minute to calm your overstimulated feelings before you made up your mind. People whose first response is to say no probably felt intruded on or easily overwhelmed when they were children. As a result, they developed a pattern of saying no without thinking, in order to protect themselves. They dug a deep line in the sand and never crossed it. But always saying no creates a gulf between you and others. Practice saying yes. Don't give up saying no, just sprinkle a few yeses here and there. One of the many advantages of being a grown-up is that we can be an innie and say yes to more opportunities. We can let in more without being hurt, shamed, or blamed. We can speak up if someone hurts us. If someone is shaming us, we can say, "It seems hard for you to understand that I need to take a couple of minutes to decide." We can deal with invasive people by direct responses: "Hey, you're stepping on my toes." No isn't the only way to remain safe. Yes opens the door and invites many good things into your life.

A sound first step toward slowing down your quick-draw no is to watch yourself for a week and notice if no is your first answer to most things. If it is, pause, take a big breath, and think about what you are feeling. You may be anxious, scared, or nervous. Your internal CD may be playing "Don't Fence Me In."

You don't have to leap from fear to the automatic no. Remind yourself that you can take a minute to consider your options. Allow for some breathing room by telling yourself that it's okay to say, "Let me think about that." (Anyone who gets irritated if you take a few moments to think over your answer is the kind of person you should use no with.) Imagine the consequences of saying yes. Would it really be that horrifying? Try

> **Say No**
>
> - Say no nicely but firmly, without apology or lengthy explanation.
> - Make your own plans top priority: "I'd love to, but I have to finish this article."
> - Acknowledge the other person: "I appreciate the invitation. You do so much good work for the hospital, but unfortunately at this time I can't. Thank you for thinking of me."
> - Consider limiting your yes, if you must say it. "I can help with the bake sale, but I can't do the phone drive."
> - Realize you don't have to accept all good offers; others will come.
> - Say yes or no without much thought occasionally, just for the heck of it, on a matter of little consequence. Yahoo!

saying yes a few times and see what happens. Remember, you can often tailor the situation to your needs: "I can't meet you right after work, but I can stop by a little later." And don't forget, you can always change your mind and say no.

Tip 5: Try No

As I have explained, while there are those of us who say no too quickly, there are others who find themselves hardly able to say no at all.

Growing up, we learned to associate saying no with conflict. Conflict makes us anxious because it increases our feeling of overstimulation. So we avoid saying no. But since we need to conserve our energy, it is important to learn to say no. We need to spend our limited energy on what we most need or want to do. If you don't establish boundaries, people may not realize they need to take us into consideration. They will walk right over us.

To begin to develop firmer parameters, notice for a week if your first answer to most things is yes. Pause and breathe. Ask yourself what you *really* want to do. Notice if you are feeling afraid. Is your fear taking over and pushing you to automatically say yes? You may feel unsure and pressured, anxious that you must respond right away. Put on your thinking cap before you reply. Remind yourself that it's okay to give yourself time; it's okay to say, "I'm not sure yet." Think about what is exactly being asked of you. Think about the impact on you if you say no. Say no a few times and see what happens. Healthy people will not abandon you. If they do, say no even more.

After you notice your patterns for a week or so, you are ready for advanced no tips. Practice some of the strategies in the box on page 247. They are at your ready when you need a response.

Why You Need Special Handling

A human being's first responsibility
is to shake hands with himself.
—HENRY WINKLER

In their book *Better Boundaries,* Jan Black and Greg Enns say that the "path to well-placed boundaries is a natural process that begins with treasuring yourself, then moves to taking steps toward owning your life and protecting it." Setting your own parameters means deciding who and what to let in and who and what to keep out. It's a process of conscious sifting and sorting. Introverts need personal privacy, fences here and there.

The more you are able to appreciate your introversion and relish it, the more you will be leaping into self-acceptance, understanding, and growth. If you feel competent and lovable as an introvert, you will be able to set your own parameters.

You are a unique individual. No other set of genes has ever been mixed together like yours, and none ever will be again. That is quite a thought! You are an "only-used-once blueprint" of you. Treat yourself well.

Points to Ponder

Remember the Three P's:

- Personal Pacing
    - Accept your limitations.
    - Notice your energy rhythms.
    - Break everything into itsy-bitsy steps.
- Personal Priorities
    - Realize you have choices.
    - Choose what has meaning to you.
    - Constantly evaluate how your choices are working for you.
- Personal Parameters
    - Protect your introverted self.
    - Set parameters by saying yes, no, and maybe.
    - Take time to think about decisions.

CHAPTER IX

Nurture
Your Nature

But your solitude will be a support
and a home for you,
even in the midst of very
unfamiliar circumstances,
and from it you will find all your paths.

—RAINER MARIA RILKE

Bustling from activity to activity and interacting with lots of people are highly valued pursuits in many societies. But they don't work well for introverts. When we try to keep up, we find ourselves overspending our energy, and in no time at all we are running on empty. Without ways to renew, we may lose sight of our special nature and the nurturing it requires. Yet it is crucial for us, in order to function well, to create the pauses, solitude, and environment we need to restore ourselves. Otherwise life is one long experience of exhaustion.

Imagine trying to drive a car that has run out of gas. The only way to make it go is to get out and push it. Introverts often try to push themselves through life. That is why they often complain of feeling fatigued. In an attempt to be more energized, like extroverts, they sometimes use anger (which pumps adrenaline), anxiety (which increases heart rate, blood pressure, and sugar and stress hormones), caffeine (which stimulates the Full-Throttle System), or drugs (usually ones like cocaine that rev up the system). If introverts don't realize they are overextending, they can become ill. They don't even realize until their bodies break down that they are running on anxiety and adrenaline.

Nurturing
Your Natural Resources

What lies behind us and
what lies before us are tiny matters,
compared to what lies within us.
—RALPH WALDO EMERSON

Nurturing yourself means giving yourself the personal specific care you need. In *The Botany of Desire*, Michael Pollan says, "The tulip is an introvert among flowers." Tulips are "naturalizers," which means they bloom better every year. But they will bloom only if they have a hibernation period each year to restore themselves. They also need to have sunlight, water, and fertilizer; to be planted at the right depth; and to be planted right side up! In this chapter, I will discuss the special conditions *you* need to thrive.

Like an elegant tulip, your nature is a bit paradoxical. This is nothing to be ashamed of. Given the right conditions, tulips are hardy and bloom longer than many other flowers. But they won't bloom at all if conditions are inhospitable. Introverts are like that, too.

Why does your nature require the special conditions? As I discussed in Chapter 3, our physiology is linked to the rest-and-digest side of the nervous system, the Throttle-Down System, so every part of our body is attempting to preserve our resources. We are made for contemplation and hibernation. Our brains fire fewer "feel good" Hap Hits. Moving our limbs takes more conscious thought. We have a tendency toward low blood sugar, low blood pressure, shallow breathing, sleep difficulties, tension headaches, and occasionally feeling drained and discombobulated.

Because we tend to have less physical energy, we must learn how to fill our tanks with superhigh octane every now and then. Plus, we must recharge ourselves by conserving our energy. One of the main ways we do this is by quieting outside stimulation and creating downtime. However, many introverts have felt so stigmatized about the private, reserved aspect of their nature that they have not allowed themselves the time to develop effective restorative practices. It's time to change that!

Trouble in River City

There's trouble in River City,
and it starts with T and ends with C.
—PROFESSOR HAROLD HILL

In the musical *The Music Man*, set in the early 1900s, Professor Harold Hill wrangles the townfolk into buying band uniforms and instruments for their children by telling them that there is "trouble" in River City. And what is that dastardly trouble? The children have too much free time on their hands. With idle time, boys and girls are easily led down the path to no good.

Today the belief that idleness is the devil's playground and the push to keep kids busy is even stronger than in the time of *The Music*

Man. But time to reflect and ponder is not only good for introverts but necessary. What's more, as Anthony Storr says in his book *Solitude,* "The capacity to be alone is also an aspect of emotional maturity." The very quality that has been thought of as troubling or as a liability is actually a sign of psychological health.

Harnessing Your Energy

Energy is the fuel we use for a well-running life. The latest research has given us valuable evidence about how to keep our fuel at optimal levels. The first step to corralling our energy is to understand how and why it ebbs and flows.

When I keep talking about energy, what do I really mean? Energy is all around us. It is usually invisible, but it makes things happen. All living things require the constant expenditure of energy. Nothing can live, move, work, or change without energy. Energy comes in many forms, including kinetic, electrical, heat, sound, light, and nuclear. Although we can't hold it in our hands, we can feel the sun's energy as it warms us and enjoy its light, and we can hear the power in a gust of wind or a rushing waterfall. After being hungry and tired, we can feel our energy and stamina return when we feast on a nutritious meal.

Thermodynamics is the branch of physics concerned with energy. The first law of thermodynamics is that energy can be transformed, but it cannot be created or destroyed. The second law is that when we use or transform energy (called "free energy"), it becomes disorganized (called "entropy") and we can't reuse it until it can be organized again. It's a continuous cycle. As a result, energy is constantly changing from a state of free energy to entropy and back again. Extroverts convert disorganized energy into free energy by going out and about in the world. By staying put, introverts transform disorganized energy into free energy. (When you feel any of the symptoms listed in the box Energy Crisis, it is a sign that your energy is disorganized—which is exactly how you may feel, as if static is coursing through your mind and body.)

Nature has given humans a multitude of ways to convert scattered energy into composed energy: We can exercise, give ourselves nourishing foods, attend to our five senses, practice meditation and yoga, have a massage, take a vacation, and create environments that are restorative. We can connect with family and friends, focus on our purpose in life, and gain peace of mind through religion or spirituality. Nature presents us with an assortment of ways to nurture ourselves.

Energy Crisis

Are you giving yourself enough downtime? When your reserves are low, you may have trouble sleeping or eating; have frequent colds, headaches, back pains, or allergies. You may also experience some of the signs and signals listed here. These red flags are telling you that you are in an energy crisis. If you feel any of the sensations listed below, take time out to restore yourself.

- anxious, agitated, irritable, and snappish
- unable to think, concentrate, or make decisions
- confused and discombobulated, as if you are dashing from thing to thing in a blur
- trapped and wondering what is the meaning of life
- drained, tired, put-upon, and pooped
- disconnected from yourself

Rekindling Energy Reserves

nergy comes in many forms: mental energy, alert energy, healing energy, calm energy, vital energy, active energy, loving energy, sensory energy, and creative energy, to name just a few. Although we all

Break Breakdown

A few suggestions for a fifteen-minute break:

- Close your eyes; relax your body; think of a beach, lake, or the wind sweeping through tall pines.
- Take a short walk.
- Stretch and yawn; take a catnap.
- Drink a cup of tea or a glass of water with a few drops of lemon juice in it.
- Stare, and think of nothing.
- Tighten your muscles and then release them; feel the difference.
- Put your feet up and put a cool or warm washcloth on your forehead.
- Think of a memory that makes you smile (anything involving my grandkids fills this bill).
- Look at a funny website.
- Play a computer game, do a crossword puzzle, leaf through a magazine, read a comic book, peruse travel brochures.
- Scribble a few lines in a journal.
- Play with one of your children's toys.

A few suggestions for a thirty-minute break:

- Take a nap.
- Take a walk.
- Read a magazine article.

use many types of energy, there are two main types that innies constantly need to nurture in themselves: calm energy and alert energy. Calm energy allows our busy minds to quiet while we collect our thoughts and feelings. Alert energy helps us when we feel tired or overloaded.

- Order something from a catalog.
- Take the scenic route to work.
- Plan a surprise for your child or partner.
- Track down an old friend on the Internet.
- Break out of your routine, and do something backward (I like to eat my dessert first sometimes, Mary Poppins–style).

A few suggestions for a two-hour break:
- Go to a bookstore and browse in a section you have never studied before.
- Take a sack lunch and a good book to a scenic place.
- Visit a museum or historical building.
- Sit in a park, garden, or pretty grounds and daydream.
- Take a hike and watch a sunset.
- Trade foot, back, or neck rubs with your partner.
- Relax with a mask, cool eye pads, and soothing music.
- Make cookies and take them to the office or give them to your child's class.
- Start a jigsaw puzzle.
- Plan your next vacation.
- Look at old photos or home movies.
- Plant flowers where you can see them out your window.
- Hit a bucket of golf balls.
- Go fly a kite.

Compose Yourself by Taking Breaks

The best remedy for a short temper is a long walk.
—JACQUELINE SCHIFF

Genetic research has shown that it takes introverts longer than extroverts to reconstitute themselves when they are depleted. The reason? The receptor sites at the end of introverts' nerves are slow to re-uptake neurotransmitters. In other words, introverts require more resting time to feel restored.

As an introvert, you can avoid getting depleted by building in breaks—even if you don't feel as if you need one. Put these breaks and short naps on your calendar. Use a bright-colored pen and write "Break"—fifteen minutes every two hours. Then adhere to your schedule; take those breaks for a week or two and see how you feel.

Ted, an introverted animation director I interviewed, said, "I used to wait until I couldn't function and *then* take some downtime. I never seemed to catch up. Now I build short breaks into my schedule, and I find I never get into that overextended funk I used to."

Breaks are the best tool to create calm or alert energy, if you know how to take them. Take a look at the box *Break Breakdown* on page 256 for suggestions.

Mini-Vacation

Because of their slower tempo, introverts often feel as if they don't accomplish enough, and as a result, they don't allow themselves to take more than a short break. When I suggest to clients that they take one day of the weekend and spend it in bed with their PJs on, doing nothing but reading, watching bad TV, and lounging, they usually eye me with skepticism and say, "Is it okay to stay in bed *all* day?" If they give it a try and don't feel too guilty, they are often surprised at how much better they feel. Doing something completely different can be energizing, too. For example:

- Rent three old movies and watch them with breaks for walks.

- Attend a daylong music festival.

- Go to a day spa and have the full treatment.

- Take a train to another town, have lunch, and take the train back.

- Spend the day with a friend or two and reminisce.

- Spend the night in a hotel in your own town or city.

- Take a hike to where wildflowers are blooming; bring a picnic, and take pictures.

- Take a long car drive, singing to your favorite CDs.

The Importance of Breathing

All day long you are inhaling and exhaling, but I bet you don't even notice your breathing for days, weeks, or even months. Oxygen is the basic stuff of life. It raises your energy level by delivering vital supplies to your muscles, keeping your mind clear, and maintaining your sense of well-being. Every cell in your body requires it. As you breathe, oxygen enters the body and carbon dioxide exits. If we don't breathe deeply enough, our oxygen level gets depleted and carbon dioxide builds up and increases acid in our blood, which results in a fuzzy head, a woozy feeling, and increased anxiety.

Set Yourself on the Sunny Side of Life

Believe it or not, scientists have found that how we get out of bed in the morning influences how we feel all day. Ideally, we sleep deeply during the night, and as morning comes, we shift into lighter sleep. If we are awakened by a blaring alarm, dose ourselves with caffeine, and race around the house before running out the door, we set our body on *tension* for the whole day. If we ease into the morning, our body is primed for more energy and less tension. Try the steps below for several mornings and see how you feel.

- Set your alarm early enough that you have a little time to yourself in the morning.
- Awaken to gentle music on your radio.
- Sit up and slide out of bed slowly.
- Look out a window with the best view and breathe in the light.
- Do some easy stretches for five minutes.

Notice, without criticizing yourself, how you breathe normally. Do you breathe shallowly or deeply? (Introverts often breathe in a shallow way because they are on the Throttle-Down System, which slows breathing.) Are your inhalations even or do you take in more air than you release? Does your chest rise as you breathe? Do you hold your breath? Do you sigh a lot?

Healthy deep breathing originates from your abdomen (right below your belly button), not your lungs. Use your increased awareness and try some of the following exercises to see if you feel more energized. Find a comfortable place to lie down on a mat or carpet. Put a folded towel under your head and a pillow under your knees. Place one hand on your abdomen and the other hand on your chest over your breastbone. Now take a roomy breath. Which hand rises and falls the most? The goal is to have the hand on your abdomen higher.

With practice, you can learn to breathe deeply from your belly so that it becomes automatic. As you continue to inhale, inflate your stomach. Exhale as you push your stomach down. Visualize your tummy as a balloon, enlarging and shrinking as you inhale and exhale. Breathe in and out through your nose in a rhythmic pattern. It may feel a little odd at first, but with practice, you can become good at belly breathing. Switching from just barely filling your lungs with air to belly breathing will increase energy and calmness. Your body will thank you.

At any time of the day you can increase your alert energy with this quick deep-breathing exercise. Close your eyes. Breathe in deeply through your nose and hold it for the count of four. Exhale through your mouth to a count of six. Repeat several times. Notice how your body feels.

Nurturing Space

Your sacred space is where you can find yourself
again and again.

—JOSEPH CAMPBELL

I have often read that introverts are not aware of their surroundings. I think it is quite the opposite. Most of them are acutely aware, so they automatically focus in on just a few specific things to help reduce their feeling of stimulation. In order to make sense of all the data they take in throughout the day, introverts need peace and quiet. Otherwise, they can't think. Imagine attempting to decide where to go on vacation while you are standing in the median strip of the New Jersey Turnpike. The noises, the whoosh of cars, the overwhelming environment would make it impossible to concentrate. You can't process information if you are overstimulated. It's what one of my clients calls the "Philco static" in her brain. All white noise. No clear reception.

The more introverted you are, the more you need a serene environment for processing stimuli and for recharging. Why is processing time so crucial? Without it, you get information overload. New input lands on top of old input, and, suddenly, your threshold is reached and you shut down. Crash. Circuits are jammed. Numbness sets in.

Many people misunderstand this phenomenon. Let me explain. I have worked with many introverts who did not think they were very smart. Ironically, about 60 percent of the intellectually gifted are introverted (Silverman, 1993). The real problem is that they have been in an overloaded state all of their lives. They think "nothing" is in their brain when actually there's "too much" in there. However, if they are not aware of the need to give themselves time to sift, sort, and contemplate, they may feel they can't think. Or, worse, they think their head is empty.

Why does this happen? Imagine that your introverted brain is like a big bank computer. All day long it takes in huge numbers of deposits, makes withdrawals, and processes various other transactions from thousands of customers, putting this here, storing that there. At night, the bank clerks handle these transactions in what they call a "batch process." (That's why it says on your bank statement that your deposit won't be reflected on your bank balance until the next day.) And in the morning. Voilà! Your deposit is posted to your account. (Hopefully.)

What would happen if the bank computer didn't operate at night? Serious congestion and backup. Accounts would be incorrect, your balance could be too high or too low. You wouldn't be able to make sense of anything. Human beings are the same. If you don't have time to process the stimuli you take in, you get backed up and congestion sets in. You can get fuzzy or go "blank."

Innies need uninterrupted time and space to let their thoughts and feelings get sorted out, to think about the pros and cons of things. Only reflective time allows them to figure out what they really feel about something and gives them access to information they have unconsciously ingested. "That idea just floated into my brain"—clients will tell me after they learn to give themselves more downtime.

After processing time, some introverts like to talk about their thoughts and feelings to another person who is a good listener. They may not need any feedback. If they do like a response, often it helps just to summarize what they said. In this way they can appreciate and clarify their own thought process. They begin to trust that they will think of useful ideas and creative solutions to problems. Trusting your process is important.

Carve Out
Your Own Nook or Cranny

When introverts spend too much time around other people, they can start to feel drained just by the physical proximity. They can feel tired in a crowd without ever talking to anyone. Carving out physical space gives them the expanse they need to regroup. Most introverts need their own personal space because they tend to be territorial. They need an actual place to call their own. It gives them a sense of controlling their own energy.

Renewing space needs to feel safe and comfortable, free from crowds, interruptions, loud noises, and demands. If it isn't protected and comfortable, it will take energy away rather than give it.

Picture what type of space feels cozy and nurturing to you. What kind of environment do you need in order to muse—mull over your problems, invent a fantasy, savor memories? My client Emma likes to putter around the house clipping dead leaves from her Boston ferns, rearranging knickknacks, and taking in the muted tones of the rag rugs on her polished hardwood floors. When you are relaxing, you are reducing outside stimulation and replenishing your energy stores.

Another client prefers to replenish her energy stores by being enveloped in a pile of fluffy feather pillows and immersing herself in a mystery novel. My client David has a busy household with four children and an extra-extroverted wife. "As long as I have my office out in the garage where I can tuck myself away for an hour, I am okay," he says. A friend of mine made a tiny Zen cubbyhole in her attic where she meditates with cushions, candles, meaningful pictures, and aromas.

Here are some things to consider when you are creating a special nook or cranny for yourself:

- Do you want an outdoor or indoor spot? One of my clients still lusts after his tree house. Many people love the feel of a hammock or chaise lounge under a cool shade tree. Others prefer comfortable furniture with soft pillows and cozy throws.

- What kind of light do you want and how much? Lots of natural light? Candles? Gentle lamp light? Cool shadows?

- What colors enhance your feeling of well-being?

- Do you want complete quiet? Music? Sounds of nature? A water fountain? Remember, you can use earplugs, sound machines, and headphones.

- Do you want pets around? (You can learn from cats, they are expert refuelers.)

If you don't have the luxury of a special room of your own, then carve out a space for yourself with a folding screen, plants, or a bookshelf. Even an area rug helps give a sense of separateness.

When my client Rochelle was in the fifth grade, she divided up the bedroom she shared with her sister by hanging a chenille bedspread. It was her attempt to have a room of her own. Still on the quest for a space of her own in junior high, she moved into the breakfast nook. She had to more or less fall into her bed (it filled up the entire nook), but it was hers. Another of my clients made a little reading loft for herself in a closet.

Remember, you may need different types of space at different times. If you have been indoors too much, you may need the feeling of the great outdoors; at other times, though, you may prefer to cozy up to a fireplace. There are many ways to create a personal space in the world.

I often suggest to clients that when they feel the world assaulting them, they should imagine a bubble or force field around them. The sense of having protection from outside stimulation increases their energy immeasurably.

Light and Air Temperature

Introverted bodies seem to be particularly attuned to fluctuations in temperature and to the rhythms of light and dark. Our systems are often harder than extroverts' to get going in the morning (that old Throttle-Down System again). We need natural light, especially bright morning light, to help us feel awake. At Harvard University, researchers studied the link between light and alertness. They found that people felt more energized all day when they had at least fifteen minutes of bright light first thing in the morning. Natural light is vital to all of us but especially to introverts, since they function on the less energized side of the nervous system. Natural light regulates levels of a hormonelike substance called melatonin, which has a powerful effect on mood, sleep, and the reproductive system. An insufficient amount of light can cause a buildup of melatonin, resulting in depression and lethargy. This situation can become quite serious during winter months and has been given an actual diagnosis, "seasonal affective disorder" (SAD).

There are ways to increase your light intake. At home or work, sit by a window. To the best jof your ability, avoid fluorescent lighting (the most unnatural form of light). Go outside for a light break. Use full-spectrum lightbulbs or a lamp that replicates daylight if you live in the northern latitudes. Bring extra lamps to work if your office only has one light source.

You may be interested to learn that introverts tend to run cool and get chilled easily. Their normal body temperature is often below the average 98.6. Their Throttle-Down System pulls blood from the extremities to help the internal organs digest food, so hands and feet receive less warming blood. If innies feel too cold, it can be even more difficult for them to get going and leave the house. At the same time, because they may not sweat as easily as extroverts—sweating is the main way humans regulate overheating—innies don't fuction well when they are overheated. Every body movement slows to a crawl and thinking grinds to a halt.

Innies have a relatively narrow range of temperatures in which they feel comfortable. In order to ensure maximum functioning, it's a good idea to:

- Dress in layers so you can adjust to the temperature.

- Bring a sweater or jacket even if you don't think it will be necessary.

- Tuck hand warmers in your pockets.

- Wear thin socks with a thicker pair over them so you can take them off after your tootsies toast up.

■ Take a portable heater or fan to work to balance the room temperature and keep the air circulating by opening a window for at least a few moments every day.

Your Nose Knows

Unlike our other senses, our sense of smell has its very own short pathway from the nose to the brain. Have you ever whiffed bubble gum and a memory of childhood floated through your head? We have an immediate reaction to fragrances because they are processed right next door to both the emotional center and the memory center of the brain.

Since our sense of smell registers on our most basic systems, it has an effect on our Throttle-Down System. When smelling fragrances we like, we take slow, deep breaths and so we also take in more oxygen. As we have seen, these two processes increase our energy level. There is evidence that fragrances may also improve concentration and learning. In one study, two groups of subjects were asked to do connect-the-dots puzzles. One group was then asked to sniff a fragrance. Then both groups were asked to redo the puzzles. The group that had sniffed the fragrance finished 30 percent faster. In another study of stress response, subjects who were showing signs of stress were given a whiff of spiced apple. This was followed by an increase of alpha brain waves, which indicated a relaxed alert state.

Outside the United States, aromatherapy is being used in conjunction with a variety of medical and nonmedical conditions. In Great Britain, for example, aromatherapy involving lavender is used to treat insomnia and jasmine is used to treat anxiety. And in a study there, when dieters selected a favorite scent to sniff, they actually lost weight easer! In Japan, lemon scent has been dispersed through the ventilation system in some office buildings to increase productivity.

You can enjoy the benefits of aromatherapy by inhaling a few drops of the essential oil fragrances you respond to best. Put a couple of drops in your bath or shower, or use with a massage or manicure. Put the scent on a tissue and whiff it several times a day. Or light several essential-oil candles and let them waft through your home.

Test various scents in perfumes, colognes, spices, and foods to determine their effects on your mood and sense of alertness. Once you discover what works best, you can use the particular scents to create a desired mood. Program your nose by training it to associate a scent to an emotion. For example, every time you are in a relaxed and alert state, sniff a tangerine aroma. Soon, each time you smell tangerine, it will evoke in you a state of alertness and relaxation.

Refreshing and Invigorating Aromas

REFRESHING	INVIGORATING
• lavender	• peppermint
• rose	• spearmint
• chamomile	• citrus
• geranium	• eucalyptus
• sandalwood	• cypress
• vanilla	• rosemary
• fresh mown grass	• orange blossom

Musical Moments

Music is your own experience,
your thoughts, your wisdom.
—CHARLIE PARKER

Since ancient times, music has been used in all cultures as a powerful force to help shift moods and improve emotional states. Studies show that many people find it more exhilarating than sex. It can energize us, relax us, or inspire us to move. Music influences our respiratory rate, blood pressure, stomach contractions, and hormone levels, which in turn affect our immune system. Heart rates slow down or speed up to synchronize with the beat of the music, and it can increase oxygenation and alter our brain waves (remember the relaxing alpha waves I mentioned earlier).

Several experiments have shown that musical preferences are extremely idiosyncratic. What is soothing to one person can be jarring to another. Your taste in music may also change from day to day. Sometimes jazz may be relaxing, and sometimes it may be irritating. Pay close attention to your differing reactions to various types of music. Note whether a particular style makes you happy or sad, relaxed or energized. If you are down in the dumps, try to pick something to match your low-key mood. Gradually, shift into a more up-tempo piece—gospel, swing, rock, reggae, new age, gunfighter ballads, or Dixieland jazz just may do it—and feel your gloom lift.

Since introverts sometimes have trouble getting going, music can help you get out of the starting gate. Music can also help you kick back and relax. It can distract you from unpleasant voices chattering in your head or from painful memories, and it can lift a blue mood. As you relax, your energy stores are converted into usable fuel.

Take time out to enjoy the notes of nature. Nature's music can be refreshing, renewing, and soothing. I like to listen to a CD of nature sounds—a mountain storm full of wind, rain, cracks of lightning, and claps of thunder. After listening to it, I feel rather electrified. Or you can put a bird feeder outside your window and listen to the various chirps and calls. Stroll by the ocean, through the woods, or around a lake, and concentrate on listening to the lively music nature is playing.

Studies show that humming, singing, and whistling can also keep us energized. They improve mood and awareness and decrease anxiety. Think about how many parents naturally croon to their babies. Singing increases oxygen and seems to affect neurotransmitters, so sing in the shower or the car or, if you're serious enough, join a choir. Notice how lighthearted singing makes you feel? And don't forget whistling. It is a lost art—bring it back by puckering up and blowing. Bet you'll feel more spirited.

Listen to Your Body Talk

A person's mood is like a symphony,
and serotonin is like the conductor's baton.
—JAMES STOCKARD

As we've seen, acetylcholine, serotonin, and dopamine are neurotransmitters our brain uses for a number of important mental and physical functions, and it's vitally important to keep the supply at optimal levels. The only way we can control our neurotransmitters, other than by taking drugs, is by maintaining our physical health. Our brains and neurotransmitters are affected by nutrition, sleep, stress levels, and exercise.

Nutritional Noshing

To eat is human; to digest, divine.
—CHARLES T. COPELAND

Because of the way our nervous system is organized, introverts metabolize food quickly. Food comes in, is converted to energy, and is used up. This makes it hard to keep our glucose level constant. Eating regularly throughout the day provides a steady stream of nutrients to keep our blood sugar stable. Grazing, as it is called, will prevent mood swings and headaches, as well as sleepiness. (Think how logy you feel after a large holiday meal.)

In *Your Miracle Brain,* Jean Carper, a highly regarded medical author, says, "Some of the most thrilling discoveries about how the brain works, and how you can influence thought and behavior with food and supplements, come from new knowledge about the activity of neurotransmitter systems." She goes on to say, "The radical conclusion: The type of neurotransmitters your neurons make and release and their ultimate destiny within the brain depends greatly on what you eat. Obviously, that makes food a very big regulator of the brain." I guess they weren't kidding when they said, "You are what you eat."

Here are some nutritional keys to neurotransmitters:

Acetylcholine is an introvert's main neurotransmitter. It improves learning, memory, and motor coordination, and it also protects against Alzheimer's disease. Estrogen increases acetylcholine, so during menopause, when acetylcholine levels drop due to the loss of estrogen, women tend to have memory problems. The best food sources for increasing acetylcholine are fish (salmon, herring, mackerel, sardines, and others), egg yolks (excellent source), wheat germ, liver, meat, milk, cheese, broccoli, cabbage, cauliflower, and lecithin.

Serotonin helps calm us. Its key building block is the amino acid tryptophan, which is produced by eating carbohydrates. Carbohydrates are sugars, and they are contained in foods like starches, refined grains, beans, vegetables, and many fruits. They come in two forms—fast release and slow release—and they affect your blood sugar and serotonin in different ways. A Milky Way is a fast-release carbo. It breaks down quickly, spiking your blood sugar and increasing serotonin. Your energy surges and then plummets. You may feel energized right after eating one and then, an hour later, you feel as if your IQ dropped fifty points. Low-fat yogurt is a slow-release carbo. It breaks down gradually and it increases your blood sugar and serotonin more like a time-release capsule. Eating slow-releasing carbohydrates at the right time of day can be calming because serotonin will then be released gently. Slow-release carbos are good in the late afternoon to soothe you and as a bedtime snack to help you sleep. Read up on how carbos work and what are the best ones to eat. I have included some good books on nutrition in the Bibliography.

Dopamine increases your alertness and makes you feel less hungry. Its key building block is the amino acid tyrosine, which is released in the bloodstream when you eat protein. Protein energizes the brain and satiates hunger quickly, so it's smart to eat some at the beginning of each meal. Fish, meats, eggs, dairy products, peanut butter, certain beans, and nuts all contain protein. Protein comes either lean or fatty. Consume smaller amounts of the leaner types of protein throughout your day to maintain alertness.

Two words on water: *Drink it.* Every part of your body needs water to function. At least 60 percent of your body is water, and bodily fluids are based on it. You lose water all day long, and if you get dehydrated, your energy will sag. So keep sipping. Nutritionists recommend eight glasses throughout the day. Your body will appreciate it, and you will keep all of your cells nice and "plumped up."

Catch Some zzzzzzz's

William Dement, M.D., Ph.D., chairman of the sleep-disorders clinic at Stanford University School of Medicine, says, "A substantial number of Americans, perhaps the majority, are functionally handicapped by sleep deprivation on any given day." Lack of sleep increases irritability and mistakes, dulls the senses, and reduces concentration. Most important, it prevents REM sleep, the state during which we dream. In REM sleep we store daily experiences in our long-term memories. If we don't get enough sleep, we can lose this crucial aspect of brain function. Then the fear many introverts have, that their brain is empty, really will come true.

One of the reasons introverts can have trouble sleeping is because they have such active brains. The blood flow to the stimulation areas of their brains is greater than in extroverts, and they are constantly bombarded by a variety of stimuli—from the inner as well as the outer world. They can't switch their minds off, shut out the world around them, or quiet their inner voices. This often makes it harder for them to simmer down, relax, and get the seven or eight hours of sleep experts say they need.

Here are some tips to help bring the Sandman:

- Introverts are usually quite sensitive to caffeine, so confine your coffee drinking to the morning.

- Put opaque shades on your bedroom windows and use earplugs or a sound machine to shut out noises.

- Take the TV out of your bedroom.

- Create a bedtime ritual that is comforting, and go to bed and get up at the same time every day.

■ Keep the bedroom cool.

■ Deep breathe, if you can't sleep, and tell yourself you are helping your body, which you are.

Have a Fit

Introverts are more sedentary than extroverts. They are not motivated to move as much, and many do not like to exercise. But it's important to find a way to stay physically fit. One reason it's important to exercise is to increase the oxygen to your brain. With more oxygen your neurotransmitters and memory function better. Also, your body is stronger and has more endurance and flexibility if the muscles are stressed a little bit. Finally, exercise strengthens your heart and lungs and improves your overall stamina, and you may feel peppier. My best suggestion about exercise is to find one or several you like and write down in your calendar your "have a fit" date with yourself. Then, as Nike says, Just Do It. I have found that some innies enjoy group activities, but most prefer a sport that is also individual. Yoga, stretching, swimming, martial arts, moderate weight lifting, dancing, in-line skating, bicycle riding, or gliding around on one of those aluminum scooters with neon wheels are all healthful. I like to walk and listen to books on tape. Manny, an introverted English professor, likes to walk with his two pups, Keats and Shelley, looking like two furballs racing down the sidewalk. Another client rows and several others golf.

Remember to pace yourself. It is better to exercise three times a week for thirty minutes than several hours once every two weeks. It's important to keep at it because it's so easy to stop exercising. Unfortunately, this is what happens to many people. Since most introverts don't get the same energy lift from exercising that extroverts do, and receive milder Hap Hits from the experience, once they fall off the wagon they may have trouble getting back on. Remember why you are doing it, to improve your body and mind. When you finish your session, reward yourself—a new book, hot shower, a computer game, or a movie.

Ya Gotta Have Friends

Introverts often feel isolated and, at times, lonely. As I have explained, there are many complex psychological and physiological reasons for this. But one explanation can't be overlooked: Many of us have a relatively small circle of friends. Unlike extroverts, who consider almost everyone they know a friend, we believe all relationships have to be "deep" and "meaningful" in order to be authentic. But seeing more acquaintances as friends, and accepting that satisfying relationships can be light as well as deep, will make the world feel like a friendlier place. Having more friends also adds spice to our life. Otherwise we can get into the same old routine.

Another reason for a potpourri of friends is for support

How to Thrive in the Friend Department

- Explain introversion to your extroverted friends; this saves hurt feelings. Explain that you may need to call or e-mail them when you feel energized and that they should not take it personally if they don't hear from you for several weeks.

- Explain introversion to your introverted friends, because they may not know much about their temperament.

- Schedule lunch with a friend at least once every two weeks.

- Invite a friend over, from time to time, clearly stating the starting and stopping time.

- Let go of any so-called friends who are negative.

insurance. If a friend is unavailable, moves away, or dies, or if some-how the relationship ends, we are left without enough emotional backup. This is especially true as we age. We need people who can talk about subjects we enjoy or find educational. We need people who can talk for hours about everything or not much. We need book friends and idea friends; friends we can be quiet with; friends we can be silly with; friends to do things with—travel, shop, see a movie. We need friends of all ages, from tots to seniors. We need introverted and extroverted friends. We need friends who understand introverts.

Grow Your Spirit

We are not human beings trying to be spiritual.
We are spiritual beings trying to be human.
—JACQUELYN SMALL

Spiritual growth is important to many introverts. Our temperament tends to be peace-loving and honest, so the tenets of many religions reflect our values. Also, many of us want to understand the meaning of life. We can get caught up in seeing life through a small lens. Spiritual beliefs help us to see the bigger picture and balance our inside world and the larger world of humanity. Religion can reduce overwhelm, as it gives practical guidelines and advice about how to live a fulfilled life. Feeling there are more possibilities can help lift any sense of depression or hopelessness and can give us energy. Often our spiritual beliefs bring the added benefit of enabling us to enjoy fellowship and community in a structured environment.

Spiritual practices can offer optimism, a way to cope, a sense of peace, and an overall sense of well-being. If you aren't currently mak-ing room for any spiritual or religious practice, and you think it's worth a try, or if you want to expand a budding interest or increase your involvement, try some of these activities: Visit a church or synagogue and consider joining. Read a devotional every morning or say a short prayer each day as you look out your window. Join a church choir. Take a class on the religions of the world. Do one kind thing for someone each day and tell no one. Hold hands and pray as a family before dinner. Read M. J. Ryan's book *Attitudes of Gratitude,* which reminds us to notice the small wonders in life. Observe the special moments in your life by writing down three things that you are grateful for each day. Give to others by buying Toys for Tots during the holidays, become a Big Brother or Sister, or send an underprivileged child to camp during the summer. These are just a few of the myriad ways to volunteer your time, money, and energy. Check in with yourself to see if you feel enriched by these practices.

In his book *The Biology of Success,* Dr. Bob Arnot says, "Scientific, not anecdotal, studies now show that prayer works wonders on health. Of the three hundred studies on spirituality in scientific journals, the National Institute of Health Research found that 75 percent showed that religion and prayer have a positive effect on health." If this is an aspect of your personality you want to nurture in order to fill up your reserves for living, then build a few spiritual habits into your life.

Create a Statement of Purpose

What we all must decide is how we are valuable
rather than how valuable we are.
—EDGAR Z. FRIEDENBERG

What gives your life meaning? How would you like to make a difference? Everyone was born with a life purpose. It may feel scary to think you don't have one or can't think of it—but you do and you can. Many introverts want to know the reason they are on this planet. (It doesn't have to be to save the world.) It helps them direct their inner strengths toward what is most fulfilling to them. A clear purpose gives meaning to life and increases energy because it provides direction. It helps to give your life shape and makes you feel more motivated and less discontented.

Since introverts may not have as much energy as extroverts for "out-in-the-world" activities, it is especially important for them to zero in on doing what holds the most meaning for them. Also, because they are so easily overwhelmed by the demands of everyday life, it may not occur to them to think about what they really want for themselves.

Perhaps you have already articulated your purpose. If not and you would like to create a statement of purpose, then follow the guidelines below. They can be useful. Keep in mind, your purpose doesn't have to be locked in; it can change over time.

Here are five questions to get you started on your statement of purpose. (If other pertinent questions occur to you, great. Use them, too.) Jot down answers, trying to capture the first thought that occurs. Play with the ideas that pop into your mind. (It might also help to refer back to the goals and priorities you set in Chapter 8.)

Don't agonize. If "I want to be happy" comes to mind, think about what in particular would make you happy. Then arrange your ideas in a single paragraph. Let it sit for a few days, and then go over it again. Remember, what you write is not carved in stone; you can expand or change it at any time.

1. What things in my life are most important to me?

2. What would I like to contribute to the world?

3. In this lifetime, I hope to _____.

4. How can I make these things happen in my life?

5. Who are the people I want to be with on my journey?

Here is what I wrote. (This is an example only, not a *right* answer.)

My Statement of Purpose

My purpose in life is to live consciously each day, making choices that stimulate growth in myself and in others. I hope my work will provide ways for people to better understand themselves with more compassion and appreciation for their humanness. I want to create meaningful relationships, built on mutuality, fun, and growth. I would like to leave memories of zany times, touching moments, and enduring wisdom with others.

Take a stab at it. It does not have to be perfect, profound, or even include an answer to all the questions listed above. (You may notice that my example does not.) It just has to be tailor-made for *you*. And you can always amend and update it later. Having a statement of purpose helps you to direct your personal energy toward what matters to you most and to live with meaning based on your own values and talents. It helps you feel fully alive.

When Your Nature Is Nurtured

Happiness is not a station to arrive at,
but a manner of traveling.
—MARGARET LEE RUNBECK

Picture yourself as the tulip I mentioned at the beginning of the chapter. See yourself as a vibrant, graceful, hardy, rich, and miraculous bloom. You need special care that only you can provide for yourself. In some ways it is frustrating to realize that for the rest of your life, you have to maintain your environment so carefully. In another way it is exciting to realize you have the power to care for yourself well. If you should occasionally fall down on the job, just read over this chapter and shift back into the nurturing-gardener mode. You can do this any time and as often as you need to.

Points to Ponder

If you do all or even some of these energy-boosting activities regularly, you'll be ready for any of the hurdles life throws onto your path. Nurturing ourselves makes us stronger, happier, and more accepting about being an introvert. You'll feel less like a fish out of water.

- Nurture your special nature.
- Notice what seems to boost your energy and also what appears to drain it.
- When you are aware of a sense of well-being and calm, you are on the right track. Feeling irritated and tired are signals that you need to change your strategies.
- Small changes have big payoffs.
- Spend your energy wisely.

CHAPTER X

Extroverting: Shine Your Light into the World

To fear is one thing. To let fear grab you by
the tail and swing you around is another.

—KATHERINE PATERSON

You have acknowledged you are an introvert, and you are well on your way to living comfortably in your own skin. Now it's time to get a little uncomfortable again—for a good reason. Nice as it would be to stay within the confines of the familiar, it's not always practical. There are things introverts have to do that call for some extrovert-like skills. For example, if you want to look for a new job, change your child's physician, or make new friends, you'll need extroverted skills. I couldn't have written this book if I hadn't been willing to push the envelope. I had to grit my teeth and make phone calls, go out and interview people, and talk to groups.

At times, we all need to do some extroverting in order to achieve our goals and dreams. We have to make forays outside our comfort zones. We can always race right back afterward.

Extroverts are like lighthouses, built to focus energy outward. Their attention is directed away from themselves; they're constantly scanning the external environment. That's where extroverts gain physical energy, and they get Hap Hits from the buzz of dopamine. No such luck for innies. We are built like lanterns, a soft glow hinting at the strength within. Our attention is always on internal clues. When we go out into the real world, we have to do things differently. We need to reduce our internal brightness, and we need to turn up another flame, focusing the beam outward.

Extroverts dive into the world at a fast clip, with a fearless attitude that exudes confidence. They are chatty, open, spontaneous, and ready to try just about anything. Just as they need to learn some skills from innies, we need to learn some of their skills.

In this chapter, I suggest strategies for making your forays into extroverting as smooth and anxiety-free as possible. You will learn to adopt aspects of the "E attitude" (extrovert attitude). It's a lighter, more carefree and confident approach to life. And in small doses and for short periods, you can use it to your advantage.

Illusion of Comfort Zone

No sooner do we think
we have assembled a comfortable life
than we find a piece of ourselves
that has no place to fit in.

—GAIL SHEEHY

From infancy forward, we find security in what is familiar. Children of all temperaments may bring along a blankie or stuffed toy to help them with their feelings of unfamiliarity. The frayed fabric reminds them of hearth and home. It calms their fears and anxieties. As adults, we continue to seek the familiar, since it helps us manage feeling overwhelmed. Introverts, even more than extroverts, notice and find safety in what they are accustomed to. To take in new outside information requires energy.

Introverts may develop a fantasy that if they are comfortable all the time they will be okay. But that fantasy can be limiting. No matter how carefully you construct your life, you will still encounter obstacles, challenges, hurdles, and unpleasant feelings, and you need to be able to deal with them. It requires trying new behaviors and tolerating the strange feeling of not quite being you.

In addition, growth means feeling a little bit new to yourself. An insulated life may protect you from unpleasant feelings, but it also limits you from having experiences and meeting people, both of which might help you   and bring you delights you never imagined or thought possible.

Remaining too comfortable causes us to lose aspects of our personalities. Just as muscles do not gain strength when they're not used, parts of our personality will not be strengthened unless you flex them every now and then. What's more, you can become bored or depressed without new information and challenges. Fears of being abandoned, rejected, or disappointed may increase unless positive outside experiences remind you that these fears are not always grounded in reality.

As an introvert, you need to remind yourself that though you are burning fuel rapidly when you are extroverting, you are also gaining new ideas, relationships, and experiences. The world is an exciting place. Unlike extroverts, you won't be able to flash your light around willy-nilly. But you can pinpoint the areas where you want to focus your "extroverting" energy.

Catching Confidence

Character consists of what you do
on the third and fourth tries.
—JAMES MICHENER

W e introverts need to feel that we can rely on ourselves to manage in an environment that is not our natural niche. Standing
up to a difficult co-worker, returning merchandise to a store, lobbying
for a promotion, complaining to your child's school, or joining a book
club can be challenging. But challenges are meant to be overcome, and
being confident in yourself is a great place to start. Remember, you can
shine like an extrovert and then reduce your flame and return to the
warmth of your lantern. Take good care of yourself as you extrovert and
take breaks. It will pay off.

Many introverts stay in their comfort zone because they aren't sure
that they can manage in the "outie world." When they are out and
about, they often feel overwhelmed and can't remember their own
abilities. They might compare themselves to extroverts and decide they
are deficient. They withdraw so they won't feel bad about themselves.
Introverts can also get caught up in the idea so pervasive in our culture
that our personal value is based on what we do—not on who we are.

In her book *Confidence: Finding It and Living It,* Barbara De
Angelis, Ph.D., explains that "when you base your confidence on *who
you are,* instead of *what you accomplish,* you have created something
that no one or no circumstance can ever take away from you."
(Emphasis in original.) This is so important for introverts because
many of our abilities aren't valued in the extroverted world.

Confidence is an often misunderstood term. People think of it
in an extroverted way: doing activities quickly, having high energy,

and racking up a host of accomplishments. But if that were true, only people like Olympic champions would have inner security. Nature didn't design the universe that way, or most people would be left out. Also, think of all the people who seem to be at the top of their game and are very accomplished, yet behave in self-destructive ways, like abusing drugs or alcohol. In addition, if your confidence rests on what you are already good at, then it's tough to do new things. To undertake novel activities you have to be a beginner and go through a learning curve and be awkward. Confidence based solely on accomplishment limits your ability to expand and tackle new interests.

Consider Sean, a new client in his early twenties. "My mind is so quick, other people can't keep up with me, and I realized when I was very young that I can outthink most adults," he said to me at our first meeting. "I'm like Wile E. Coyote; I can twirl around almost everyone." Some people heard Sean's bravado and mistook it for confidence. Actually, Sean was frightened, impulsive, and driven. He had little confidence and depended instead on his quickness, equating it with knowledge and intelligence. In his professional life, Sean was having difficulty getting along with authority figures, and his career was stalled. He was *doing* a lot, but he was getting nowhere fast.

If you can feel confident only when you are participating in an activity you do well, what happens when you *aren't* doing that activity? If you feel secure about your abilities only when you are parenting, how do you manage when your kids don't need you? Or, if you are in a helping profession, what becomes of your sense of yourself when you are not giving to someone else? If you become ill, for instance, are you now worthless because you can't accomplish anything?

There is a difference between confidence based on accomplishment and confidence based on your inner qualities. This is why achieving a specific goal, like graduating from school, buying a fancy car, getting that promotion, or having a certain amount in the bank, feels good but wears off relatively fast. Research indicates that increased satisfaction from a big promotion lasts, at the most, about six months. In order to feel self-assurance we need something that is always with us. Confidence needs to come from what is *inside* us, not what we do *outside.*

Confidence rests on an inner pledge. It's an agreement you make with yourself to learn or do whatever you need to do in order to attain your goals. It's the ability to be determined, curious, tolerant of mistakes, and kind to yourself as you learn new skills. No one can take your persistence or any of these qualities away from you.

Introverts, especially, need to think about their internal abilities, since they may not have as many external accomplishments to lean on as extroverts do. Unlike Sean, they can't even fool themselves that they feel confident. Here are some of the advantages they do have going for them: the ability to focus well for long periods of time, to be persistent, to take many factors into account, to master new information, to strive to do a good job, to contemplate, and to create in imaginative ways. These are just a few qualities on a pretty impressive list, I might add. Usually if I tell clients some of the qualities I see in them, they are surprised. "I never thought of those aspects of myself as valuable," they often say.

So how can you boost your introverted confidence account? It only takes some of your observation skills. Imagine you have a bank account for confidence. Credit your account whenever you take an action that moves you toward a goal or a priority. Visualize yourself depositing some "confidence coin" in your account. Better yet, keep a confidence notebook and tally your "deposits." When you are fearful but you are able to make a difficult phone call anyway, make another deposit. Add another coin to your account whenever you trust and value your emotions. If someone criticizes you and you are able to consider their feedback objectively without overvaluing (they are right; I was despicable to do that) or undervaluing (they are way off the mark; I am right), drop a few coins in your account. After you decide how to respond to the criticism, "I can see your point, but I think you misunderstood me; I meant . . . ," make another deposit. Whenever you are hopeful, put in more confidence coins. If you have a disappointment—you don't get the new job you really wanted—allow yourself to feel sad and discouraged for a few days. Remind yourself it was only one job and then deposit a wad of dough into your account as you send out another résumé.

Imagine how you would feel about yourself if you really put in a deposit every time you demonstrated a confident attitude. In no time, you would have built up a hefty account.

Now, when you go out extroverting, you can either glance over your notebook or visualize a huge balance. The

> ## Shake Off That Pattern
>
> Many clients I have worked with tense up when they are anxious. Their bodies get as tight as skins drawn over kettledrums in a marching band. Telling themselves to stop feeling anxious doesn't help. Nor does criticizing themselves. It only makes them tense up even more. So I suggest that they do the opposite of what they usually do. For example, when our body feels tense, we usually attempt to make ourselves relax. But this doesn't always work. So change the pattern. On purpose, tense up your whole body. Then let go with a big sigh. Now shake like a golden retriever after a run through the sprinklers on a scalding summer day. Shake, shake, shake. Visualize beads of water raining in the air all around you. How do you feel now?

big balance is a constant reminder that you have the ability to work for what you want and that you can rely on yourself. You are resilient. You can ask for help if you need it, and you can bounce back after experiencing an obstacle or disappointment.

One Is Enough

When you discover you are riding a dead horse,
the best strategy is to dismount.

—DAKOTA SAYING

In general, extroverts don't spend much time stuck in a rut. They are up and going before they even think about it. But for introverts, getting going can be like scaling Mt. Everest. Because they know it takes extra energy to climb out of their well-worn path and because they aren't rewarded with Hap Hits from moving their bodies, it is easy to stay sedentary. Less energy is needed to confront the familiar. And, if innies aren't in the world enough, they can assume they have more problems than other people, reinforcing the notion that something is wrong with them. They feel even more ashamed and increase their isolation. Innies often don't realize that life has built-in stresses and strains and that everyone struggles in one way or another.

So what's an innie to do if he or she gets stuck in a rut? This may surprise you. But doing just *one* thing differently can help you make any change you want to make. It's like throwing one stone in a pond. Various ripples undulate across the water, altering the entire surface. Try the following:

1. Pinpoint the pattern you want to change.

2. Do *any* part of it differently.

3. Try a solution you have used successfully in another situation.

4. Use paradox. Think of how you could make the problem worse. New solutions may occur.

5. Focus your attention on what you would like to have happen, not on what is happening.

6. Congratulate yourself for succeeding. There is something freeing about doing something out of your usual routine.

Here's how this technique can work in practice: My client Alex goes home every night from work and watches TV, but he would like to change this pattern and go out at least one night a week. (1) Since it's hard for him to blast himself out of his home once he's ensconced, I suggested that he go somewhere else straight from work—a movie or a museum exhibit, a café with a co-worker, the mall to window-shop. (2) Then I asked him to imagine how he would feel if he could-n't go out for the next three weeks. (3) This is often a surprising motivator. It dislodges fear. Suddenly he could think of lots of places he would like to go. Next, I encouraged him to imagine himself at a driving range hitting a bucket of balls, or at one of the other fun places on his list, which included the planetarium, the bookstore, the Thursday-night art walk. I asked him to jot all of them down on a page entitled Weekend Capers and keep it at work or in his car so he could refresh his memory about his options. (4) He actually went to a reading at the library and had fun.

Many introverts feel anxious during transitions, which they experience as periods of uncertainty. When they leave their home, they get especially nervous. They anticipate what could go wrong, and they know that will require more energy. Also, they're concerned with their ability to handle themselves in an unfamiliar environment. Frequently, they're afraid they will leave behind something they might need. For example, my introverted client Holly told me that when she is getting ready to go out, she often can't find her keys and her Palm Pilot. Or she forgets various important items and has to dash back into the house several times. Both of these situations make her extremely anxious. Holly and I talked about how she could change this situation.

I asked her to notice all of the steps she went through as she prepared to leave her home. When she came back the next week, she talked about all the things that went wrong. I asked her if there were ever times when the process seemed to flow better. She told me how she gets ready for the gym: "I walk around the house; I pick up my gym clothes, my Walkman, water bottle, and the rest of my gear, and put them in my gym bag next to my purse by the front door. Then all I have to do is check the bag and go." I asked her if she could use any of those steps in other situations. Then she came up with the idea of setting up a "staging area" near the front door. "The night before I go out, I can walk around the house collecting the things I need," and then tell her kids not to move them. She thought this would lessen her anxiety about forgetting important items. Finally, I asked her to picture herself leaving her home in a relaxed state of mind, reminding her she had everything she needed. Holly reported that over the next few weeks she found more ways to short cut her "staging" and she felt less frazzled leaving her home.

When innies do any part of an exiting routine differently, it heightens their awareness. This prevents them from cruising on automatic anxiety pilot.

Play Spontaneously with Life

"Life is just a chair of bowlies," author and artist Mary Engelbreit writes. Extroverts are often thought of as fun-loving, and being out and about in the world is entertaining for them. Introverts, on the other hand, often take themselves too seriously. As children, they may have been criticized for being silly, and so they don't show that side of themselves. Also, since innies are self-conscious and don't like to draw attention to themselves, they may associate being playful with feeling foolish, overstimulated, and exhausted. However, play and spontaneity can actually increase our vitality, bring people together, make life more rewarding, and expand our horizons. Without joie de vivre we can be too solemn and apathetic.

To play means to give yourself a space where anything is possible. Notice how children stack up blocks until they fall over and scatter on the floor in some unlikely pattern. The children are thrilled. Something new has happened. Infant research has shown that one of the most important bonding qualities between parents and babies is playfulness. It's the glue that holds people together. Play also releases tension. It can unlock your thinking by creating new links between ideas, and it can air out your brain cobwebs.

When I give presentations, I begin by thanking the group for the invitation and then I say, "Hold on a minute, midlife eyes, you know," and I dive into my purse and slip on my Groucho Marx glasses. When I look out into the audience, most people smile or laugh. Our spirits lift a little, and we feel a sense of group cohesiveness.

Much as we introverts need play, a spontaneous space may also feel threatening because it means uncertainty. Yet life is uncertain, and many of the goodies of life come from that very fact. Many things happen out of serendipity. Walk a new route and you might meet your future spouse. Extroverting requires the ability to lighten up and enjoy the surprises in life.

I have found most introverts have a playful side, even if they aren't aware of it. A playful attitude helps introverts lessen fear and energy drain. To help you get in touch with your more playful side, write down five things you have secretly always wanted to do—things outside your normal routine. Think outside the box.

Here are some suggestions:

- At a restaurant, order a food you have never tried before, like snails (I mean escargots!).

- On a Saturday, stay up very late, or get up very early, whichever is different for you.

- Watch some old musical you have never seen: *Singin' in the Rain, Music Man, Oklahoma*, or *Daddy Longlegs*.

- Close your eyes, throw a penny in a fountain, and make a wish.

- With your family or a group of close friends, play a game like Taboo, Twister, or Charades.

- Take a fantasy trip to Nepal, Tahiti, Russia, or the Amazon. Imagine what it would smell, feel, look, and sound like. Think of a bizarre food you might eat there. How about roasted snake? Imagine what it would taste like.

- Do one thing you always wanted to do as a kid but that you were too young for or your parents wouldn't let you or you couldn't afford. For me it was getting a playhouse. Use the experience to create what you want for yourself.

You can find playful ways to do ordinary things. I have a pink pen that lights up on the top when I write with it. I also have an orange carrot pen that wiggles. It never ceases to amaze me how people—even serious people—suddenly become quite animated when they see my goofy pens. They always laugh and ask me about them. It adds zip to my life—and, I think, to theirs, too.

Take time out to play, and don't take things so seriously. Appreciate yourself for your strengths as well as your limitations. Enjoy your impromptu side.

Seven Strategies for Extroverting

You must always do the thing you think you cannot do.
—Eleanor Roosevelt

By boosting your confidence, getting out of your rut, and learning to play, you'll have prepared yourself to face the external world. Here are seven strategies that can make the adventure more rewarding.

Strategy 1: Shoot from the Lip

Extroverts like to talk (and as a result are listened to more than introverts). Extroverts don't like to listen for very long and may stop listening to innies if they talk slowly or hesitantly. Some extroverts think innies aren't very smart or are wishy-washy because of their soft voices and their ability to see both sides of an issue. If you have had years of experience feeling ignored or overlooked when you speak, or if you think getting people's ear requires too much effort, this may have discouraged you from expressing yourself. It may also have made you feel isolated. What is amazing is that a few simple tricks will make a huge difference. Try out this exercise twice a week for three weeks on days when you feel fully fueled. Remember you need only to fire up your lips for a short visit to Extrovertland.

Go out and speak to a stranger or two. Pick a person in your immediate area who looks friendly and say anything that relates to the location you are in. "Aren't those scarlet leaves on the maple tree just magnificent?" "The service is sooooo slow here." "I just love the honey wheat bread in this bakery." Speak a little quicker and a little louder than you usually do. Use short sentences. Say only one thing. Then go on with whatever you are doing, shopping, sitting, or standing in line. See how it goes. Notice if you feel a little agitated. For many introverts, just the experience of speaking to a stranger is highly stimulating. Remind yourself you can feel stirred up and still say something simple. Picture yourself speaking without effort.

Notice if the people you talk to join in easily and say something back to you. If they don't say anything, just imagine they might be uncomfortable. Don't take it personally. If, on the other hand, they follow your lead and start to chat, remind yourself that short, pleasant little conversations help us feel linked to other human beings. This experience can give you the incentive to expend a little extra energy when you want to reach out to other people.

After you have practiced talking to strangers in small bursts, it is time to gather your firepower for a longer mission—something that you find a little daunting, like the dreaded merchandise return. (Often introverts hate returning merchandise.) If returning isn't a bugaboo for you, try something else that is—like straightening out a discrepancy on your bill with the telephone company or getting a bid on carpet cleaning. Pick a high-anxiety mission. Introverts often fear the quick pace required for these

---

Put on a Happy Face

Smiling lifts your innergy; it elevates your mood. Moving your facial muscles affects various neurotransmitters, directing where blood flows to the brain. Try this brief experiment. First, raise your eyebrows and smile wide, showing your teeth and holding the pose for thirty seconds. What kind of thoughts or feelings go through your mind? Now bring your eyebrows together and clench your jaw. Hold this pose for thirty seconds. What thoughts and feelings are going through your mind now? If you look happier, you might feel happier. So fake it if you have to, until your neurotransmitters kick in.

experiences, which are unpredictable, may require immediate decisions, and where conflicts lurk at every turn. Many introverts end up feeling very anxious and discombobulated. But don't let yourself be scared off.

When you are ready to tackle this adventure, rehearse what you want to say—something like, "I would like to return this sweater. Unfortunately, it didn't fit my daughter. Here's my receipt." After a few practice runs you are ready.

Research shows that people are perceived as smart if they speak quickly, in a loud voice, and they avoid slang words and phrases. Whether you are talking in a classroom to your child's teacher, in a meeting at the office with your colleagues, or at home at a family gathering, speak in short, decisive sentences in a firm, strong, and clear voice, making direct eye contact. If you are in a group, always make a firm, short, connecting statement: "I would like to add . . ." Or "As Jim said, I think . . ." Always reward yourself with a small treat after you completed your mission.

Strategy 2: Quick-Calm Your Inner Irritations

Bankruptcy stared me in the face,
but one thought kept me calm;
soon I'd be too poor to need an anti-theft alarm.
—GINA ROTHFELS

Upsetting things happen to us each day. You are cut off as you are driving; you are late for an important engagement; the computer locks up; you are criticized by your boss; you can't think of your customer's name; you spill something on your favorite shirt . . . the list goes on.

The irritations of life usually upset introverts more than extroverts. Since they are more alert to their internal world, they notice their reactions to stress sooner and more intensely. As their inner upset increases, it is harder to soothe themselves. (Since extroverts are less focused on their inner world, bad news often rolls off them like water off a duck's back.)

Neuroscience tells us it is better to address reactions as they arise rather than let them build up. And in his book *High Energy Living*, Robert Cooper, Ph.D., offers a method to cool down in any situation. I have adapted his method into what I call the Quick-Calm Plan. Unlike many other techniques for handling stress, it takes only a few minutes and five steps, and you can practice it anywhere.

The Quick-Calm Plan

1. Keep breathing.
2. Make your eyes calm and alert.
3. Let go of your tension.
4. Notice uniqueness.
5. Call upon your sage.

1. *Keep breathing:* When you feel stress, you often hold your breath. If you don't interrupt this process and start breathing normally, you will be propelled toward anxiety, anger, and frustration. Breathing increases blood flow and oxygen to your brain and muscles, thus reducing tension and increasing your sense of well-being.

2. *Make your eyes calm and alert:* Practice this at home, in front of a mirror. Change your expression so that you are smiling with a relaxed, alert, focused gaze. Attempt to match the expression of someone who is enjoying listening to music or watching children at play. Say to yourself, "I am alert, and my body is calm." Following your lead, your neurochemistry will shift to cheer you up.

3. *Let go of your tension:* Under stress we tend to collapse or tense up. Notice your posture and where your body is holding tension. Are your shoulders tight? Is your tummy upset? Is your jaw clenched? Distribute your weight on both feet. Bounce slightly to make sure you have done this. Now, imagine that someone is gently pulling you up by the top of your head. Grow an inch. Open and lift your chest. Picture a relaxing emerald liquid flowing through your veins, warming and easing away tensions.

4. *Notice uniqueness:* When we are conscious and alert, we are aware that every situation is different. However, brains like to clump experiences together and then make snap judgments, slapping a prepackaged solution on the problem in an attempt to reduce our anxiety. So instead of immediately organizing an experience into a familiar category—for example, "Oh, my wife is criticizing me again"—take a moment to notice how this situation is unique. "My wife cares about me. Her voice doesn't sound critical; perhaps she is attempting to help me with her comment." Now you can respond appropriately to the situation.

5. *Call upon your sage:* Appeal to your inner sage, the wise part we all have inside ourselves. Acknowledge that you are facing a problem, and let your sage remind you about another time when you handled a similar situation successfully. Recall how you felt and step into that feeling state. It's like trying on a suit of confidence. The more you rely upon your inner sage, the more you can trust she or he will be there when you are in need. (And remember, if you ignore a problem or deny that it exists, it does not go away and usually gets worse.)

Strategy 3: Be Kind, Don't Rewind

Extroverts don't review everything they say. In fact, often they don't give their utterances a second thought. And that's part of the reason many of them have such a carefree attitude. Introverts, on the other hand, constantly evaluate what they have said. They have that active internal voice in the Broca's area of the brain, which controls speech and understanding language. It is on the pathway with other areas of the brain that assess reactions and compare the past, present, and future. Sometimes this internal voice can become critical.

Extroverts can have a critical internal voice, too, but it's more focused on what they do rather than on what they say. Introverts' internal voice often focuses on what they say, which can have the unfortunate effect of reducing their speaking out loud. Are you aware of your internal voice? Is it friend or foe? Is it encouraging? Discouraging? Often, if introverts feel bad after venturing out into the extrovert world, it is the voice in their head, not something that actually happened, which is the source of the problem.

My client Barry gave me a perfect example of how this works. He told me how embarrassed and stupid he felt after he made a presentation. When I asked him how the audience reacted, he acknowledged that people enjoyed the talk and he had received many compliments. But still he felt awful because when a woman in the audience asked him the title of a book he had mentioned, the name flew right out of his head. As we reviewed the experience, he realized that the inner voice in his head was giving him a hard time for forgetting. He needed to tell that critical voice to put a sock in it.

Think about the accusatory voices in your head. What do they say before and after you go out into the world? Who do they sound like? If the message is: "You should be different, you should be more outgoing," who do you think is speaking? Your mother? Your father? Your older sister? Your grandmother? Your boyfriend from high school? If a voice says, "This shouldn't be hard for you," who is that? Though the voices in your head may seem like you, they are more likely to be created from people in your past who wanted you to behave in a certain way. And you know what? Their disparaging comments came from the things *they* were uncomfortable about, not about who *you* are.

Unfortunately, the voices in our heads can affect our ability to manage in the hustling, bustling, fast-talkin' real world. Since we are already reluctant to venture out of our comfort zone and are burning fuel every second, critical voices deplete us and discourage us even more.

In order to gain a new perspective on your inner voices, I suggest that you find a cute picture of yourself as a young child. Sit and look at it for a least five minutes. The world often feels like a big and frightening place to kids, especially if they are introverted. Write down five things that little child needed when venturing out in an extroverted world. For instance, my list reads:

- She needs a hand to hold.
- She needs a kind, encouraging voice.
- She needs to be reminded that she sometimes feels uncomfortable.
- She needs to know ways to soothe herself.
- She needs to know that feelings always pass.

What she doesn't need is criticism.

The next time you have an embarrassing or uncomfortable experience, try not to evaluate what you said. Just hush up your critical voices. Make it clear that you aren't going to listen. Picture yourself as a child and tell yourself everything you said is fine.

Strategy 4: Pack Your Survival Kit

Many introverts are more sensitive to their surroundings and to anything that's unpleasant or discomforting than extroverts are. Outdoor environments can be especially challenging because they may feel exposed and bombarded by sensory stimuli. Combine that sensory onslaught with the energy they are expending, which drains out of them like bathwater when the plug is pulled. To top it off, add the fact that they are metabolizing food at a higher rate than extroverts, which means their blood sugar can easily plummet. These conditions make it vitally important for introverts to lay in some supplies before they go extroverting. Their coping capacity will increase if their physical

---

An Introvert's Survival Kit

Having what you need to reduce the onslaught of the world can sometimes make the difference between feeling fine and feeling frazzled. Here are some items you may want to keep in your tote, purse, briefcase, or car:

1. Earplugs to block street noises.

2. Snacks (nuts, protein bars, and any other protein snacks). These will boost your blood sugar when you feel it plummet.

3. Bottled water. Remember to keep drinking.

4. A Walkman or a Discman with soothing music.

5. A note card with an affirmation on it like "Today I will relax and enjoy what comes."

6. A soothing scent on a cotton ball. Sniff it if unpleasant odors bother you. (It's especially useful in August on the streets of New York!)

7. Medication for motion sickness, which can sometimes be caused by movies or unexpected movements.

needs are attended to. See the box "An Introvert's Survival Kit" for a list of items that will make this easier.

Make extroverting as pleasant and comfortable as possible. Dress in soft fabrics and comfortable shoes. Wear layered clothing so you can adjust to varying temperatures. Make any outing a more positive experience by adding beauty and nature. Walk through a park or take a stroll through an art gallery. (When I go to my institute, I park a block away so I can walk past picturesque homes.)

Turn off your cell phone or pager unless you absolutely need to be available. Keep a small book of uplifting poems, quotes, or sayings in your bag and read a few as you stand in line or have a break at work. Whenever possible, adjust the lighting to suit you. In crowds, imagine

8. An umbrella or parasol, if the sun bothers you. Children's umbrellas aren't as intrusive as large ones, and they can also shut out the feeling of large crowds. Lots of people comment on what a great idea it is when I walk around with my umbrella on a sunny day.

9. Sunscreen, handcream, and lip balm. Many innies have sensitive skin.

10. A battery fan, a small spray bottle, or, better yet, a combination of both. (These have the benefit of being conversation starters. I have made lots of pals while standing in long lines in hot weather or sitting at a baseball game sharing squirts from my bottle.)

11. Hats with big brims and sunglasses.

12. A sweater or blanket.

13. Those slick little pocket packets that radiate heat.

14. Earmuffs or a colorful ski headband, if the wind hurts your ears.

a bubble or shield around you. You can extrovert longer if you take good care of yourself.

Strategy 5: Refill Your Tank

Extroverting is a gas guzzler. Extroverts' tanks are pumped with glucose and adrenaline, so no wonder they don't want to stay home long. Introverts' energy, on the other hand, may well dip below the optimal level. As soon as you are aware of this drop, do the following exercise to increase your fuel level.

You are going to create an imaginative getaway. You can enter your getaway with a key word. Think of a word you associate with a relaxing respite, for example: Hawaii, garden, beach, pond, woods. Picture the location in your head. Then add your five senses to it. What would it look like, smell like, sound like, taste like, feel like? My client Kelly uses the word *glen*. Her little clearing has moss and grass and wildflowers surrounded by shady trees. The birds are twittering; the air is crisp. She visualizes herself sinking into the grass by the bank of a stream and dipping her toes into the chilly water. The sun warms her back. Kelly can feel her body relax and her energy revive.

Close your eyes and think of your word several times during the day. Imagine you are *there*. Apply your senses to your word. Practice this technique until you can think of your word and transport yourself in an instant. It's a quick and effortless refueler.

Here are some other ways to give yourself a quick fill-up:

- Run cold water on your wrists, or alternate hot and cold, ten seconds each.
- Fill a small spray bottle with water and squeeze in a dash of lemon juice. Use it occasionally to mist your face.

- Stand up; bend at the waist so your arms are dangling near the floor and you are looking at your knees. Relax and breathe for a few seconds; rise up slowly.

- Stand up; lift your chin slightly; bring your head forward and nod slightly. Rest in the nod. Repeat this several times during the day.

- Turn off the lights and sit in the dark for a few minutes.

- Stare out a window, watch people, and let your mind wander.

- Sit down, close your eyes, put your head back, and think of a fun experience from your past.

- Buy a hot (or cold) neck wrap, put in microwave (or freezer), and apply it for five minutes on any area of your body where you feel tension.

Strategy 6: Stay on the Funny Side of Life

A laugh at your own expense
costs you nothing.
—MARY WALDRIP

When you go out into the extrovert world, don't leave home without your sense of humor. Humor is the fastest way to keep our perspective, reduce stress, and strengthen our bodies, increase enjoyment in everyday living, and connect with other people. Since introverts focus inward on their own experience, they can sometimes lose sight of the bigger picture. Sometimes they think irritating things happen only to them. They imagine if they were extroverting *correctly,* everything would go well. Humor helps us step outside of ourselves and see our lives from a broader viewpoint. It's like suddenly looking at your life from the top of a mountain. It's easy to identify the crucial landmarks. Humor reduces anxiety. It reminds us that this too shall pass. It helps us manage the minor annoyances so we can save being upset for what really matters—big-ticket items like life and death. Remember that your energy supply is limited, so don't waste any of it by becoming grouchy. Arnold Glasow said, "Laughter is a tranquilizer with no side effects."

My client Alice told me how a sense of humor helps her. "Whenever something really frustrating happens, like arriving in snowy Chicago and my baggage doesn't, I keep thinking, 'Boy, wait till I tell my friends about standing here at two A.M. in freezing O'Hare airport with no baggage in my California cotton capris.' " Ironically, lots of wonderful experiences occur out of aggravation. Alice continued, "In this instance, a guy came over and said he was in Chicago for an ice-cream convention and his company was going to give away jackets at its booth and he had extras. Would I like one? I said sure. He pulled a huge jacket with black and white cow heads staring out with somber eyes. You could almost hear them mooing. On the shuttle to the hotel, my cow jacket gave lots of strangers a good laugh. It's impossible to be in a funk and laugh at the same time. I ended up wearing the cow jacket all weekend because so many people started chatting with me about it."

When babies are about ten weeks old, they begin to laugh, and in another six weeks they chuckle once an hour. By the time they are four years old, they giggle every four minutes. But by the time we reach adulthood, something sad happens. We laugh, on the average,

---

Strictly Speaking

Here's what the dictionary says about laughing. It "is a rhythmic spasmodic reflex with expiration from an open glottis and vibration of the vocal cords, often accompanied by a baring of teeth and facial grimaces." Doesn't that sound like fun?

only about fifteen times a day (even less for many adults). We lose an important part of our natural stress-relieving arsenal.

Remember that full-flavored euphoria you feel after a good laugh? A hearty laugh gives the muscles of your face, shoulders, diaphragm, and tummy a good workout. Your breathing revs up, and your blood pressure and heart rate temporarily rise as oxygen races through your bloodstream. Researchers speculate that laughing, like jogging, releases endorphins. Endorphins produce high-level alertness and reduce pain. Research shows that laughing reduces stress and increases immunity. In one study, participants were shown funny videotapes and then given increasingly harder math problems to solve. (That would definitely spike my stress response.) Watching funny tapes reduced the subjects' stress but—here's the interesting part—*only for those who were used to laughing a lot.* It seems that to receive the physiological benefits of laughter, you need to keep that funny bone well oiled.

Another study found that people who reported that they consistently used humor to cope with stress had a higher baseline level of antibodies that safeguard against illness. Yet another study showed that the immune response of people with a good sense of humor didn't drop when exposed to stress. Even those who use humor only infrequently have higher levels of antibodies in their saliva after watching a humorous video.

The Benefits of Laughter

Laughter is the shortest distance between two people.
—VICTOR BORGE

Besides being just plain fun, laughter:

- increases a sense of well-being
- increases enjoyment of social interactions
- increases oxygen, endorphins, antibodies, and pain thresholds
- lowers stress
- reduces anxiety, overwhelm, depression, frustration, and anger

My husband, Mike, has had several jobs that offered us the opportunity to travel. Unfortunately, our talent for travel disasters seemed to be an added bonus. We call it the "curse of the rolling black cloud." One time we had just belted ourselves into our United Airlines seats, thanking our lucky stars that nothing had gone wrong. Yet. At that moment, the pilot came on the speaker and said in a deadpan voice, "We will be delayed due to a swarm of bees attached to our back wheel. A beekeeper has been called to come and capture the queen. We are hoping the rest of the hive will fly away when the queen is removed. We will notify you of the progress." I looked at Mike with a blank face. "Do you think he's kidding?" I said. Mike returned my blank stare. The captain wasn't kidding. It was time for us to switch into humor mode. "Nobody is going to believe this, even coming from us," we said, laughing.

Here are a few ideas for bringing more laughter into your life:

- On your next car ride with your family, listen to an audio book by a humorous author like Bill Cosby, Paul Reiser, Art Buchwald, or Dave Barry.

- Cut out cartoons, jokes, and/or funny sayings and post them around your home and office.

- Remember to laugh at other people's jokes and funny stories.

- Make an effort to notice your own foibles and to have empathy with the human condition.

- Exaggerate something that happens. When clients are stuck in complaining and helplessness, I overstate what they are saying. "Oh My God, That Sounds Dreadful. What In The World Will You Do?" I don't intend to make fun of them, but sometimes it helps put the situation in perspective, and we both laugh. Solutions come much easier after a hearty chuckle.

■ Use humor in a strained situation, when it's appropriate. There's a now famous story that when President Reagan was taken to the hospital after he was shot by a would-be assassin, he said to his wife, Nancy, "Honey, I should've ducked."

One word of caution. Not all humor is healthful. Scorn, sarcasm, ridicule, and contempt originate from fear, anger, and/or envy, and they are harmful. If someone sends a hostile remark in your direction, do not laugh—it will only encourage them. It's better to say something like, "Wow, that was a zinger. Hold on a minute, let me get the arrow out of my chest." Then continue the conversation by changing the subject or asking someone else a question. If you find yourself being sarcastic, think about why you may be mad at the person at whom you directed the sarcasm. Don't use humor in situations where someone is severely depressed or has suffered the loss of a loved one. While humor can sometimes be injected in these types of situations, it's not always easy to tell what may give offense, even to close friends or relatives.

> **Laughing Last**
>
> A bird lands on a turtle's shell. The turtle is crying. The bird says, "Now what's wrong?"
>
> "I'm a failure," the turtle says.
>
> "Why?"
>
> "I'm so slow," says the turtle.
>
> "You're supposed to be slow, you're a turtle and turtles are slow."
>
> "I wish I was fast," said the turtle.
>
> "Why?"
>
> "Hares are always laughing at me."
>
> "What's your life expectancy?"
>
> "A hundred and fifty years," says the turtle.
>
> "—and the hare's?"
>
> "Five years," says the turtle.
>
> The bird walked off the turtle's back.
>
> "Well, just think, you get a hundred and forty-five years of last laughs."

However, humor in tragic situations can help us cope. In one award-winning episode of the *Mary Tyler Moore Show,* Mary attends the funeral of Chuckles the Clown, who—while dressed as a peanut—was trampled to death by an elephant. That episode was one of the best examples of gallows humor ever filmed.

Strategy 7: Shine Your Light Into the World

Although introverts may feel uncomfortable in groups, ironically they also usually long for a sense of community. Seeing relationships in all-or-nothing terms may interfere with creating their own community. They may think people are either totally busy with social commitments all the time or completely isolated. But you don't have to be a social butterfly in order to enjoy a greater sense of fellowship. Whether you are married, single, raising a family, or on the verge of retirement, you may wish for more personal relationships. Many of my introverted clients who want to meet more people usually make the same comment: "I have no idea how to get started."

Here's one way: On a blank piece of paper, write your name in the middle with a colored pen and draw a circle around it. Now write down your present social network, using colored pens to identify different groups. Blue could be your best friends, red could be your family, orange could be your work relationships, and purple could be any other groups you belong to. Think about the people and groups you have interacted with during your lifetime. Pay attention to those you once liked but who are no longer in your life. Think back. If there is an old activity you enjoyed, like taking photographs, which you would like to start again, add it to your list. Green might be a good choice for new connections, as it symbolizes growth.

Think about the following statements and see if any apply to you. If they do, start thinking about how you can incorporate the ideas they represent into your network. Perhaps there are people already in your network who could help.

- I would like to have more good friends with whom I feel comfortable.
- I would like to join or start a group with others who have similar interests, values, backgrounds, professions, hobbies, spiritual beliefs, or political views.
- I would like to broaden my life experiences by joining a group with different backgrounds, interests, or ideas than mine.
- I would like to be involved with a group that is improving the world.
- I would like to be involved with a group that lends support and assistance to its members, like a group for newly retired people.
- I would like to be active in a community group such as Friends of the Library, PTA, a mentoring organization like Big Brothers or Big Sisters, or the docent program in my local museum.
- I would rather join an established group.
- I don't want to join a group. I would rather just increase my network of friends.

Now comes the part that can be tricky for innies: overcoming fears, anxieties, and resistances. "I will feel uncomfortable and anxious." "I don't have the energy." "I might get hurt or rejected." "I hate that getting-to-know-you phase." "I'll end up having all the responsibility." These are some common introvert fears.

To allay them, try to think through what apprehensions they are masking. For example, are you afraid of being rejected, embarrassed, or hurt? Or just plain old frightened of the new and unknown? Then, remind yourself that fears aren't real or predictive. They are just electrical energy to which you have assigned a specific meaning. Most things we worry about never come to pass. Finally, decide to enjoy yourself no matter what.

Here are five strategies that may help you venture out:

1. Pick one connection you want to make or one group with which you want to develop more community, and take one step. For example, go to a church singles meeting, take a salsa dance class, attend a meeting of your local tree commission, ask a friend to go with you to a book group, or volunteer for your child's school fair committee. Start small and congratulate yourself for any progress you make.

2. Have a regular weekly date or phone conversation with a friend. It might be a good idea to formalize this relationship by asking the person to make a regular commitment of time. If one friend doesn't want to, ask another.

3. Invite two friends over for a discussion of a topic of mutual interest.

4. Remember, Rome wasn't built in a day, so several forays into extroverting may fizzle. That's to be expected. If you have given a new group or person several tries and it doesn't seem to be clicking, then move on and attempt another connection. No one fits in everywhere. Eventually, you will find people and organizations you enjoy and feel included in and stimulated by.

Also bear in mind that the Internet community can be a good place for introverts to connect with friends and family, as well as make new cyber relationships. Even though there have been many dire predictions about how computers cause alienation, reduce personal interaction, and diminish a sense of community, the Internet appears actually to increase people connections for introverts. It also permits people who are ill, isolated, live on the other side of the world, or can't meet in person to check in with each other on a consistent basis. And when you e-mail someone, you can give yourself plenty of time to think about what you want to say and revise all you want before you hit the send or reply button.

I am constantly amazed that well-known authors and researchers in fields I am investigating will e-mail me with information and express their willingness to be helpful. It has left me feeling *less* alienated, not more alienated. Strangers are more caring and responsive than I could have imagined. Often I think they are friendlier than they might be in person because they feel safe and more in control.

You can use the Internet to join chat rooms with people who have similar interests, read bulletin boards to find out information about various organizations, and so on. Believe it or not, several of the psychoanalysts at my institute and some of my clients have found partners on (fee-based) dating sites on the Internet.

One word of caution. A study by the British Psychological Society in 1998 regarding Internet addiction found that the most frequent cyber surfers were thirty-something introverts, male or female, and that they were likely to be suffering from depression. So, if you are spending more time on the Internet than in other parts of your life, if friends or relatives complain to you about your Internet use, and you feel depressed, think about seeing a physician for an evaluation. Depression is a condition that is highly treatable with a combination of psychotherapy and medication.

Lighthouses
Point the Way Home

This above all:
To thine own self be true . . .
—William Shakespeare

I t is easier to think of extroverting in the fast-paced world if you know you have a supply of strategies to rely on, and if you know your foray away from home base is limited in time. From your effort and courage to practice new techniques will come new friends, career options, romance, recognition from others, and—the most important of all—a solid sense of your own inner advantages and strengths. The world will benefit from your contributions. Leisure time at home will feel doubly refreshing because you won't feel so isolated or guilty that you are avoiding life. A well-earned repose.

Points to Ponder

- Sometimes you need to flex your outie muscles.
- You won't always be comfortable extroverting.
- Learn what helps you while extroverting and do it!
- Be a confident introvert.
- Believe the extroverted world will benefit from your contributions.

Final Farewell

In all things of nature
there is something of the marvelous.
—ARISTOTLE

I hope this book has helped you understand being an introvert in an extroverted world. I believe that by accepting your introverted temperament, you will be able to take better care of yourself and lessen any guilt or embarrassment you may have about being an introvert. The world is better off when introverts feel comfortable living in their own skin and following their own path. Sharing your advantages brightens the lives of everyone you meet. Spread the word to friends, family, and co-workers that introverts are much more than okay.

I would love to hear from you. My address is Marti Laney, P.O. Box 8993, Calabasas, California 91372 USA. My e-mail is martilaney@sbcglobal.net. Please visit my website at www.theintrovertadvantage.com.

Words for Introverts to Live By

Be playful.

Take breaks.

Appreciate your inside world.

Be authentic.

Enjoy curiosity.

Stay in harmony.

Revel in solitude.

Be grateful.

Be you.

Remember, let your light shine.

Selected Bibliography and Suggested Reading

Prelude and Overture

Aron, Elaine N. *The Highly Sensitive Person: How to Thrive When the World Overwhelms You.* New York: Broadway Books, 1996.

Jung, Carl G. *Psychological Types.* New York: Harcourt Brace & Company, 1923.

Kroeger, Otto, and Janet M. Thuesen. *Type Talk: The 16 Personality Types That Determine How We Live, Love, and Work.* New York: Delta, A Tilden Press Book, 1988.

_____. *Type Talk at Work: How the 16 Personality Types Determine Your Success on the Job.* New York: Delta, A Tilden Press Book, 1992.

Myers, David G. *The Pursuit of Happiness: Who Is Happy—and Why.* New York: William Morrow and Company, 1992.

Myers, Isabel Briggs, with Peter B. Myers. *Gifts Differing.* Palo Alto, Calif.: Consulting Psychologists Press, 1980.

Chapter 1:
What's an Innie? Are You One?

Goleman, Daniel. *Emotional Intelligence: Why It Can Matter More Than IQ.* New York: Bantam Books, 1997.

Hirsh, Sandra, and Jean Kummerow. *Life Types: Understand Yourself and Make the Most of Who You Are.* New York: Warner Books, 1989.

Segal, Nancy L. *Entwined Lives: Twins and What They Tell Us About Human Behavior.* New York: Plume Books, 1999.

Chapter 2:
Why Are Introverts an Optical Illusion?

Brian, Denis. *Einstein: A Life.* New York: John Wiley & Sons, 1996.

Bruno, Frank J. *Conquer Shyness.* New York: Macmillan Books, 1997.

Carducci, Bernardo J. *Shyness, a Bold New Approach.* New York: HarperCollins Publishers, 2000.

_____. *Psychology of Personality: Viewpoints, Research, and Applications.* Pacific Grove: Brookes/Cole, 1998.

Zimbardo, Philip G. *Shyness, What It Is, What to Do About It.* Reading, Mass.: Perseus Publishing, 1989.

Chapter 3:
The Emerging Brainscape: Born to Be Introverted

Acredolo, Linda, and Susan Goodwyn. *Baby Signs: How to Talk with Your Baby Before Your Baby Can Talk.* Lincolnwood, Ill.: NTC/Contemporary Publishing Group, 1996.

Carter, Rita. *Mapping the Mind.* Berkeley: University of California Press, 1998.

Conlan, Roberta, ed. *States of Mind: New Discoveries About How Our Brains Make Us Who We Are.* New York: Dana Press, 1999.

Hammer, Dean, and Peter Copland. *Living with Our Genes: The Groundbreaking Book About the Science of Personality, Behavior, and Genetic Destiny.* New York: Anchor Books, 1999.

Hobson, J. Allan. *The Chemistry of Conscious States: How the Brain Changes Its Mind.* New York: Little, Brown & Co., 1994.

Kosslyn, Stephen M., and Oliver Koenig. *Wet Mind: The New Cognitive Neuroscience.* New York: Free Press, 1995.

Kotulak, Ronald. *Inside the Brain: Revolutionary Discoveries of How the Mind Works.* Kansas City, Mo.: Andrews and McMeel, 1996.

Pert, Candace B. *Molecules of Emotion: The Science Behind Mind-Body Medicine.* New York: Touchstone, 1997.

Ridley, Matt. *Genome: The Autobiography of a Species in 23 Chapters.* New York: HarperCollins Publishers, 1999.

Schore, Allan N. *Affect Regulation and the Origin of the Self: The Neurobiology of Emotional Development.* Hillsdale, N.J.: Lawrence Erlbaum Associates, 1994.

Springer, Sally, and Georg Deutsh. *Left Brain, Right Brain: Perspective from Cognitive Neuroscience.* New York: W. H. Freeman & Company, 1997.

Chapter 4:
Relationships: Face the Music and Dance

Avila, Alexander. *Love Types: Discover Your Romantic Style and Find Your Soul Mate.* New York: Avon Books, 1999.

Emberley, Barbara. *Drummer Hoff.* New York: Simon & Schuster, 1967.

Gottman, John M., and Nan Silver. *The Seven Principles of Making Marriage Work.* New York: Three Rivers Press, 1999.

Hendricks, Harville. *Keeping the Love You Find.* New York: Pocket Books, 1992.

Jones, Jane, and Ruth Sherman. *Intimacy and Type: A Practical Guide for Improving Relationships.* Gainesville, Fla.: Center for Applications of Psychological Type, 1997.

Tieger, Paul D., and Barbara Barron-Tieger. *Just Your Type: Create the Relationship You've Always Wanted Using the Secrets of Personality Type.* Boston: Little, Brown & Co., 2000.

Chapter 5:
Parenting: Are They Up from Their Nap Already?

Bourgeois, Paulette. *Franklin the Turtle* series for children 4 to 8. *Franklin's New Friend; Franklin's School Play; Hurry Up, Franklin; Franklin Forgets;* and *Franklin in the Dark* are just a few of the books in this charming series that would be helpful for introverted children. They are also available in Spanish. New York: Scholastic Books.

Brazelton, T. Berry, and Stanley I. Greenspan. *The Irreducible Needs of Children: What Every Child Must Have to Grow, Learn, and Flourish.* Reading, Mass.: Perseus Publishing, 2000.

Galbraith, Judy, and Pamala Espeland. *You Know When Your Child Is Gifted When . . . A Beginner's Guide to Life on the Bright Side.* Minneapolis: Free Spirit Publishing, 2000.

Greenspan, Stanley I., with Jacqueline Salmon. *The Challenging Child: Understanding, Raising, and Enjoying the Five "Difficult" Types of Children.* Reading, Mass.: Perseus Publishing, 1995.

Nolte, Dorothy Law, and Rachel Harris. *Children Learn What They Live: Parenting to Inspire Values.* New York: Workman Publishing, 1998.

Swallow, Ward. *The Shy Child: Helping Children Triumph Over Shyness.* New York: Warner Books, 2000.

Tieger, Paul D., and Barbara Barron-Tieger. *Nurture by Nature: Understand Your Child's Personality Type—and Become a Better Parent.* New York: Little, Brown & Co., 1997.

Chapter 6:
Socializing: Party Pooper or Pooped from the Party?

Branch, Susan. *Girlfriends Forever: From the Heart of the Home.* New York: Little, Brown & Co., 2000.

Dimitrias, Jo-Ellen, and Mark Mazzarella. *Put Your Best Foot Forward: Making a Great Impression by Taking Control of How Others See You.* New York: Simon & Schuster, 2001.

Gabor, Don. *How to Start a Conversation and Make Friends.* New York: Simon & Schuster, 2000.

Garner, Alan. *Conversationally Speaking: Tested New Ways to Increase Your Personal and Social Effectiveness.* Licolnwood, Ill.: NTC/Contemporary Publishing Group, 1997.

Horn, Sam. *Tongue Fu: Deflect, Disarm, and Diffuse Any Verbal Conflict.* New York: St. Martin's Press, 1997.

Stoddard, Alexandra. *Daring to Be Yourself.* New York: Avon Books, 1990. Stoddard has written many wonderful books with introverted hearts.

Chapter 7:
Working: Hazards from 9 to 5

Balzamo, Frederica J. *Why Should Extroverts Make All the Money: Networking Made Easy for the Introvert.* Chicago: Contemporary Books, 1999.

Cooper, Robert K. *High Energy Living: Switch on the Sources to Increase Your Fat-Burning Power, Boost Your Immunity and Live Longer, Stimulate Your Memory and Creativity, Unleash Hidden Passions and Courage.* Emmaus, Pa.: Rodale Books, 2000.

Deep, Sam, and Lyle Sussman. *Smart Moves for People in Charge: 130 Checklists to Help You Be a Better Leader.* Reading, Ill.: Addison-Wesley Publishing, 1995.

_____. *Smart Moves: 14 Steps to Keep Any Boss Happy, 8 Ways to Start Meetings on Time, and 1600 More Tips to Get the Best from Yourself and the People Around You.* Reading, Ill.: Addison-Wesley Publishing, 1990.

Gelb, Michael J. *Present Yourself! Transforming Fear, Knowing Your Audience, Setting the Stage, Making Them Remember.* Torrance, Calif.: Jalmer Press, 1988.

Kroeger, Otto, and Janet M. Thuesen. *Type Talk at Work: How the 16 Personality Types Determine Your Success on the Job.* New York: Delta, A Tilden Press Book, 1992.

Morley, Carol, and Liz Wilde. *Destress: 100 Natural Mood Improvers.* London: MQ Publications, 2001.

Murphy, Thomas M. *Successful Selling for Introverts: Achieving Sales Success Without a Traditional Sales Personality.* Portland, Oreg.: Sheba Press, 1999.

Nelson, Bob. *1001 Ways to Reward Employees.* New York: Workman Publishing, 1994.

Tieger, Paul D., and Barbara Barron-Tieger. *Do What You Are: Discover the Perfect Career for You Through the Secrets of Personality Type.* New York: Little, Brown & Co., 2001.

Chapter 8:
Three P's: Personal Pacing, Priorities, and Parameters

Black, Jan and Greg Enns. *Better Boundaries: Owning and Treasuring Your Life.* Oakland: New Harbinger Publications, 1997.

Fadiman, James. *Unlimit Your Life: Setting and Getting Goals.* Berkeley: Celestial Arts, 1989.

Lamott, Anne. *Bird by Bird: Some Instructions on Writing and Life.* New York: Pantheon Books, 1994.

Levine, Stephen. *A Year to Live: How to Live This Year As If It Were Your Last.* New York: Random House, 1998.

Patrone, Susan. *Maybe Yes, Maybe No, Maybe Maybe.* New York: Orchard Books, 1993.

Sark. *A Creative Companion: How to Free Your Creative Spirit.* Berkeley: Celestial Arts, 1991. Her other titles are great, too!

Wildsmith, Brian, and Jean De La Fontaine. *The Hare and the Tortoise.* London: Oxford University Press, 2000.

Chapter 9:
Nurture Your Nature

Arnot, Robert. *The Biology of Success: Set Your Mental Thermostat to High with Dr. Bob Arnot's Prescription for Achieving Your Goals!* Boston: Little, Brown & Co., 2000.

Carper, Jean. *Your Miracle Brain: Maximize Brain Power, Boost Your Memory, Lift Your Mood, Improve IQ and Creativity, Prevent and Reverse Mental Aging.* New York: HarperCollins Publishers, 2000.

Carson, Richard. *Taming Your Gremlin: A Guide to Enjoying Yourself.* New York: HarperPerennial, 1983.

Gardner, Kay. *Sounding the Inner Landscape: Music as Medicine.* Rockport, Mass.: Element Books, 1990.

Lee, Vinny. *Quiet Places: How to Create Peaceful Havens in Your Home, Garden, and Workplace.* Pleasantville, N.Y.: Reader's Digest Association, 1998.

Moore, Thomas. *Care of the Soul: How to Add Depth and Meaning to Your Everyday Life.* New York: HarperCollins Publishers, 1998.

Pollan, Michael. *The Botany of Desire: A Plant's-Eye View of the World.* New York: Random House, 2001.

Seton, Susannah. *Simple Pleasures of the Home: Cozy Comforts and Old-Fashioned Crafts for Every Room in the House.* Berkeley: Conari Press, 1999.

Sobel, David S., and Robert Ornstein. *The Healthy Mind Healthy Body Handbook*. New York: Patient Education Media, Inc., 1996.

Storr, Anthony. *Solitude: A Return to the Self.* New York: Ballantine Books, 1988.

Chapter 10:
Extroverting: Shine Your Light into the World

Axelrod, Alan, and Jim Holtje. *201 Ways to Deal with Difficult People: A Quick Tip Survival Guide*. New York: McGraw Hill, 1997.

Cooper, Robert K. *High Energy Living: Switch on the Sources to Increase Your Fat-Burning Power, Boost Your Immunity and Live Longer, Stimulate Your Memory and Creativity, Unleash Hidden Passions and Courage*. Emmaus, Pa.: Rodale Books, 2000.

DeAngelis, Barbara. *Confidence: Finding It and Living It.* Carlsbad, Calif.: Hay House, 1995.

Freeman, Criswell. *When Life Throws You a Curveball . . . Hit It! Simple Wisdom for Life's Ups and Downs*. Nashville: Walnut Grove Press, 1999.

Shaffer, Carolyn R., and Kristin Anundsen. *Creating Community Anywhere: Finding Support and Connection in a Fragmented World*. New York: Tarcher/Putnam, 1993.

Tieger, Paul, and Barbara Barron-Tieger. *The Art of SpeedReading People.* New York: Little, Brown & Co., 1998.

Tourels, Stephanie. *365 Ways to Energize Body, Mind and Soul*. Pownal, Vt.: Storey Publishing, 2000.

Warner, Mark. *The Complete Idiot's Guide to Enhancing Self-Esteem*. New York: Alpha Books, 1999.

Index

A

accomplishment, confidence and, 285–86

acetylcholine, 65
  introverts and, 72, 74
  Locked-in Syndrome and, 66
  nutrition and, 271
  parasympathetic nervous system and, 76
  self-nurturing and, 270
  unconscious information processing and, 245–46

acetylcholine pathway, 84

Adler, Alfred, 26

adrenaline, 71. *See also* noradrenaline

advisor class, 12–13

Affect Regulation and the Origin of the Self (Schore), 74–76

affirmation note-card, 300

alertness, Quick-Calm Plan and, 296

Allen, Joan, 39

Alzheimer's disease, 72

antisocialness, 45, 46. *See also* reclusiveness myth; socializing

anxiety
  confidence and, 287
  Quick-Calm Plan and, 297

Arnot, Bob, 277

aromas
  effects of, 267–68
  in introvert's survival kit, 300

Aron, Elaine, 12, 45

Attitudes of Gratitude (Ryan), 277

autonomic nervous system. *See also* parasympathetic nervous system; sympathetic nervous system
  hypothalamus and, 74
  neurotransmitters and, 73

B

battery fans, 301

Berry, Diane, 77

Better Boundaries (Black and Enns), 248

Biology of Success, The (Arnot), 277

Bird by Bird (Lamott), 228

Black, Jan, 248

blankets, 301

body-brain circuits, 84–85

bosses, introverted, 214–16

boundaries. *See* parameters

brain. *See also* left brain; neurotransmitters; parasympathetic nervous system; right brain; sympathetic nervous system
  delayed processing puzzle, 2
  functional mapping of, 61
  parts of, 87–88
  processing by extroverts, 86–87
  processing by gifted and talented introverts, 262–63
  processing by introverts, 83, 86
  unconscious information processing in, 245–46

brain locking/overload, 11. *See also* overwhelmed feelings; pacing
  external stimulation and, 23
  long-term memory and, 80–81
  repartee and, 162
  socializing and, 160

breadth, extroverts and, 23–24

break suggestions, 256–57

breathing
  overwhelmed feelings and, 212
  Quick-Calm Plan and, 296
  self-nurturing with, 259–61

Brian, Denis, 41

Briggs, Katharine C., 12